Lecture Notes in Computer Science   10068

Commenced Publication in 1973
Founding and Former Series Editors:
Gerhard Goos, Juris Hartmanis, and Jan van Leeuwen

More information about this series at http://www.springer.com/series/7407

Aske Plaat · Walter Kosters
Jaap van den Herik (Eds.)

Computers and Games

9th International Conference, CG 2016
Leiden, The Netherlands, June 29 – July 1, 2016
Revised Selected Papers

Editors
Aske Plaat
Leiden Institute of Advanced Computer
 Science (LIACS)
Leiden University
Leiden, Zuid-Holland
The Netherlands

Jaap van den Herik
Leiden Institute of Advanced Computer
 Science (LIACS)
Leiden University
Leiden, Zuid-Holland
The Netherlands

Walter Kosters
Leiden Institute of Advanced Computer
 Science (LIACS)
Leiden University
Leiden, Zuid-Holland
The Netherlands

ISSN 0302-9743   ISSN 1611-3349 (electronic)
Lecture Notes in Computer Science
ISBN 978-3-319-50934-1   ISBN 978-3-319-50935-8 (eBook)
DOI 10.1007/978-3-319-50935-8

Library of Congress Control Number: 2016959640

LNCS Sublibrary: SL1 – Theoretical Computer Science and General Issues

Printed on acid-free paper

This Springer imprint is published by Springer Nature
The registered company is Springer International Publishing AG
The registered company address is: Gewerbestrasse 11, 6330 Cham, Switzerland

Preface

This book contains the papers of the 9th Computer and Games Conference (CG 2016) held in Leiden, The Netherlands. The conference took place from June 29 to July 1, 2016, in conjunction with the 19th Computer Olympiad and the 22nd World Computer-Chess Championship.

The Computers and Games Conference series is a major international forum for researchers and developers interested in all aspects of artificial intelligence and computer game playing. During the Leiden conference, a Workshop on Neural Networks in Games was organized; the exciting results on Go from 2015–2016 were in everybody's mind. Moreover, there was an invited talk by Aja Huang (Google DeepMind) on Alpha Go, titled "Alpha Go: Combining Deep Neural Networks with Tree Search." Earlier conferences took place in Tsukuba (1998), Hamamatsu (2000), Edmonton (2002), Ramat-Gan (2004), Turin (2006), Beijing (2008), Kanazawa (2010), and Yokohama (2013).

The Program Committee (PC) was pleased to see that so much progress was made in new games and that new techniques were added to the recorded achievements. In this conference, 30 papers were submitted. Each paper was sent to at least three reviewers. If conflicting views on a paper were reported, the reviewers themselves arrived at a final decision. With the help of external reviewers (see after the preface), the PC accepted 20 papers for presentation at the conference and publication in these proceedings. As usual we informed the authors that they submitted their contribution to a post-conference editing process. The two-step process is meant (a) to give authors the opportunity to include the results of the fruitful discussion after the lecture in their paper, and (b) to maintain the high-quality level of the CG series. The authors enjoyed this procedure.

The aforementioned set of 20 papers covers a wide range of computer games and many different research topics. We grouped the topics into the following four main classes, which determined the order of publication: Monte Carlo Tree Search (MCTS) and its enhancements (seven papers), concrete games (seven papers), theoretical aspects and complexity (five papers), and cognition model (one paper). The paper "Using Partial Tablebases in Breakthrough" by Andrew Isaac and Richard Lorentz received the Best Paper Award.

We are sure that the readers will enjoy the research efforts presented by the authors. Below, we introduce them in the topics investigated by brief characterizations of the papers largely paraphrased by ideas as submitted by the authors, in particular in the abstract. The aim is to show a connection between the contributions and to provide insights into the research progress.

Monte Carlo Tree Search

The seven topics discussed in the area of MCTS are as follows (the game area is mentioned in brackets); Partial Tablebases (Breakthrough), Deep Convolutional Neural Network (Go), Parameterized Poker Squares (Poker), Robust Exploration (Go), Pruning Playouts (Havannah), Fast Seed Learning (Go), and Heuristic Function Evaluation Framework (several games).

"Using Partial Tablebases in Breakthrough" is written by Andrew Isaac and Richard Lorentz. In the game of Breakthrough the endgame is reached when there are still many pieces on the board. This means that there are too many possible positions to be able to construct a reasonable endgame tablebase on the standard 8×8 board, or even on a 6×6 board. The fact that Breakthrough pieces only move forward allows researchers to create partial tablebases on the last n rows of each side of the board. The authors show how this construction results in a much stronger MCTS-based 6×6 player and even allows positions to be solved that would otherwise be out of reach.

"Using Deep Convolutional Neural Networks in Monte Carlo Tree Search" is authored by Tobias Graf and Marco Platzner. Deep Convolutional Neural Networks have revolutionized Computer Go. Large networks have emerged as state-of-the-art models for move prediction and are used not only as stand-alone players but also inside MCTS to select and bias moves. Using neural networks inside the tree search is a challenge due to their slow execution time even if accelerated on a GPU. In this paper the authors evaluate several strategies to limit the number of nodes in the search tree in which neural networks are used. All strategies are assessed using the freely available cuDNN library. The authors compare the strategies against an optimal upper bound that can be estimated by removing timing constraints. They show that the best strategies are only 50 ELO points worse than this upper bound.

"Monte Carlo Approaches to Parameterized Poker Squares" is written by Todd Neller, Zuozhi Yang, Colin Messinger, Calin Anton, Karo Castro-Wunsch, William Maga, Steven Bogaerts, Robert Arrington, and Clay Langley. Parameterized Poker Squares (PPS) is a generalization of Poker Squares where players must adapt to a point system supplied at play time and thus dynamically compute highly varied strategies. The authors detail the top three performing AI players in a PPS research competition, all three of which make use of a variety of Monte Carlo techniques.

"Monte Carlo Tree Search with Robust Exploration" is authored by Takahisa Imagawa and Tomoyuki Kaneko. This paper presents a new MCTS method that focuses on identifying the best move. By minimizing the cumulative regret, UCT has achieved remarkable success in Go and other games. However, recent studies on straight-forward regret reveal that there are better exploration strategies. To improve the current performance, a leaf to be explored is determined not only by the mean but also by the whole reward distribution. The authors adopt a hybrid approach to obtain reliable distributions. A negamax-style backup of reward distributions is used in the shallower half of a search tree, and UCT is adopted in the rest of the tree. Experiments on synthetic trees show that the presented method outperformed UCT and other similar methods, except for trees having uniform width and depth.

"Pruning Playouts in Monte Carlo Tree Search for the Game of Havannah" is written by Joris Duguépéroux, Ahmad Mazyad, Fabien Teytaud, and Julien Dehos. MCTS is a popular technique for playing multi-player games. In the paper, the authors propose a new method to bias the playout policy of MCTS. The idea is to prune the decisions that seem "bad" (according to the previous iterations of the algorithm) before computing each playout. Thus, the method evaluates the estimated "good" moves more precisely. The improvement is tested for the game of Havannah and compared with several classic improvements. The method outperforms the classic version of MCTS (with the RAVE improvement) and the different playout policies of MCTS that have been submitted to experiments.

"Fast Seed-Learning Algorithms for Games" is authored by Jialin Liu, Olivier Teytaud, and Tristan Cazenave. Recently, a methodology was presented for boosting the computational intelligence of randomized game-playing programs. The authors propose faster variants of these algorithms, namely, rectangular algorithms (fully parallel) and bandit algorithms (faster in a sequential setup). They check the performance on several board games and card games. In addition, in the case of Go, they check the methodology when the opponent is completely distinct to the opponent used in the training.

"Heuristic Function Evaluation Framework" is written by Nera Nešić and Stephan Schiffel. The authors present a heuristic function evaluation framework that allows one to quickly compare a heuristic function's output with benchmark values that are pre-computed for a subset of positions in the state space of the game. The framework reduces the time to evaluate a heuristic function drastically while also providing some insight into where the heuristic is performing well or below par. The authors analyze the feasibility of using MCTS to compute benchmark values instead of relying on game theoretic values that are hard to obtain in many cases. They also propose several metrics for comparing heuristic evaluations with benchmark values and discuss the feasibility of using MCTS benchmarks with those metrics.

Concrete Games

Seven papers discussed six concrete games. They are: 2048, Werewolf Game (two articles), Mastermind, Domineering, Reverse Hex, and Computer-Aided Go.

"Systematic Selection of N-tuple Networks for 2048" is authored by Kazuto Oka and Kiminori Matsuzaki. The puzzle game 2048 is a single-player stochastic game played on a 4×4 grid. It is the most popular game among similar slide-and-merge games. One of the strongest computer players for 2048 uses temporal difference learning (TD learning) with N-tuple networks. Here, it matters a great deal how to design the N-tuple networks. In the paper, the authors thoroughly study the N-tuple networks for the game 2048. In the first set of experiments, they conduct TD learning by selecting 6- and 7-tuples exhaustively, and evaluate the usefulness of those tuples. In the second set of experiments, they conduct TD learning with high-utility tuples, varying the number of tuples. The best player with ten 7-tuples achieves good results. It utilizes no game-tree search and plays a move in about 12 microseconds.

"Human-Side Strategies in the Werewolf Game Against the Stealth Werewolf Strategy" is written by Xiaoheng Bi and Tetsuro Tanaka. The werewolf game contains unique features, such as persuasion and deception, which are not included in games that have been previously studied in AI research. The authors concentrate on a werewolf-side strategy called "stealth werewolf." With this strategy, each of the werewolf-side players behaves like a villager, and the player does not pretend to have a special role. Even though the strategy is thought to be suboptimal, this has not been proved. The authors restrict the human-side strategies such that (1) the seer reveals his/her role on the first day, (2) the bodyguard never reveals his/her role, and (3) the advantage of the werewolves in determining the player to be eliminated by vote is nullified. They calculate the ε-Nash equilibrium of strategies for both sides under these three restrictions, and discuss implications.

"Werewolf Game Modeling Using Action Probabilities Based on Play Log Analysis" is authored by Yuya Hirata, Michimasa Inaba, Kenichi Takahashi, Fujio Toriumi, Hirotaka Osawa, Daisuke Katagami, and Kousuke Shinoda. In the study, the authors construct a non-human agent that can play the werewolf game (i.e., AI wolf) with the aims of creating more advanced intelligence and acquiring more advanced communication skills for AI-based systems. They build a behavioral model using information regarding human players and the decisions made by such players; all such information is obtained from play logs of the werewolf game. To confirm the model, simulation experiments are conducted of the werewolf game using an agent based on the proposed behavioral model, as well as a random agent for comparison. An 81.55% coincidence ratio of agent behavior versus human behavior is obtained.

"Nash Equilibrium in Mastermind" is written by François Bonnet and Simon Viennot. Mastermind is a famous two-player deduction game. A Codemaker chooses a secret code and a Codebreaker tries to guess this secret code in as few guesses as possible, with feedback information after each guess. Many existing works have computed optimal worst-case and average-case strategies of the Codebreaker, assuming that the Codemaker chooses the secret code uniformly at random. However, the Codemaker can freely choose any distribution probability on the secret codes. An optimal strategy in this more general setting is known as a Nash Equilibrium. In the current research, the authors compute such a Nash Equilibrium for all instances of Mastermind up to the most classic instance of four pegs and six colors, showing that the uniform distribution is not always the best choice for the Codemaker. They also show the direct relation between Nash Equilibrium computations and computations of worst-case and average-case strategies.

"11 × 11 Domineering Is Solved: The First Player Wins" is authored by Jos Uiterwijk. The author has developed a program called MUDoS (Maastricht University Domineering Solver) that solves Domineering positions in a very efficient way. MUDoS enables the solution of currently known positions (up to the 10 × 10 board) much quicker (measured in number of investigated nodes) than has happened to date. More importantly, MUDoS enables the solution of the 11 × 11 Domineering board. This board was until now far out of reach of previous Domineering solvers. The solution needed the investigation of 259,689,994,008 nodes, using almost half a year of computation time on a single simple desktop computer. The results show that under optimal play the first player wins, irrespective of whether Vertical or Horizontal starts the game. In addition, several other boards hitherto unsolved are also solved.

"A Reverse Hex Solver" is written by Kenny Young and Ryan Hayward. The authors present Solrex, an automated solver for the game of Reverse Hex. Reverse Hex, also known as Rex or Misère Hex, is the variant of the game of Hex in which the player who joins his/her two sides loses the game. Solrex performs a mini-max search of the state space using Scalable Parallel Depth First Proof Number Search, enhanced by the pruning of inferior moves and the early detection of certain winning strategies. Solrex is implemented on the same code base as the Hex program Solver, and can solve arbitrary positions on board sizes up to 6 × 6, with the hardest position taking less than four hours on four threads.

"Computer-Aided Go: Chess as a Role Model" is authored by Ingo Althöfer. Recently, computers have gained strength in the Asian board game Go. Similar to the experience in Chess some 15–30 years ago, teams with humans and computers may be much stronger than each of their Go components. The paper claims that time is ripe for computer-aided Go on a large scale, although so far neither most users nor the Go programmers have thought about it. A main part of the paper describes successful pioneers in playing Go with computer help. Progress in computer-aided Go may also lead to progress in human Go and in computer Go itself.

Theory and Complexity

The five topics discussed are: Polyhedral Uncertainty Set (two-person zero-sum games), A Class Grammar (General Games), the Number of Legal Go Positions (Go), A Googleplex of Games (Go), and Majority Systems (Subtraction Game).

"Quantified Integer Programs with Polyhedral Uncertainty Set" is written by Michael Hartisch, Thorsten Ederer, Ulf Lorenz, and Jan Wolf. Quantified Integer Programs (QIPs) are integer programs with variables being either existentially or universally quantified. They can be interpreted as a two-person zero-sum game with an existential and a universal player, where the existential player tries to meet all constraints and the universal player intends to force at least one constraint to be not satisfied. Originally, the universal player is only restricted to set the universal variables within their upper and lower bounds. This idea is extended by adding constraints for the universal variables, i.e., restricting the universal player to some polytope instead of the hypercube created by bounds. It is also shown how this extended structure can be reduced from a polynomial-time algorithm to a QIP.

"A Class Grammar for General Games" is authored by Cameron Browne. While there exist a variety of game description languages (GDLs) for modeling various classes of games, the GDLs discussed are aimed at game playing rather than the more particular needs of game design. The paper describes a new approach to general game modeling that arose from this need. A class grammar is automatically generated from a given library of source code, i.e., from the constructors and associated parameters found along its class hierarchy, to give a context-free grammar that provides access to the underlying code while hiding its implementation details.

"The Number of Legal Go Positions" is written by John Tromp. The number of legal 19×19 Go positions has been determined as

```
20816819938197998469947863334486277028652245
38845305484256394568209274196127380153785256
48451698519643907259916015628128546089888314
42712971531931755773662039724706484093535
```

which is approximately $2 \cdot 10^{170}$. This is roughly 1.2% of the total number of positions, being $3^{19 \times 19}$. The proof uses a correspondence between legal positions and paths through a graph of so-called border states. It requires considerable computing power, taking over 250,000 CPU-hours and 30 PB of disk IO.

"A Googolplex of Go Games" is authored by Matthieu Walraet and John Tromp. The authors establish the existence of $10^{10^{100}}$ Go games on the 19×19 board. Players can produce very long games: They fill in their eyes and continue capturing each other, restricted only by the superko rule that forbids repeating the whole board position. The challenge in proving a lower bound is to make a single game as long as possible, by visiting as many of the roughly $2 \cdot 10^{170}$ legal positions as possible. It will then turn out that there are sufficient choices along the way to lift the game length into the exponent.

"An Analysis of Majority Systems with Dependent Agents in a Simple Subtraction Game" is written by Raphael Thiele and Ingo Althöfer. It is common knowledge that a majority system is typically better than its components, when the components are stochastically independent. However, in practice the independency assumption is often not justified. The authors investigate systems of experts that are constituted by couples of dependent agents. Based on recent theoretical work, they analyze their performance in a simple two-player subtraction game. It turns out that systems with negatively correlated couples perform better than those with a positive correlation within the couples. From computer chess practice, it was known that systems of very positively correlated bots were not so successful.

Cognition Model

One paper is classified under the heading Cognition Model. Still, it is an important topic that clearly belongs to this conference.

"Do People Think Like Computers?" is authored by Bas van Opheusden, Zahy Bnaya, Gianni Galbiati, and Wei Ji Ma. From computer-chess practice it is known that systems of rather positively correlated bots are not always successful, since they run the risk of missing an important variation. At first, human cognition inspired the earliest algorithms for game-playing computer programs. Then, however, the studies of human and computer game play quickly diverged: the artificial intelligence (AI) community focused on theory and techniques to solve games, while behavioral scientists empirically examined the specific topic of simple decision-making in humans. In this paper, the authors combine concepts and methods from the two fields to investigate whether human and AI players take similar approaches in an adversarial combinatorial game. The authors develop and compare several models that capture human behavior, and demonstrate that the models can predict behavior in two related tasks. At the end, they use the models to describe what makes a strong human player.

The book would not have been produced without the help of many persons. In particular, we would like to mention the authors and the reviewers for their help. Moreover, the organizers of the three events in Leiden (see the beginning of this preface) have contributed substantially by bringing the researchers together. Without much emphasis, we recognize the work by the various committees of CG 2016 as essential for this publication. One exception is made for Joke Hellemons, who is gratefully thanked for all services to our games community. Finally, the editors happily recognize the generous sponsors: NWO Exact Sciences, Museum Naturalis, Surf-SARA, Municipality of Leiden, Digital Games Technology, Faculty of Science, ICGA, ISSC, the Leiden Institute of Advanced Computer Science, and the Leiden Centre of Data Science.

September 2016   Aske Plaat
                                                    Jaap van den Herik
                                                       Walter Kosters

Organization

Executive Committee

Editors

Aske Plaat	Universiteit Leiden, The Netherlands
Jaap van den Herik	Universiteit Leiden, The Netherlands
Walter Kosters	Universiteit Leiden, The Netherlands

Program Co-chairs

Aske Plaat	Universiteit Leiden, The Netherlands
Jaap van den Herik	Universiteit Leiden, The Netherlands
Walter Kosters	Universiteit Leiden, The Netherlands

Organizing Committee

Johanna Hellemons	Universiteit Leiden, The Netherlands
Abdel El Boujadanyni	Universiteit Leiden, The Netherlands
Marloes van der Nat	Universiteit Leiden, The Netherlands
Aske Plaat	Universiteit Leiden, The Netherlands
Jan van Rijn	Universiteit Leiden, The Netherlands
Jaap van den Herik	Universiteit Leiden, The Netherlands
Jonathan Vis	Universiteit Leiden, The Netherlands

Program Committee

Ingo Althöfer	Friedrich Schiller Universität Jena, Germany
Yngvi Björnsson	Reykjavik University, Iceland
Bruno Bouzy	Université Paris Descartes, France
Ivan Bratko	University of Ljubljana, Slovenia
Cameron Browne	Queensland University of Technology, Australia
Tristan Cazenave	Université Paris-Dauphine, France
Bo-Nian Chen	Institute for Information Industry, Taiwan
Jr-Chang Chen	Chung Yuan Christian University, Taiwan
Paolo Ciancarini	University of Bologna, Italy
Rémi Coulom	Lille, France
Omid David	Bar-Ilan University, Israel
Diogo Ferreira	University of Lisbon, Portugal

Erik van der Werf   GN Hearing, The Netherlands
Mark Winands   Maastricht University, The Netherlands
Thomas Wolf   Brock University, Canada
I-Chen Wu   National Chiao Tung University, Taiwan
Shi-Jim Yen   National Dong Hwa University, Taiwan

Sponsors

NWO (Netherlands Organization of Scientific Research)
Museum Naturalis
SurfSARA
Leiden Institute of Advanced Computer Science
Leiden Centre of Data Science
Leiden Faculty of Science
ISSC
ICGA
Digital Games Technology
The Municipality of Leiden

The Advances in Computer Chess/Games Books

The series of Advances in Computer Chess (ACC) Conferences started in 1975 as a complement to the World Computer-Chess Championships, for the first time held in Stockholm in 1974. In 1999, the title of the conference changed from ACC into ACG (Advances in Computer Games). Since 1975, fourteen ACC/ACG conferences have been held. Below we list the conference places and dates together with the publication; the Springer publication is supplied with an LNCS series number.

London, England (1975, March)
Proceedings of the 1st Advances in Computer Chess Conference (ACC1)
Ed. M.R.B. Clarke
Edinburgh University Press, 118 pages.

Edinburgh, UK (1978, April)
Proceedings of the 2nd Advances in Computer Chess Conference (ACC2)
Ed. M.R.B. Clarke
Edinburgh University Press, 142 pages.

London, England (1981, April)
Proceedings of the 3rd Advances in Computer Chess Conference (ACC3)
Ed. M.R.B. Clarke
Pergamon Press, Oxford, UK, 182 pages.

London, England (1984, April)
Proceedings of the 4th Advances in Computer Chess Conference (ACC4)
Ed. D.F. Beal
Pergamon Press, Oxford, UK, 197 pages.

Noordwijkerhout, The Netherlands (1987, April)
Proceedings of the 5th Advances in Computer Chess Conference (ACC5)
Ed. D.F. Beal
North Holland Publishing Comp., Amsterdam, The Netherlands, 321 pages.

London, England (1990, August)
Proceedings of the 6th Advances in Computer Chess Conference (ACC6)
Ed. D.F. Beal
Ellis Horwood, London, UK, 191 pages.

Maastricht, The Netherlands (1993, July)
Proceedings of the 7th Advances in Computer Chess Conference (ACC7)
Eds. H.J. van den Herik, I.S. Herschberg, and J.W.H.M. Uiterwijk
Drukkerij Van Spijk B.V., Venlo, The Netherlands, 316 pages.

Maastricht, The Netherlands (1996, June)
Proceedings of the 8th Advances in Computer Chess Conference (ACC8)
Eds. H.J. van den Herik and J.W.H.M. Uiterwijk
Drukkerij Van Spijk B.V., Venlo, The Netherlands, 332 pages.

Paderborn, Germany (1999, June)
Proceedings of the 9th Advances in Computer Games Conference (ACG9)
Eds. H.J. van den Herik and B. Monien
Van Spijk Grafisch Bedrijf, Venlo, The Netherlands, 347 pages.

Graz, Austria (2003, November)
Proceedings of the 10th Advances in Computer Games Conference (ACG10)
Eds. H.J. van den Herik, H. Iida, and E.A. Heinz
Kluwer Academic Publishers, Boston/Dordrecht/London, 382 pages.

Taipei, Taiwan (2005, September)
Proceedings of the 11th Advances in Computer Games Conference (ACG11)
Eds. H.J. van den Herik, S-C. Hsu, T-s. Hsu, and H.H.L.M. Donkers
Springer Verlag, Berlin/Heidelberg, LNCS 4250, 372 pages.

Pamplona, Spain (2009, May)
Proceedings of the 12th Advances in Computer Games Conference (ACG12)
Eds. H.J. van den Herik and P. Spronck
Springer Verlag, Berlin/Heidelberg, LNCS 6048, 231 pages.

Tilburg, The Netherlands (2011, November)
Proceedings of the 13th Advances in Computer Games Conference (ACG13)
Eds. H.J. van den Herik and A. Plaat
Springer Verlag, Berlin/Heidelberg, LNCS 7168, 356 pages.

Leiden, The Netherlands (2015, July)
Proceedings of the 14th Advances in Computer Games Conference (ACG14)
Eds. A. Plaat, H.J. van den Herik, and W. Kosters
Springer, Heidelberg, LNCS 9525, 266 pages.

The Computers and Games Books

The series of Computers and Games (CG) Conferences started in 1998 as a complement to the well-known series of conferences in Advances in Computer Chess (ACC). Since 1998, nine CG conferences have been held. Below we list the conference places and dates together with the Springer publication (LNCS series number).

Tsukuba, Japan (1998, November)
Proceedings of the 1st Computers and Games Conference (CG98)
Eds. H.J. van den Herik and H. Iida
Springer Verlag, Berlin/Heidelberg, LNCS 1558, 335 pages.

Hamamatsu, Japan (2000, October)
Proceedings of the 2nd Computers and Games Conference (CG2000)
Eds. T.A. Marsland and I. Frank
Springer Verlag, Berlin/Heidelberg, LNCS 2063, 442 pages.

Edmonton, Canada (2002, July)
Proceedings of the 3rd Computers and Games Conference (CG2002)
Eds. J. Schaeffer, M. Müller, and Y. Björnsson
Springer Verlag, Berlin/Heidelberg, LNCS 2883, 431 pages.

Ramat-Gan, Israel (2004, July)
Proceedings of the 4th Computers and Games Conference (CG2004)
Eds. H.J. van den Herik, Y. Björnsson, and N.S. Netanyahu
Springer Verlag, Berlin/Heidelberg, LNCS 3846, 404 pages.

Turin, Italy (2006, May)
Proceedings of the 5th Computers and Games Conference (CG2006)
Eds. H.J. van den Herik, P. Ciancarini, and H.H.L.M. Donkers
Springer Verlag, Berlin/Heidelberg, LNCS 4630, 283 pages.

Beijing, China (2008, September)
Proceedings of the 6th Computers and Games Conference (CG2008)
Eds. H.J. van den Herik, X. Xu, Z. Ma, and M.H.M. Winands
Springer Verlag, Berlin/Heidelberg, LNCS 5131, 275 pages.

Kanazawa, Japan (2010, September)
Proceedings of the 7th Computers and Games Conference (CG2010)
Eds. H.J. van den Herik, H. Iida, and A. Plaat
Springer Verlag, Berlin/Heidelberg, LNCS 6515, 275 pages.

Yokohama, Japan (2013, August)
Proceedings of the 8th Computers and Games Conference (CG2013)
Eds. H.J. van den Herik, H. Iida, and A. Plaat
Springer, Heidelberg, LNCS 8427, 260 pages.

Leiden, The Netherlands (2016, July)
Proceedings of the 9th Computers and Games Conference (CG2016)
Eds. A. Plaat, H.J. van den Herik, and W.A. Kosters
Springer, Heidelberg, LNCS 10068, 225 pages.

Contents

Using Partial Tablebases in Breakthrough

Andrew Isaac and Richard Lorentz[✉]

Department of Computer Science, California State University,
Northridge, CA 91330-8281, USA
andrew.isaac.37@my.csun.edu, lorentz@csun.edu

Abstract. In the game of Breakthrough the endgame is reached when there are still many pieces on the board. This means there are too many possible positions to be able to construct a reasonable endgame tablebase on the standard 8×8 board, or even on a 6×6 board. The fact that Breakthrough pieces only move forward allows us to create partial tablebases on the last n rows of each side of the board. We show how doing this enables us to create a much stronger MCTS based 6×6 player and allows us to solve positions that would otherwise be out of reach.

1 Introduction

Recently the game of Breakthrough has been attracting attention among researchers [1,4,6,7]. It has a simple set of rules, an interesting mix of strategy and tactics, and scales easily to different sizes. In this work we describe the construction of endgame tablebases for Breakthrough, focusing on boards of size 6×6.

Endgame tablebases are usually full board databases of a game at a stage when very few pieces remain and are typically constructed using retrograde analysis [8]. For example, in chess Nalimov tablebases have been used and expanded for many years now [5]. In Breakthrough, however, the endgame is reached while there are still many pieces on the board. Breakthrough is normally played on an 8×8 board and typically the endgame is reached while more than half the pieces are still on the board. With 8 or fewer pieces per player on a 64 square board there are simply too many legal positions to consider constructing a normal tablebase. In fact, even on a 6×6 board it is already impractical.

The rules of Breakthrough require that pieces always move towards the goal. Because of the forward running of pieces it is possible to recognize forced wins in positions by just looking at rows near the goal, that is, rows near the end of the board. The forward running also allows for a kind of iterative retrograde approach to constructing the tablebase. Given a tablebase containing all wins for White in the last $n-1$ rows we can use it to construct wins for White from the last n rows. Once constructed we can use the tablebases to improve the play of a Breakthrough playing program and use them to solve positions on smaller boards by simply applying the game playing program enhanced with the tablebase.

In Sect. 2 we briefly describe Breakthrough and give some examples of the endgame. Section 3 is where we describe our notion of tablebases, how we build them, and how we use them in an MCTS based Breakthrough player. In Sect. 4

© Springer International Publishing AG 2016
A. Plaat et al. (Eds.): CG 2016, LNCS 10068, pp. 1–10, 2016.
DOI: 10.1007/978-3-319-50935-8_1

we show what we were able to accomplish using tablebases in 6×6 Breakthrough and Sect. 5 summarizes our results and points towards future directions of research.

2   The Game of Breakthrough and Its Endgame

Breakthrough is usually played on an 8×8 board but our studies will focus on the smaller 6×6 board. Each player begins with 12 pieces as shown on the left of Fig. 1. White pieces move one square at a time either diagonally or vertically to unoccupied squares and towards row 6, the goal row. White may capture a black piece if the piece is located where a diagonal legal move could be made – as a chess pawn might capture. A white piece cannot move straight forward if that square is occupied by either a white or a black piece. Black moves similarly in the other direction. The first player to have a piece reach the goal row or to capture all of the enemy pieces is the winner. White plays first.

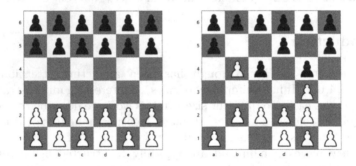

Fig. 1. Sample 6×6 breakthrough positions.

The right of Fig. 1 shows a position in the middle of a game. If it is White's turn to play, the piece on square b4 can capture the black piece on a5 or move to b5 or c5. If Black is to move, the black piece on square e4 can move to either d3 or f3 but not e3.

To get a feel for the number of endgame positions possible in Breakthrough we consider situations with six or fewer pieces for each player, with White to move, and note that we are only interested in positions where there is no white piece on either of the last two rows (else the game is over or White has a win-in-1) and there is no black piece on the first row (else Black has already won). In the case of a 6×6 board, for each placement of 1 through 6 white pieces in the first 4 rows, we place 6 black pieces on the last 5 rows on the unoccupied squares. We underestimate the true total by assuming that all white pieces occupy squares that a black piece might also occupy, even though this is not true if a black piece is on one of its first two rows. It leads us to Eq. (1) as an estimate of the number of positions possible with six or fewer pieces of each color.

$$\sum_{i=1}^{6} \left(\binom{24}{i} \times \sum_{k=1}^{6} \binom{30-i}{k} \right) \approx 4.03 \times 10^{10} \tag{1}$$

Similarly, Eq. (2) estimates the number of endame positions on an 8 × 8 board with no more than 8 pieces of any color.

$$\sum_{i=1}^{8} \left(\binom{48}{i} \times \sum_{k=1}^{8} \binom{56-i}{k} \right) \approx 2.25 \times 10^{17} \tag{2}$$

Both of the above counts include illegal positions, e.g., all of the white pieces are on the first 3 rows of column a and b. However, the number of illegal positions is quite small given how few pieces are on the board and so the estimates given above are reasonable.

3   Endgame Tablebases

Any board configuration with White to move that has a white piece on row 5 is a win-in-1 because White can simply move to the goal row. An effective win-in-3 is a board configuration where White can make a move that preserves a win-in-1 against any black defense. This either means that Black has no defense and White will win on the next move or Black can prevent the immediate win but White can follow with a move that restores it.

For example, in the position on the left of Fig. 2 White has a win-in-3 by moving 1. d4–d5. Black must continue to defend the win-in-1 by capturing the advanced piece, which White in turn recaptures until White finally lands on row 5 and is invulnerable to capture. Thus the win-in-3 actually takes a total of 7 moves.

The position in the middle of Fig. 2 shows an effective win-in-5 that actually requires 9 moves to complete. The idea is that White must clear the Black d6 piece so that White will be able to play f3–f4–e5–f6. After 1. c3 × b4 Black is forced to play 2. c5 × b4 else White wins by moving to or capturing a5. White then plays 3. c4–c5, Black is forced to capture and White wins with the f4 piece. Since Black must reply to White's first two moves, it is an effective win-in-5.

The rightmost position of Fig. 2 shows an effective win-in-9. It is a win-in-9 because two preparatory moves need to be made in the process of advancing to the goal. The main line is: 1. b3 × c4, 2. e5 × d4, 3. c3 × d4, 4. a5–a4, 5. f3–e4, 6. f5 × e4, 7. e3–f4, 8. a4–a3, 9. f4–f5, 10. e6 × f5, 11. d4–d5, 12. c6 × d5, 13. c4 × d5, 14. a3–a2, 15. d5–e6. We can see that most of the moves are either forcing moves or moves advancing towards the goal, but moves 1 and 7 are extra moves needed to prepare for the breakthrough at d5.

Using this concept of a forced win, where defensive moves by the opponent are not counted towards the move count, board configurations can be stored in a tablebase along with their effective number of moves required to win. During game play a player can consult the tablebase to determine if a forced win exists

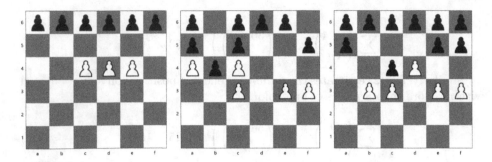

Fig. 2. Forced wins.

and in how many effective moves. By comparing any forced wins White or Black may have it is possible to determine who will win the game even with a significant portion of the game left to play.

The rules of Breakthrough require pieces to move in one direction up or down the board, so once an opponent's piece has progressed beyond a certain row, it is no longer defensively relevant to a win involving pieces in rows that it has already passed. For example, a forced win that only requires White to use pieces in the top 3 rows is certain to be an effective forced win-in-3 because every move threatens a win-in-1 and so must be responded to. A forced win that requires White to use pieces in the top 4 rows must be at least a forced win-in-5, since there will be at least one time when white moves from row 3 to row 4 and after Black answers at best a win-in-3 will have been created. In this case if Black has an effective win-in-3 moves (or less) after White makes its move, Black will have the winning position.

Any board configuration can be represented as an integer using Gödel numbering, so if a certain configuration can be identified as a forced win, the integer value of that configuration can be added to a database of forced wins, along with any other information related to the configuration, such as the effective number of moves required or the next move the player needs to make to achieve the forced win. If every forced win can be identified, the game itself would be solved. To limit the size of the tablebase of forced wins to be solely resident in RAM and to be able to construct the tablebase in a reasonable amount of time, only forced wins that involve pieces located on the last n rows, for some suitable n, are included. During game play, the current board state in those n rows can be converted to its integer value and the endgame tablebase can be consulted to determine if a forced win has been achieved.

3.1   Building an Endgame Tablebase for Breakthrough

Below we discuss the following three topics. Building an endgame tablebase for Breakthrough in Sect. 3.1; n x 6 tablebases in Sect. 3.2; using endgame tablebases in Sect. 3.3.

To construct a tablebase for 6×6 Breakthrough that is limited in size and can be quickly queried, the top 3 rows are first examined to identify any effective forced wins-in-3. This is done by iterating through all valid configurations of pieces that may exist in the top 3 rows. Assuming White to move, any white pieces in row 6 can be skipped, since that is already a win, as well as any white pieces in row 5 as that is a trivial win-in-1. Only configurations where there are some white pieces on row 4 and Black pieces on any of the top 2 rows need to be examined as possible forced wins. We start with 1 white piece and build up to more pieces. Configurations that either have White to move to row 5 and where it is invulnerable to capture, or that will eventually lead to White being able to move to row 5 and be invulnerable to capture as the result of responses by Black get added to the tablebase until all possible forced wins in 3 moves are found.

Once all forced wins only requiring pieces that belong to the top three rows are found, this process is repeated for the all possible combinations within the top 4 rows, skipping any forced wins already found in the top 3 rows from the previous step. We repeat the process similarly for the top five rows.

The order the pieces are placed goes from fewer to more white pieces and within a fixed number of white pieces from higher numbered to lower numbered rows. This allows us to fill the tablebase in a single pass.

In order for a configuration to be added to the tablebase it has to be determined if White has a forced win. For every possible white move, all possible black responses are tested. For every black response, if White has a forced win that is already in the tablebase the configuration is added to the tablebase.

To determine the total number of moves required for the forced win once it is identified it is assumed that White will choose the move that leads to the shortest previously found forced win, while Black will choose the move that leads to longest inevitable loss. In order to determine the effective number of moves of a forced win, an imaginary offensive move by Black is applied. If making the offensive move by Black results in a better forced win for White, it is assumed that Black instead will choose to make a defensive move. If the effective number of moves for a forced win is the same whether Black makes a defensive or offensive move, it is assumed that Black will use the opportunity to make an offensive move over a defensive move.

For every board configuration entered into the tablebase, the symmetric configuration is added as well. An important feature of this optimization when combined with the order that white pieces are added to the board as described above is that all forced wins get added to the tablebase in a single run. Without the addition of symmetries or by using a poor ordering of positions, forced wins may go undetected when the forced win testing program is run a single time, requiring a second run (or more) to find the remaining wins.

3.2 $n \times 6$ Tablebases

A summary of the complete tablebase that we created for 6×6 Breakthrough can be seen in Table 1. Notice that there are no wins-in-3 for the 4-row tablebase.

Table 1. Tablebase contents

Rows	3	4
Wins-in-3	227,547	0
Wins-in-5	0	19,888,955
Wins-in-7	0	642,417
Wins-in-9	0	6,170
Wins-in-11	0	190
Wins-in-13	0	5
Wins-in-15	0	0
Total forced wins	227,547	20,537,737
Time to generate	15 s	2.5 h

This is because it is impossible for a White piece on row 3 or lower to affect such a fast win.

In contrast, it is possible to have a win-in-5 that involves row 2 or 1. Consider the first diagram in Fig. 3. After White has moved d2–d3 Black is in zugzwang and once Black moves White has a straightforward short win. It is because of the zugzwang that White is suddenly presented with a shorter win than was available before Black moved.

The right side of Fig. 3 shows one of the longest wins in the tablebase. Being a win-in-13 means that White will make a total of 7 moves. Three of the moves advance the piece from row 3 to row 6 and the other 4 moves aid in this advancement.

It is worth pointing out that Black actually has a shorter win in this position but the tablebase only reports wins for White. When the tablebase is actually used, after finding the win-in-13 for White it will make White's first move and query the database to see if Black indeed has a faster win. Here is a summary of White's win-in-13 with a shorter win for Black pointed out. 1. e3–e4, (the key to the winning attack is to breakthrough using the c4 square) 2. f5 × e4, 3. f3 × e4,

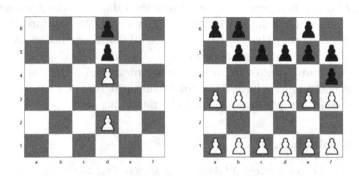

Fig. 3. 5 row win-in-5 (left) and 5 row win-in-13 (right).

4. f4–f3, 5. a3–a4, 6. c5–d4, 7. a4 × b5, 8. a6 × b5, (a forced move by Black
and does not count towards the mate count) 9. b3–b4, (as far as the tablebase is
concerned, Black is now in zugzwang, but in this particular board position Black
can make a move that threatens a win that is shorter than White's) 10. d4–e3,
11. b4–a5, 12. b6 × a5, (forced) 13. d3–d4, and now White has an obvious win-
in-3 that completes the original win-in-13, though Black has an equally obvious
win-in-3 and so would actually win this game.

3.3 Using Endgame Tablebases

There are a number of natural places in an MCTS based program one might
use tablebases. We have an EPT (early playout termination [3]) program named
WANDERER [4] that plays the game of Breakthrough and we use it to study the
various options.

In the spirit of EPT it makes sense to access the tablebases during the random
playouts. The simplest approach would be to augment the evaluation function
to test if either player has a faster forced win than the other and if so, return
accordingly. In contrast, if at any time during the playout, not just at the end
when the evaluation is invoked, it can be determined that a player has a forced
win it would be a shame to ignore this important information. But it is not cheap
to query the tablebase so the multiple queries could prove to be too expensive. As
it turns out the advantage of immediately recognizing the forced win overshadows
the cost of the queries and so checking the tablebase after every move in the
playout is to be preferred. This is not entirely surprising because in a similar
way with both Havannah and Breakthrough we have shown it is preferable to
detect a win-in-1 and make that move during a playout rather than just make a
random move [2,4].

The other place to consider querying the tablebase is during tree expansion.
When expanding a node in the MCTS tree, if the tablebase shows that a child
node allows a forced win by the opponent there is no need to add the node to
the tree as a player will never select a move that allows the opponent to win.
A simplified version of this is already done in WANDERER in order to aid the
MCTS solver: if a position is found that allows a win-in-1 by the opponent (or
an easy to see win-in-3) then that child is not added to the tree.

But querying the tablebase at every node creation can be very slow. Our
tests show that given a fixed amount of time the size of the tree we are able to
create when doing these queries is less than half the size than when we do not
make the queries. Further, the tests show that this is too high a price to pay and
the version of WANDERER without the queries easily outperforms the one with
them under normal time constraints (see Table 2 in Sect. 4).

It is possible that a forced win for White requiring pieces in the top 5 rows
can actually be a shorter effective win than a forced win for White only requiring
pieces in the top 4 rows, and likewise an effective forced win requiring all 6 rows
can be a shorter forced win than a forced win requiring fewer rows. Since the
tablebase only holds entries for all forced wins located 5 rows or less from the
winning row, it is possible that a forced win requiring all 6 rows, which is not

contained within the tablebase due to size and time limitations, could be a better effective forced win. The best forced win requiring pieces located 6 rows from winning would be at least an effective win in nine moves, so only effective forced wins in the tablebase that are nine moves or less are considered to be reliable forced wins when the tablebase is queried.

We are also interested in solving Breakthrough positions with an ultimate goal of solving 6×6 Breakthrough. So far the best results along these lines are by [6] where they solve 5×6 Breakthrough. When trying to solve positions the faster we can eliminate nodes, the better. In this case it is more important to prove and remove nodes quickly than to find promising moves. Our tests show that by querying the tablebase at the time of node creation and not adding losing nodes we can solve positions eight or more times faster and use comparably less RAM.

4   Results

In order to gauge any change in performance we ran a number of tests that are summarized in Table 2. TB$n$rows denotes a version of Breakthrough using a tablebase that checks n or fewer rows and noTB represents a version of Breakthrough using no tablebases at all. TBtree denotes a version of WANDERER that queries the 4-row tablebase both in the random playouts and when adding nodes to the tree. None of the other versions check during node expansion.

Tests showed that versions of WANDERER that use the tablebase performed considerably better than the version that did not. Additionally we found that, despite the slowdown required to make additional queries to the tablebase, WANDERER performed best when making use of the 4 or 5-row tablebase, while the 5-row tablebase did not seem to show significant game playing improvement over the 4-row tablebase.[1] Test #7 shows that querying the tablebase when building the tree is too expensive for real-time play.

When trying to solve positions, however, querying the tablebase when building the tree is fruitful. In order to aid in the solving, we made some plain modifications to WANDERER (mainly in terms of its evaluation function) and found that adding tablebase queries as the tree is being built reduces the solving times by at least a factor of six. We have been able to solve every position we have tried 6 moves from the beginning of the game, most positions 5 moves from the start of the game, and many from 4 moves. We have not found any positions after just 3 moves that we can solve, indicating we are still some distance from actually solving 6×6 Breakthrough. Our hope is to be able to solve 6×6 Breakthrough by simply using existing tools of tablebases and WANDERER.

---

[1] Time and space requirements prevented us from creating a complete 5-row tablebase so we created an abbreviated version where we further restricted the number of pieces on the board.

Table 2. Test results with 6×6 breakthrough

Test #	Player A	Player B	Player A white	Player B white	Player A vs. player B
1	noTB	noTB	124–76	127–73	197–203
2	TB3rows	noTB	157–43	65–135	292–108
3	TB4rows	noTB	173–27	38–162	335–65
4	TB5rows	noTB	182–18	35–165	347–53
5	TB4rows	TB3rows	175–25	77–123	298–102
6	TB5rows	TB4rows	132–68	127–73	205–195
7	TB4rows	TBtree	159–41	96–104	263–137

5   Conclusions and Future Work

We have shown that incomplete tablebases can significantly improve the performance of a 6×6 Breakthrough playing program. Even a straightforward 3-row tablebase provides significant improvement and adding a 4th row improves quite a bit more. We were unable to complete a full 5-row tablebase, but we were still a bit surprised that adding the partial 5th row did not improve the program. This point requires further research.

Ultimately we want to extend these ideas to 8×8 Breakthrough and improve WANDERER, our competitive program. The increase in size from 6×6 to 8×8 provides some difficulties. We can produce a 3-row tablebase and expect some improvement from that, but a complete 4-row tablebase is just too big. As a result, we plan to create a 4×6 tablebase and query that on both sides of the 8×8 board.

Finally, though we are still some distance from solving 6×6 Breakthrough we conjecture that it is a win for White since all reasonable positions that we have solved after 4 or 5 opening moves have proven to be wins for White. This goes against the opinion of most Breakthrough players because (1) 5×5 Breakthrough is a win for Black and (2) there are a number of common positions reached in competitive 8×8 Breakthrough games where Black has the forced win.

References

1. Finnsson, H., Björnsson, Y.: Game-tree properties and MCTS performance. In: IJCAI Workshop on General Game Playing (GIGA11) (2011)
2. Lorentz, R.: Experiments with Monte-Carlo tree search in the game of Havannah. ICGA J. **34**(3), 12–21 (2011)
3. Lorentz, R.: Early playout termination in MCTS. In: Plaat, A., Herik, J., Kosters, W. (eds.) ACG 2015. LNCS, vol. 9525, pp. 12–19. Springer, Heidelberg (2015). doi:10.1007/978-3-319-27992-3_2
4. Lorentz, R., Horey, T.: Programming breakthrough. In: Herik, H.J., Iida, H., Plaat, A. (eds.) CG 2013. LNCS, vol. 8427, pp. 49–59. Springer, Heidelberg (2014). doi:10.1007/978-3-319-09165-5_5

5. Nalimov, E.V., Haworth, G.M., Heinz, E.A.: Experiments with Monte-Carlo tree search in the game of Havannah. ICGA J. **23**(3), 148–162 (2000)
6. Saffidine, A., Jouandeau, N., Cazenave, T.: Solving breakthrough with race patterns and job-level proof number search. In: Herik, H.J., Plaat, A. (eds.) ACG 2011. LNCS, vol. 7168, pp. 196–207. Springer, Heidelberg (2012). doi:10.1007/978-3-642-31866-5_17
7. Skowronski, P., Björnsson, Y., Winands, M.H.M.: Automated discovery of search-extension features. In: Herik, H.J., Spronck, P. (eds.) ACG 2009. LNCS, vol. 6048, pp. 182–194. Springer, Heidelberg (2010). doi:10.1007/978-3-642-12993-3_17
8. Thompson, K.: Retrograde analysis of certain endgames. ICGA J. **9**(3), 131–139 (1986)

Using Deep Convolutional Neural Networks in Monte Carlo Tree Search

Tobias Graf[✉] and Marco Platzner

University of Paderborn, Paderborn, Germany
tobiasg@mail.upb.de, platzner@upb.de

Abstract. Deep Convolutional Neural Networks have revolutionized Computer Go. Large networks have emerged as state-of-the-art models for move prediction and are used not only as stand-alone players but also inside Monte Carlo Tree Search to select and bias moves. Using neural networks inside the tree search is a challenge due to their slow execution time even if accelerated on a GPU. In this paper we evaluate several strategies to limit the number of nodes in the search tree in which neural networks are used. All strategies are assessed using the freely available cuDNN library. We compare our strategies against an optimal upper bound which can be estimated by removing timing constraints. We show that the best strategies are only 50 ELO points worse than this upper bound.

1 Introduction

Deep Convolutional Neural Networks (DCNNs) have changed Computer Go substantially [5,11,12,14]. They can predict expert moves at such a high quality that they even can play Go themselves at a reasonable level [14]. Used in Monte Carlo Tree Search (MCTS) [2] to select and bias moves they can increase playing strength by hundreds of ELOs. During the writing of this paper Google DeepMind has released their program AlphaGo [12] which uses neural networks not only for move prediction but also for positional evaluation. For the first time in Computer Go their program has beaten a professional player and is going to challenge one of the best players in the world.

DCNNs achieved remarkable improvements but they pose a challenge for MCTS as their execution time is too slow to be used in the whole search tree. While a remedy is to use several GPUs [12] this paper focuses on single GPU scenarios where not all nodes in the search tree can use the DCNN as a move predictor. To decide which nodes profit the most from DCNN knowledge several strategies are possible. This paper evaluates four typical strategies to replace knowledge from fast classifiers with DCNN predictions. All strategies are assessed within the same Go program to decide which is best. Moreover, we construct an upper bound on playing strength by using an equal test environment but removing timing constraints. We then compare the strategies with this upper bound to show the loss in playing strength resulting from the use of replacement strategies.

© Springer International Publishing AG 2016
A. Plaat et al. (Eds.): CG 2016, LNCS 10068, pp. 11–21, 2016.
DOI: 10.1007/978-3-319-50935-8_2

The contributions of our paper are as follows.

- We demonstrate that replacing traditional move prediction knowledge in Computer Go programs can yield remarkable improvements in playing strength.
- We investigate the scalability of knowledge in MCTS, i.e., in how far do better neural networks lead to stronger MCTS-players.
- As DCNNs are too slow to be used in the complete search tree we explore several strategies to decide which nodes profit the most from DCNNs.
- We look into technical aspects of using GPUs inside MCTS.

The remainder of this paper is structured as follows: In Sect. 2 we describe the settings and architectures of the deep convolutional neural networks we use in the paper. In Sect. 3 we outline several replacement strategies for an efficient application of slow knowledge in MCTS. In Sect. 4 we show the results of several experiments regarding the quality of DCNNs and replacement strategies. In Sect. 5 we present related work. Finally, in Sect. 6 we draw our conclusion and point to future directions.

2 Deep Convolutional Neural Networks

In this section we outline the Deep Convolutional Neural Networks which are used in this paper. The architecture of our DCNNs is similar to [11]. We use several convolutional layers (3, 6 or 12) with 5×5 filter in the first one and 3×3 in the others. The width of each layer is 128, 192 or 256. After all convolutional layers we add an extra 3×3 convolutional layer with one output feature followed by a softmax layer. The position is encoded with black to move (if white moves the colors of the stones are reversed). The 20 input features of the neural network are:

- Black, White, Empty, Border
- Last 5 moves
- Legality
- Liberties (1, 2, 3, ≥4)
- Liberties after move (1, 2, 3, 4, 5, ≥6)

We used the Caffe framework [10] to train all DCNNs. We trained the networks with plain SGD with mini-batch size 128 for 3 million iterations (one iteration is one mini-batch). The learning rate is 0.05 for the first 1.5 million iterations and then halved for the rest of the training every 500,000 iterations. We used a weight decay of 1e-6 and initialized all weights with the msra-filler [8]. As dataset of Go games we used KGS games[1] with players having at least 4 dan strength using only no-handicap games which have at least 150 moves. The positions are split into a validation set with 1,280,000 positions and a training set with 60,026,402 positions. Positions of both sets are from distinct games. The positions in the training set are randomly rotated and mirrored to one of 8 possible orientations.

---

[1] http://u-go.net/gamerecords-4d/.

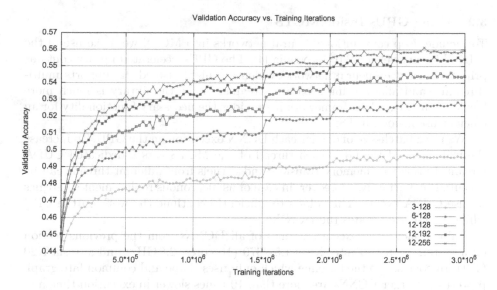

Fig. 1. Accuracy on validation set during training

Figure 1 shows the accuracy on the validation set during training. Accuracy is the percentage of positions where the top model prediction equals the move of the expert. After 1.5, 2.0 and 2.5 million iterations sharp increases in accuracy due to the learning-rate schedule can be observed. The achieved validation accuracy after training is comparable to those reached in [11].

3   Integration of DCNNs into MCTS

Deep Convolutional Neural Networks need considerably more computing time than conventional models used in MCTS. This section surveys several techniques to include DCNNs into MCTS without hampering the speed of the search.

3.1   Selection Formula

To include knowledge into MCTS we use the following formula which includes RAVE [6] and progressive bias [3].

$$(1 - \beta) \cdot Q_{\text{Uct}}(s, a) + \beta \cdot Q_{\text{Rave}}(s, a) + K \frac{\pi(s, a)}{\sqrt{\text{visits}(s, a)}}$$

where $\pi(s, a) \in [0, 1]$ is the output of the move prediction model.

3.2   Using GPUs Inside MCTS

To include deep convolutional neural networks into MCTS we make use of the cuDNN library version 3.0^2 of Nvidia [4]. The GPU-accelerated library contains primitives for deep neural networks which are highly tuned. It supports multithreading and allows using separate streams. While the library is much more low level than the Caffe framework it provides the necessary functionality for an efficient use inside MCTS.

We use a batch-size of one for each DCNN execution on the GPU. To increase the utilization of the GPU each thread of the MCTS gets a dedicated CUDA stream. In this way memory transfers and kernels from different threads can be executed concurrently. Moreover, in case of asynchronous replacement strategies we use CUDA events. This allows to efficiently continue the work on the CPU while the GPU evaluates the DCNN.

Table 1 shows the execution times of all DCNNs from the previous section on a system with two Intel Xeon E5-2670 (16 cores, 2.6 GHz) and a Tesla K20 GPU. In contrast to the baseline which only uses shape and common fate graph patterns [7] larger DCNNs are more than 10 times slower in execution time and achieve less than half the playout-rate.

Table 1. Execution time, playout-rate in MCTS and accuracy

	Execution time	Playout-rate MCTS	Accuracy validation-set
Baseline	0.38 ms	11552 p/s	42.1%
DCNN-3-128	0.94 ms	10734 p/s	49.6%
DCNN-6-128	1.70 ms	8939 p/s	52.7%
DCNN-12-128	3.23 ms	5458 p/s	54.4%
DCNN-12-192	7.52 ms	3111 p/s	55.4%
DCNN-12-256	10.07 ms	2338 p/s	55.9%

3.3   Replacement Strategies

In this paper we explore four replacement strategies for knowledge inside MCTS. We assume that a fast move predictor (e.g., [7,13]) is available in addition to the slower DCNN. This allows to specify different strategies to decide which knowledge can be used. All replacement strategies try to predict which nodes inside the search tree are important. In these nodes they apply the slow knowledge as soon as possible. All strategies can be formulated in a synchronous and an asynchronous version. On the one hand, the advantage of the synchronous version is that MCTS does not waste iterations with low quality knowledge. On the other hand, asynchronous versions can continue with the search. They will use more low quality knowledge in the beginning but in return can search faster and build a deeper search tree.

---

[2] We also tested the release candidate of version 4. We observed faster single execution times but a small slowdown when used in parallel MCTS.

Replace by Depth. This strategy decides which node gets DCNN knowledge by the depth of each node in the search tree. We specify a parameter D and every node with depth $\leq D$ gets DCNN knowledge while all others nodes only use the fast classifier. At an extreme with $D = 0$ only the root node receives DCNN knowledge. The reasoning behind this strategy is that decisions near the root are the most important and should use the best knowledge available. Disadvantages are that the parameter D is highly dependent on the overall time spent for the search and thus has to be changed for different thinking times. Moreover, MCTS builds up a very irregular search tree where some promising branches are searched very deeply while others are not. On the one hand, specifying an overall depth threshold cannot capture this important aspect of MCTS. On the other hand, this strategy does its decision at node initialization so that knowledge can be fully utilized.

The strategy can be turned into an asynchronous version by initializing each node with fast knowledge and for nodes with depth $\leq D$ immediately a request is sent to the GPU. Once the DCNN execution has been finished it replaces the fast knowledge of the node.

Replace in Principal-Variation. Beginning from the root node we can follow in each node of the search tree the move which has been investigated most. The sequence of moves resulting from this is called the principal variation and represents best play from both sides. The following strategy tries to identify the principal variation of the search and initializes all nodes of this variation with slow DCNN knowledge. All other nodes are interpreted as less important and are using fast knowledge. In MCTS the principal variation changes during the search quite often so we also want to include variations which are close. This leads to the following strategy with the parameter $\epsilon \in [0, 1]$: When starting MCTS at the root we set a flag $PV \leftarrow true$. If the move a is selected and the count of the move n_a is smaller than $\epsilon \cdot max_a n_a$ then $PV \leftarrow false$ else it is unchanged. When a new node is expanded we initialize the node with DCNN knowledge if PV is true. Otherwise, the node is initialized with the fast classifier. Moreover, if we encounter nodes during tree traversal which do not have DCNN knowledge we replace it with DCNN knowledge if PV is true. In the synchronous version we wait until the knowledge is available. In the asynchronous version we continue the work.

The advantage of the strategy is that DCNN knowledge can be utilized early in the search as important nodes are identified before expansion. In contrast to the depth-replacement strategy it is also independent of the overall search time and adapts to the irregular shape of the search tree. The disadvantage is that if the principal variation is not followed early on in the search, abrupt changes can occur. Then all nodes in the new principal variation do not have the DCNN knowledge and are thus promoted only now which can be very late in the search.

Replace by Threshold. This strategy initializes the knowledge in each node with the fast classifier. If a node is searched more than T times the fast knowledge is replaced by the DCNN. In the synchronous version a node is locked for other threads and the current thread waits for the GPU to finish the DCNN execution. In the asynchronous version a node is not locked for other threads and the current thread just sends a request to the GPU and continues the MCTS. Once the GPU has finished work the DCNN knowledge is used in the node.

The advantage of this strategy is that the threshold is mostly independent of the overall search time and can thus be easily tuned. Moreover, the more a node is searched by MCTS the more important it is. So this strategy identifies all significant nodes. The disadvantage is that this only happens quite late so that DCNN knowledge cannot be fully utilized in early stages.

Increase Expansion Threshold. MCTS expands nodes after a certain amount of simulations have passed through the node. The default value of ABAKUS is 8, i.e., if a move has more than 8 simulations a new node is expanded. While the value of 8 is optimized for a fast classifier we can increase the value to fit the slow DCNN. The synchronous version of this strategy initializes each node by DCNN knowledge and controls the rate at which nodes are expanded with a threshold E. The asynchronous version initializes each node with the fast classifier and immediately sends a request to the GPU and replaces the knowledge once the DCNN data is available.

The disadvantage of this strategy is that smaller trees are searched when the expansion threshold E is set too high. However, the DCNN knowledge can be exploited in each node from the beginning.

4   Experiments

In this section we show the results of our experiments. We run several tournaments of our program ABAKUS against the open source program PACHI [1]. ABAKUS makes use of RAVE [6], progressive widening [9], progressive bias [3] and a large amount of knowledge (shape and common fate graph patterns [7]) in the tree search part. With the addition of DCNNs it holds a 5-Dan rank on the internet server KGS[3].

As PACHI is weaker than ABAKUS we used handicap games to level the chances. One challenge for the experiments was the great range of strength which results from using DCNNs. Therefore, we used a handicap of 7 stones and komi of 0.5 in all the experiments.

In our first experiments we wanted to illustrate the raw strength improvement one can get by using DCNNs. The DCNN knowledge is used whenever a new node in the search tree is expanded. In this way the shallow knowledge is never used. To achieve a direct comparison we performed games with a fixed amount of playouts. This can also be seen as the maximum strength improvement possible by using the specific DCNN. In practice, these gains cannot be achieved as application of DCNNs; they need considerably more time than the shallow knowledge.

---

[3] www.gokgs.com.

Table 2. Playing strength of ABAKUS (white) against PACHI (black, 7 handicap stones), 512 games played for each entry, 95% confidence intervals, ABAKUS 11,000 playouts/move, PACHI 27,500 playouts/move

	Winrate vs. PACHI	ELO vs. PACHI	ELO vs. baseline	Average speed
Baseline	9.8% ±2.6	−386 [−444, −341]	0	12,092 Playouts/s
DCNN-3-128	49.3% ±4.3	−5 [−35, 25]	381	11,349 Playouts/s
DCNN-6-128	67.4% ±4.1	126 [95, 159]	512	9,277 Playouts/s
DCNN-12-128	78.9% ±3.5	229 [194, 269]	615	5,661 Playouts/s
DCNN-12-192	81.9% ±3.3	263 [226, 305]	649	3,258 Playouts/s
DCNN-12-256	85.6% ±3.0	310 [271, 358]	696	2,456 Playouts/s

The number of playouts per move was chosen as 11,000 for ABAKUS and 27,500 for PACHI. This is approximately the same amount of playouts which each program can achieve in 1 s on an empty board. In this way the experiments are comparable to later experiments which use 1 s thinking time.

The results are shown in Table 2. The better the DCNN is the stronger the program plays against PACHI. But we can also see that the strength improvement declines for the last DCNNs. Moreover, the average speed reduces quickly as more powerful networks are used (which here is not taken into account as the number of playouts is fixed per move).

The next experiments evaluate the four replacement schemes by using a fixed amount of time. We used 1 s per move so that the above results give an approximate upper bound on the playing strength. As the gain by large networks diminishes we used the DCNN-12-128 for the following experiments as it gives a good trade-off between quality and execution time.

In Table 3 we see the results for the replacement scheme depth. The column "DCNN Apply/Coun" shows the average number of simulations of a node when the DCNN knowledge is applied and how often this is done during a search. The depth replacement strategy applies knowledge once a node is expanded but as the search-tree is reused on the next move several old nodes are upgraded with the knowledge. This explains the quite high number of $D = 0$ for apply, whereas the application only uses knowledge in the root.

In Table 4 we see the results for the strategy to increase the expansion threshold to lower the rate of new nodes in the search tree. As long as E is not set too high this strategy achieves as good results as the threshold strategy. It's advantage is that knowledge is applied very early (at about 8 simulations on average) but the search tree is not as big as usual.

In Table 5 we see the results for the principal variation replacement scheme. While the scheme tries to use the DCNN as soon as possible knowledge is often applied quite late (e.g., in the synchronous case for $\epsilon = 0.5$ if the DCNN is used

Table 3. Replace by depth: evaluation with DCNN-12-128 and various parameters D, playing strength of ABAKUS against PACHI, 512 games played for each entry, 95% confidence intervals, 1 s/move

	D	Winrate	ELO	ELO vs UB	DCNN apply/count	Playouts/s
Upper bound		78.9% ± 3.5	229 [194,269]	0		
Synchronous	0	42.6% ± 4.3	−52 [−83, −22]	−281	2169.1/1.2	12077 p/s
	4	59.6% ± 4.3	67 [37, 99]	−162	28.8/201	10892 p/s
	8	63.4% ± 4.2	95 [65, 127]	−134	3.0/539	7694 p/s
	12	60.4% ± 4.2	74 [43, 105]	−155	0.6/629	6125 p/s
Asynchronous	0	41.2% ± 4.3	−62 [−93, −31]	−291	2233.3/1.2	12109 p/s
	4	64.7% ± 4.1	106 [75, 138]	−123	35.9/228	11804 p/s
	8	68.2% ± 4.0	132 [101, 166]	−97	10.7/637	9180 p/s
	12	62.5% ± 4.2	89 [58, 121]	−140	8.1/704	7252 p/s

in a node on average 46 simulations have already passed through it) which shows that the principal variation often changes during a search.

In Table 6 we see the results for the replacement scheme threshold. As soon as the threshold is sufficiently high to not disturb the search the winrate stays quite high. Only for large thresholds the winrate starts to drop as knowledge is applied too late in the nodes.

In conclusion, the strategies to replace knowledge by a simulation threshold or to increase the expansion threshold of MCTS achieve the best results. The depth replacement scheme cannot adapt to the search tree which results in worse playing strength. Using knowledge exclusively in the principal variation accomplished better results but it seems difficult to identify the final principal variation in a search. All strategies performed better when executed asynchronously.

Table 4. Increase expansion-threshold: evaluation with DCNN-12-128 and various parameters E, playing strength of ABAKUS against PACHI, 512 games played for each entry, 95% confidence intervals, 1 s/move

	E	Winrate	ELO	ELO vs UB	DCNN apply/count	Playouts/s
Upper bound		78.9% ± 3.5	229 [194, 269]			
Synchronous	8	58.1% ± 4.3	57 [27, 88]	−172	0.0/634	5513 p/s
	16	64.8% ± 4.1	106 [75, 139]	−123	0.0/449	9551 p/s
	24	69.1% ± 4.0	140 [109, 174]	−89	0.0/313	10743 p/s
	32	72.2% ± 3.9	166 [133, 201]	−63	0.0/236	11167 p/s
Asynchronous	8	67.1% ± 4.1	124 [93,157]	−105	7.5/710	6669 p/s
	16	72.7% ± 3.9	170 [137, 205]	−59	7.4/531	12002 p/s
	24	70.4% ± 4.0	151 [119, 185]	−78	8.1/344	12329 p/s
	32	65.8% ± 4.2	114 [82, 148]	−115	9.1/252	12443 p/s

Table 5. Replace in principal-variation: evaluation with DCNN-12-128 and various parameters ϵ, playing strength of ABAKUS against PACHI, 512 games played for each entry, 95% confidence intervals, 1 s/move

	ϵ	Winrate	ELO	ELO vs UB	DCNN apply/count	Playouts/s
Upper bound		78.9% ± 3.5	229 [194,269]	0		
Synchronous	0.1	63.1% ± 4.2	93 [62, 125]	-136	3.1/590	6827 p/s
	0.2	68.1% ± 4.0	131 [100, 165]	−98	8.3/473	8514 p/s
	0.3	63.6% ± 4.2	97 [66, 129]	−132	15.8/338	9838 p/s
	0.4	67.3% ± 4.1	125 [94, 159]	−104	27.3/228	10639 p/s
	0.5	68.2% ± 4.0	132 [101, 166]	−97	46.0/148	11180 p/s
Asynchronous	0.1	61.7% ± 4.2	83 [52,115]	−146	11.6/691	7947 p/s
	0.2	65.6% ± 4.1	112 [81, 145]	−117	17.8/592	9728 p/s
	0.3	71.3% ± 3.9	158 [126, 193]	−71	26.0/447	10810 p/s
	0.4	66.6 ± 4.1	120 [89, 153]	−109	36.7/317	11375 p/s
	0.5	64.3% ± 4.2	102 [71, 134]	−127	51.2/219	11707 p/s

Table 6. Replace by threshold: evaluation with DCNN-12-128 and various parameters T, playing strength of ABAKUS against PACHI, 512 games played for each entry, 95% confidence intervals, 1 s/move

	T	Winrate	ELO	ELO vs UB	DCNN apply/count	Playouts/s
Upper bound		78.9% ± 3.5	229 [194,269]			
Synchronous	0	58.1% ± 4.3	57 [27, 88]	−172	0.0/634	5513 p/s
	8	67.0% ± 4.1	123 [92, 156]	−106	8.0/493	8026 p/s
	16	70.3% ± 4.0	150 [118, 184]	−79	16.0/382	9174 p/s
	32	67.6% ± 4.1	128 [96, 161]	−101	32.0/256	10052 p/s
	64	66.5% ± 4.1	119 [88, 152]	−110	64.0/153	10678 p/s
	128	68.8% ± 4.0	137 [105, 171]	−92	128.0/85	11195 p/s
Asynchronous	0	67.1% ± 4.1	124 [93, 157]	−105	7.5/710	6669 p/s
	8	73.2% ± 3.8	175 [142, 211]	−54	16.1/653	10886 p/s
	16	69.0% ± 4.0	139 [108, 173]	−90	23.5/484	11711 p/s
	32	71.5% ± 3.9	160 [127, 195]	−69	40.6/307	11981 p/s
	64	70.8% ± 3.9	154 [122, 189]	−75	74.8/175	12066 p/s
	128	66.9% ± 4.1	122 [91, 155]	−107	141.7/94	12118 p/s

5   Related Work

Deep Convolutional Neural Networks have been first used as stand-alone players [5] without using MCTS. Later DCNNs were used inside MCTS [11] with the help of asynchronous node evaluation. A large mini-batch size of 128 taking 150ms for evaluation is used and every node in the search tree is added to the mini-batch in FIFO order. Once the mini-batch is complete it is submitted to the GPU. The disadvantage of the method is a large lag due to using a big mini-batch. According to the authors the main reason for using such a large mini-batch size was that reducing the size was not beneficial in their implementation. As shown in this paper using the freely available cuDNN library of Nvidia allows to reduce the mini-batch size to one which substantially reduces the lag.

The DARKFOREST [14] program uses a synchronized expansion. Whenever a node is added the GPU evaluates the DCNN while the MCTS waits for the result and only then expands the search tree (Synchronous Replace by Threshold with T = 0).

ALPHAGO [12] uses the strategy which we call in our paper Increase-Expansion-Threshold. Knowledge inside the MCTS is initialized with a fast classifier and asynchronously updated once the GPU has evaluated the DCNN. They use a threshold of 40 which in relation to our experiments is quite large but they use DCNNs for move prediction and positional evaluation which results in twice as many neural networks to evaluate.

6   Conclusions and Future Work

In this paper we demonstrated that using Deep Convolutional Neural Networks in Monte Carlo Tree Search yields large improvements in playing strength. We showed that in contrast to the baseline program which already uses a great deal of knowledge DCNNs can boost the playing strength by several hundreds of ELO. Ignoring execution time better move predictors led to better playing strength with improvements close to 700 ELO.

Because DCNNs have slow execution times we suggested to use the cuDNN library of Nvidia to accelerate them on the GPU. Using different CUDA streams for each MCTS search thread fully utilizes the GPU. CUDA events allowed to asynchronously execute the DCNN on the GPU while continuing with the tree search on the CPU.

To decide which nodes in the search tree profit most from DCNN knowledge we investigated several replacement strategies. The results show that the best strategy is to initialize the knowledge used inside MCTS with a fast classifier and when sufficient simulations have passed through a node in the search tree replace it with the DCNN knowledge. A second possibility is to increase the expansion threshold inside MCTS. As long as the threshold is not large the results were close to the best strategy. In the experiments in all replacement schemes asynchronous execution on the GPU yielded better results than synchronous execution. This shows that it is important to not disturb the speed of search even if DCNN knowledge is of much higher quality than the initial knowledge.

All replacement strategies in this paper focus on using neural networks for move predictions inside MCTS. Future work includes extending these schemes for positional evaluation as well. As the amount of work for the GPU doubles strategies for the efficient use of DCNNs get even more important.

References

1. Baudiš, P., Gailly, J.: PACHI: state of the art open source go program. In: Herik, H.J., Plaat, A. (eds.) ACG 2011. LNCS, vol. 7168, pp. 24–38. Springer, Heidelberg (2012). doi:10.1007/978-3-642-31866-5_3
2. Browne, C., Powley, E., Whitehouse, D., Lucas, S., Cowling, P., Rohlfshagen, P., Tavener, S., Perez, D., Samothrakis, S., Colton, S.: A survey of Monte Carlo tree search methods. IEEE Trans. Comput. Intell. AI Games **4**(1), 1–43 (2012)
3. Chaslot, G., Winands, M., Uiterwijk, J., van den Herik, H., Bouzy, B.: Progressive strategies for Monte-Carlo tree search. New Math. Nat. Comput. **4**(3), 343–357 (2008)
4. Chetlur, S., Woolley, C., Vandermersch, P., Cohen, J., Tran, J., Catanzaro, B., Shelhamer, E.: cuDNN: efficient primitives for deep learning (2014). http://arxiv.org/abs/1410.0759
5. Clark, C., Storkey, A.: Training deep convolutional neural networks to play go. In: Proceedings of The 32nd International Conference on Machine Learning, pp. 1766–1774 (2015)
6. Gelly, S., Silver, D.: Combining online and offline knowledge in UCT. In: Proceedings of the 24th International Conference on Machine Learning (ICML 2007), New York, NY, USA, pp. 273–280 (2007)
7. Graf, T., Platzner, M.: Common fate graph patterns in monte carlo tree search for computer go. In: 2014 IEEE Conference on Computational Intelligence and Games (CIG), pp. 1–8, August 2014
8. He, K., Zhang, X., Ren, S., Sun, J.: Delving deep into rectifiers: surpassing human-level performance on imagenet classification. In: IEEE International Conference on Computer Vision (2015)
9. Ikeda, K., Viennot, S.: Efficiency of static knowledge bias in Monte-Carlo tree search. In: Herik, H.J., Iida, H., Plaat, A. (eds.) CG 2013. LNCS, vol. 8427, pp. 26–38. Springer, Heidelberg (2014). doi:10.1007/978-3-319-09165-5_3
10. Jia, Y., Shelhamer, E., Donahue, J., Karayev, S., Long, J., Girshick, R., Guadarrama, S., Darrell, T.: Caffe: convolutional architecture for fast feature embedding. arXiv preprint arXiv:1408.5093 (2014)
11. Maddison, C., Huang, A., Sutskever, I., Silver, D.: Move evaluation in go using deep convolutional neural networks. In: International Conference on Learning Representations (2015)
12. Silver, D., Huang, A., Maddison, C.J., Guez, A., Sifre, L., van den Driessche, G., Schrittwieser, J., Antonoglou, I., Panneershelvam, V., Lanctot, M., Dieleman, S., Grewe, D., Nham, J., Kalchbrenner, N., Sutskever, I., Lillicrap, T., Leach, M., Kavukcuoglu, K., Graepel, T., Hassabis, D.: Mastering the game of Go with deep neural networks and tree search. Nature **529**(7587), 484–489 (2016)
13. Stern, D., Herbrich, R., Graepel, T.: Bayesian pattern ranking for move prediction in the game of go. In: Proceedings of the 23rd International Conference on Machine Learning, pp. 873–880 (2006). http://dx.doi.org/10.1038/nature16961
14. Tian, Y., Zhu, Y.: Better computer go player with neural network and long-term prediction. In: International Conference on Learning Representations (2016)

Monte Carlo Approaches
to Parameterized Poker Squares

Todd W. Neller[1](✉), Zuozhi Yang[1], Colin M. Messinger[1], Calin Anton[2],
Karo Castro-Wunsch[2], William Maga[2], Steven Bogaerts[3],
Robert Arrington[3], and Clay Langley[3]

[1] Gettysburg College, Gettysburg, PA, USA
tneller@gettysburg.edu
[2] MacEwan University, Edmonton, AB, Canada
antonc@macewan.ca
[3] DePauw University, Greencastle, IN, USA
stevenbogaerts@depauw.edu

Abstract. Parameterized Poker Squares (PPS) is a generalization of Poker Squares where players must adapt to a point system supplied at play time and thus dynamically compute highly-varied strategies. Herein, we detail the top three performing AI players in a PPS research competition, all three of which make various use of Monte Carlo techniques.

1 Introduction

The inaugural EAAI NSG Challenge[1] was to create AI to play a parameterized form of the game Poker Squares. We here describe the game of Poker Squares, our parameterization of the game, results of the competition, details of the winners, and possible future directions for improvement.

2 Poker Squares

Poker Squares[2] (a.k.a. Poker Solitaire, Poker Square, Poker Patience) is a folk sequential placement optimization game[3] appearing in print as early as 1949, but likely having much earlier origins. Using a shuffled 52-card French deck, the rules of [7, p. 106] read as follows.

> Turn up twenty-five cards from the stock, one by one, and place each to best advantage in a tableau of five rows of five cards each. The object is to make as high a total score as possible, in the ten Poker hands formed by the five rows and five columns. Two methods of scoring are prevalent, as follows:

---

[1] Whereas DARPA has its "grand challenges", ours are not so grand.
[2] http://www.boardgamegeek.com/boardgame/41215/poker-squares,
http://cs.gettysburg.edu/~tneller/games/pokersquares.
[3] http://www.boardgamegeek.com/geeklist/152237/sequential-placement-optimization-games.

© Springer International Publishing AG 2016
A. Plaat et al. (Eds.): CG 2016, LNCS 10068, pp. 22–33, 2016.
DOI: 10.1007/978-3-319-50935-8_3

Hand	English	American
Royal flush	30	100
Straight flush	30	75
Four of a kind	16	50
Full house	10	25
Flush	5	20
Straight	12	15
Three of a kind	6	10
Two pairs	3	5
One pair	1	2

The American system is based on the relative likelihood of the hands in regular Poker. The English system is based on the relative difficulty of forming the hands in Poker Solitaire.

You may consider that you have "won the game" if you total 200 (American) or 70 (English).

Note that the single remaining Poker hand classification of "high card", which does not fit any of the above classifications, scores no points.

3 Parameterized Poker Squares

As David Parlett observed, "British scoring is based on the relative difficulty of forming the various combinations in this particular game, American on their relative ranking in the game of Poker." [9, pp. 552–553] We observe that different point systems give rise to different placement strategies.

For example, in playing with British or American scoring, one often has a row and column where one dumps unwanted cards so as to form higher scoring combinations in the other rows and columns. However, a very negative score (i.e., penalty) for the "high card" category would discourage leaving any such row or column without a high probability of alternative scoring.

In our parameterization of Poker Squares, we parameterize the score of each of the 10 hand categories as being an integer in the range $[-128, 127]$. Given a vector of 10 integers corresponding to the hand classification points as ordered in the table above, the player then plays Poker Squares according to the given point system.

The goal is to design Poker Squares AI with high expected score performance across the distribution of possible score parameters.

4 Point Systems

Contest point systems consisted of the following types.

- Ameritish - a randomized hybrid of American and English (a.k.a. British) point systems; includes American and English systems (given above)
- Random - points for each hand category are chosen randomly in the range [−128, 127]
- Hypercorner - points for each hand category are chosen with equal probability from {−1, 1}
- Single Hand - only one hand category scores 1 point; all other categories score no points

Hand categories are decided according to the rules of Poker, with higher ranking hand categories taking precedence. Note that the high card hand category may be awarded points in non-Ameritish systems.

4.1 Contest Structure and Results

For each point system tested in contest evaluation, each Java player program was given the point system and 5 min to perform preprocessing before beginning game play. For each game, each player was given 30 s of total time for play decision-making. A player taking more than 30 s of total time for play decision-making or making an illegal play scored 10 times the minimum hand point score for the game.

For each point system tested, each player's scores were summed to a total score and this total was normalized to a floating point number ranging from 0 (lowest score of all players) to 1 (highest score of all players). Players were ranked according to the sum of their normalized scores across all point system tests. All testing was performed on a Dell Precision M4800 running Windows 7 (64-bit) with and Intel Core i7-4940MX CPU @ 3.1 GHz, 32 GB RAM, and running Java version 1.8.0_51. Results of the contest can be seen in Fig. 1.

Players	Mean Scores by Point System											
	American	Ameritish	British	Hypercorner	Random	High Card	One Pair	Two Pair	3 of a Kind	Straight	Flush	Full House
BeeMo	125.27	105.54	54.50	1.10	437.77	9.37	9.12	4.46	3.20	2.97	3.43	1.82
DevneilPlayer	14.36	15.27	7.51	-9.52	-86.92	5.22	4.10	0.45	0.21	0.04	0.05	0.03
Gettysburg	123.94	110.28	53.38	1.24	429.89	9.37	9.17	4.47	3.02	2.71	3.46	1.93
SRulerPlayer	51.83	55.39	30.29	-5.10	242.85	9.34	8.84	4.04	2.10	1.58	1.98	0.61
JoTriz	116.75	109.03	53.59	-0.78	351.07	9.31	9.15	4.59	3.03	2.59	3.36	1.67
Tiger	116.12	111.26	53.92	-2.20	411.78	9.35	9.16	4.52	2.89	2.94	3.41	1.82
MonteCarloTreePlayer	15.47	15.31	7.61	-9.30	-86.83	4.80	4.53	0.45	0.20	0.05	0.02	0.00
RandomPlayer	14.25	15.67	7.71	-9.66	-106.80	5.20	4.31	0.42	0.23	0.01	0.01	0.01
Max	125.27	111.26	54.50	1.24	437.77	9.37	9.17	4.59	3.20	2.97	3.46	1.93
Min	14.25	15.27	7.51	-9.66	-106.80	4.80	4.10	0.42	0.20	0.01	0.01	0.00

Normalized Scores													Total
BeeMo	1.00	0.94	1.00	0.99	1.00	1.00	0.99	0.97	1.00	1.00	0.99	0.94	11.821
DevneilPlayer	0.00	0.00	0.00	0.01	0.04	0.09	0.00	0.01	0.00	0.01	0.01	0.02	0.190
Gettysburg	0.99	0.99	0.98	1.00	0.99	1.00	1.00	0.97	0.94	0.91	1.00	1.00	11.763
SRulerPlayer	0.34	0.42	0.48	0.42	0.64	0.99	0.93	0.87	0.63	0.53	0.57	0.32	7.149
JoTriz	0.92	0.98	0.98	0.81	0.84	0.99	1.00	1.00	0.94	0.87	0.97	0.87	11.170
Tiger	0.92	1.00	0.99	0.68	0.95	1.00	1.00	0.98	0.90	0.99	0.99	0.94	11.334
MonteCarloTreePlayer	0.01	0.00	0.00	0.03	0.04	0.00	0.08	0.01	0.00	0.01	0.00	0.00	0.192
RandomPlayer	0.00	0.00	0.00	0.00	0.00	0.09	0.04	0.00	0.01	0.00	0.00	0.01	0.153

Fig. 1. Results of Contest Evaluation

Non-fixed point systems were generated with contest random seed 34412016. The twelve point systems used for contest evaluation included American, Ameritish, British,

Hypercorner, Random, and the following seven Single-Hand systems: High Card, One Pair, Two Pairs, Three of a Kind, Straight, Flush, and Full House.

Detailed performance information is available online[4]. Final contest standings were as follows:

1. Score: 11.821; Player: BeeMo; Students: Karo Castro-Wunsch, William Maga; Faculty mentor: Calin Anton; School: MacEwan University
2. Score: 11.763; Player: GettysburgPlayer; Students: Colin Messinger, Zuozhi Yang; Faculty mentor: Todd Neller; School: Gettysburg College
3. Score: 11.334; Player: Tiger; Students: Robert Arrington, Clay Langley; Faculty mentor: Steven Bogaerts; School: DePauw University
4. Score: 11.170; Player: JoTriz; Student: Kevin Trizna; Faculty mentor: David Mutchler; School: Rose-Hulman Institute of Technology
5. Score: 7.149; Player: SRulerPlayer; Student: Zachary McNulty; Faculty mentor: Timothy Highley; School: La Salle University
6. Score: 0.192; Player: MonteCarloTreePlayer; Student: Isaac Sanders; Faculty mentor: Michael Wollowski; School: Rose-Hulman Institute of Technology
7. Score: 0.190; Player: DevneilPlayer; Student: Adam Devigili; Faculty mentor: Brian O'Neill; School: Western New England University

As a benchmark, a random player was evaluated alongside contestants, scoring 0.153 tournament points. We first note that a cluster of 4 players scored close to the tournament maximum possible score of 12. The two bottom entries scored only slightly better than random play.

In the following sections, we will provide details of the top three performing players.

5 BeeMo

BeeMo implements a parallel flat Monte Carlo search guided by a heuristic which uses hand patterns utilities. These utilities are learned through an iterative improvement algorithm involving Monte Carlo simulations and optimized greedy search. BeeMo's development process was focused on three domains: game state representation, search, and learning. For each of these domains, we investigated several approaches. In the following subsections, we present the best combination of approaches according to empirical evaluations. For a more detailed description of all designs, see [4].

5.1 Game State Representation

We used a simple array representation for the tableau of face up cards and a bit packed representation for the deck of face down cards. We implemented a hand encoding scheme based on hand patterns, which are a representation of hands which retains only the relevant hand information:

- if the hand contains a flush - 1 bit;
- if the hand contains a straight - 1 bit;

---
[4] http://cs.gettysburg.edu/~tneller/games/pokersquares/eaai/results/.

- number of cards in the hand without a pair - 3 bits;
- number of pairs in the hand - 2 bits;
- if the hand contains three of a kind - 1 bit;
- if the hand contains four of a kind -1 bit;
- if the hand is a row - 1 bit.

The hand pattern encoding was extended with contextual information about the number of cards of the primary rank and secondary rank remaining in the deck. These are the ranks with the largest and second largest number of repetitions in the hand, respectively. We also added information about the number of cards in the remaining deck that can make the hand a flush. Instead of actual number of cards we used a coarse approximation with three values: not enough cards, exactly enough cards, and more than enough cards remaining to complete a certain hand. The approximation is represented on 2 bits, and so the contextual information adds 6 extra bits to the hand pattern, for a total of 16 bits for hand pattern and contextual information. The extra information increases the number of empirically observed unique patterns by a factor of 10. Our experiments indicate that this added complexity is overcome by the significant improvement in training accuracy.

5.2 Search

We implemented several game tree search algorithm classes: rule based, expectimax, greedy, and Monte Carlo. We compared their performance using a crafted heuristic for the American scoring system. Our empirical analysis indicated that the best search algorithms belong to the Monte Carlo and Greedy classes. As the final agent uses a combination of flat Monte Carlo and optimized greedy, we will present our implementation of these algorithms.

Optimized Greedy implements a greedy strategy based on hand pattern utilities. Every new card placed on the tableau of face up cards, influences only two hands: the column and the row in which the card is placed. Thus, the value of placing the card in any position can be estimated by the sum of the changes of the values for the column hand and for the row hand. The change in every hand is the difference of the hand pattern utility after and before placing the card. The optimized greedy algorithm places the card in the position that results in the largest value. Computing these values is very fast as it needs four look ups in a hash table of hand pattern utilities, two subtractions and an addition. It is exactly this simplicity that makes the algorithm very fast.

The algorithm plays ten of thousand of games per second, has impressive performances (consistently scores over 115 points on the American scoring), and it is essentially the same for any scoring system - the only changes are in the hand pattern utilities' hash table entries.

Flat Monte Carlo is a variation of the imperfect information Monte Carlo [5]. At a given node, the algorithm evaluates each child by averaging the scores of a large number of simulated games from that child, and then selects a move that results in the child with the largest value. Any search algorithm can be used to guide the simulated games, but a fast one is preferable. For this reason we used the optimized greedy search for the simulated games.

The resulting algorithm consistently outperformed optimized greedy by a margin of 10 points on the American scoring. However, the time efficiency of the algorithm was significantly worse than that of optimized greedy. Parallelization improved the algorithm speed significantly. In its final implementation the algorithm creates several threads of game simulations which are run in parallel on all available cores. Despite being an order of magnitude slower than the greedy algorithm, the parallel flat Monte Carlo is fast and has the best score performances of all the algorithms we tried.

5.3   Learning

Because the scoring scheme is not known, learning the partial hand utilities is the most important part of the agent. We used Monte Carlo simulations for learning the hand pattern utilities. The learning algorithm uses rounds of 10,000 Monte Carlo simulations, 5,000 for training and 5,000 for evaluation.

All hand pattern utilities are initialized to zero. At the end of a training game, the value of each final hand is recorded for every hand pattern which resulted in the hand. For example, if a partial hand has only a 5♥ and at the end of the game results in a flush with a score of 20, then a value of 20 is recorded for the pattern which encodes a hand with only 5♥. The utility of a hand pattern is estimated as the average of all recorded values. The updated hand pattern utility set is used in the next simulated game.

Using flat Monte Carlo search for the training phase, the agent learned hand pattern utilities which for the American scoring resulted in performance comparable to those obtained using the crafted hand pattern utilities, and reduced running time.

While simple and fast, flat Monte Carlo search suffers from lack of specialization. When used for learning hand pattern utilities this drawback negatively affects the accuracy of the estimations. For example, low frequency patterns with high utilities are rarely updated and thus the learned values may be unreliable. To check if our learning algorithm has such a pitfall we implemented a UCT evaluation scheme inspired by the UCB1 variation of the Upper Confidence Bound [2]. We used a small exploration parameter which was optimized empirically. UCB1 slightly increased the number of discovered patterns, but its influence on agent's performance was positive only for the American and British scoring systems. For the final agent we decided to use both evaluation schemes by alternating them with different frequencies.

In the evaluation phase, 5,000 simulated games are played using the set of hand pattern utilities learned in the training phase. The average of the games' scores is used to evaluate the overall utility of a set of patterns. The set with the highest overall utility is used by the final agent. The agent consistently completes 180 rounds of learning during the allowed 300 s. However, most of the improvements are done in the first 10 rounds, after which the performance evolution is almost flat.

As indicated in the contest results, the final agent played strongly under all scoring systems. Given that (1) players employed various heuristics and differing uses of Monte Carlo techniques, and (2) players achieved similar peak performance, we conjecture that these top players closely approximate optimal play.

6 GettysburgPlayer

The GettysburgPlayer uses a static evaluation, which abstracts game states and attempts to assess their values given any scoring system, in combination with expectimax search limited to depth 2.

6.1 Static Evaluation

The total state space is too large to evaluate in advance, so the state space is abstracted and on-policy Monte Carlo reinforcement learning is applied in order to simultaneously improve estimates of the abstracted game and improve play policy that guides our Monte Carlo simulations.

Abstracting Independent Hands. Our Naïve Abstract Reinforcement Learning (NARL) player abstracts the state of each independent row/column and learns the expected value of these abstractions through Monte Carlo ϵ-greedy reinforcement learning. Each hand abstraction string consists of several features which we considered significant.

- Number of cards played in the game so far
- Indication of row ("-") or column ("|")
- Descending-sorted non-zero rank counts and how many cards are yet undealt in each of those ranks appended to each parenthetically
- Indication of whether or not a flush ("f") is achievable and how many undealt cards are of that suit
- Indication of whether or not a straight ("s") is achievable
- Indication of whether or not royal flush ("r") is achievable

For example, "14|1(3)1(2)1(2)f(8)s" represents a column hand abstraction after the 14th move. There is one card in each of three ranks, two of which have two of that rank undealt and one has three undealt. A flush is achievable with eight cards undealt in that suit. A straight is achievable and a royal flush is not.

During Monte Carlo reinforcement learning, such hand abstractions are generated and stored in a hash map. Each abstraction maps to the expected hand score and number of occurrences of the hand. These are continuously updated during learning. By storing the expected scores of each row/column complete/partial hand, the hash map allows us to sum scoring estimates for each row and column, providing a very fast estimate of the expected final score of the game grid as a whole. Note that this naïvely assumes the independence of the hand scoring estimates.

Raising Proportion of Exploration Plays. During the Monte Carlo reinforcement learning stage, we use an ϵ-greedy policy with a geometric decay applied to the ϵ parameter. Thus for most of time the player chooses an action that achieves a maximal expected score, but also makes random plays with probability ϵ.

In our initial application of ϵ-greedy play, $\epsilon = 0.1$ with geometric ϵ-decay $\delta = 0.999975$ per simulated game iteration. However, we empirically observed that if we significantly raise the initial value of ϵ to 0.5, increasing initial exploration, the player has a better performance.

In addition, the time cost for random play is much less than greedy play, so increasing the proportion of random plays increases the number of overall learning iterations per unit time. Empirically, this relatively higher ϵ will not only raise the number of exploration plays but also will be able to leave sufficient time for exploitation plays. However, purely random play makes certain types of hands highly improbable (e.g., royal flush, straight), so sufficient exploitation-heavy play time is necessary to learn the value of long-term attempts to achieve such hands.

Considering Frequency of Partial Hand Sizes. We observed our player's behavior and found that it tended to spread cards evenly among rows and columns in the early and middle stages of the game. The reason for this behavior is that the player is making greedy plays that maximize expected score gain. In a pre-evaluation between NARL and another player developed earlier that performed better under the single-hand Two Pairs point system, we observed that with same card dealt, NARL tended to set up one pair evenly among rows and columns according to the assumption of hand independence, while the comparison player appeared to gain an advantage by preferring to focus on developing a row/column with a pair and two single cards early.

Based on this observation, we added the current distribution of hand sizes to the abstraction. The number of cards played in each row and column are tallied, and we summarize the distribution in a hand size frequency vector represented as a string. For instance, the string "721000" represents a grid hand size distribution after the 2nd move. (The number of cards dealt can be inferred from the abstraction.) The zero-based index of the string corresponds to hand size in a row/column. Thus, "721000" indicates that there are seven empty hands, two with one card, one with two cards, and none with more than two.

The previous grid hand abstraction is trained together with hand size abstraction to learn the difference between the final score and expected score at each of the 25 states across the game. In practice, we find that adding this abstraction feature generally improves performance for some simpler point systems.

Experiments and Data. We experimented with 3 players, all of which used ϵ-decay $\delta = 0.999975$. The first used an initial epsilon $\epsilon_0 = 0.1$, whereas the second and third used $\epsilon_0 = 0.5$. Only the third player incorporated the hand size frequency abstraction feature.

For each random point system (the Ameritish point system, Random point system, Hypercorner point system) we generated a sample of 500 systems and measured the average greedy-play performance of 2000 games for each player and system. For fixed point systems, we collected average performance of 2000 games for each player and system. For each point system, performance was scaled between 0 and 1 as with the previously described tournament scoring (Fig. 2).

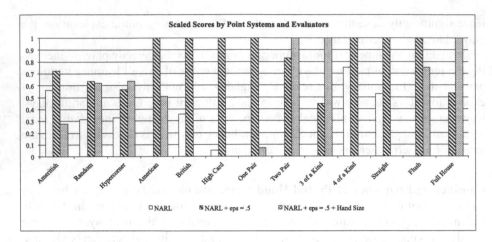

Fig. 2. Comparison of learning evaluation performance. NARL with $\epsilon_0 = 0.5$ performed best for most point systems.

6.2 Search Algorithm

Using the NARL static evaluation, we compared three search algorithms: (1) Flat Monte Carlo [3, Sect. 2.3] limited to depth 5, (2) Flat UCB1 limited to depth 5 and multiplying the exploration term $\sqrt{2ln(n)/n_j}$ by 20 to encourage greater exploration[5], and (3) expectimax with a depth limit of 2.

The three algorithms were paired with the three static evaluators and tested against each other using the contest software, 8 scoring systems, and the seed 21347. Each player ran 100 games per point system. The final comparison was based upon each player's total normalized score. A combination of depth 2 expectimax and the NARL evaluator ($\epsilon_0 = 0.5$) received the highest total score and was submitted for competition.

Significance testing of the various player components revealed that our static evaluation function was most significant to the player's performance [8]. Space limitations preclude the full set of alternative designs considered. However, these and relevant experimental data are available in [8] as well.

7 Tiger: A Heuristic-Based MCTS Player

This summary is based on a more detailed discussion available in [1]. The player uses Monte Carlo Tree Search (MCTS) [3] with added domain knowledge to select moves.

7.1 Design and Application of the State Heuristic

This player includes a state heuristic that can accommodate any scoring system. It can be framed as ten applications of a hand heuristic, corresponding to the ten rows and

---

[5] The factor of 20 was chosen through limited empirical performance tuning. It is not necessarily optimal for this problem.

columns in the game. Five-card hands are simply scored according to the current scoring system. One to four card hands, however, are evaluated with probability estimates.

In four-card hands, for each hand type, a *weight* in [0, 1] is calculated, representing an estimated likelihood of obtaining that hand type with the next card draw given the cards remaining in the deck. For example, suppose a 4-card hand contains a 6♥, 6♣, 6♠, and 7♠, while the deck contains only a 6♦, 7♥, and 8♥. Here, three-of-a-kind is given a weight of 1/3 because among the remaining cards only 8♥ would result in three-of-a-kind. Once these weights are calculated for every hand type, each weight is multiplied by the hand type value according to the current scoring system, and added together to form a weighted sum. Note that this ignores the fact that the ten hands in the grid are dependent on each other, both spatially and in "competition" for cards.

This approach gets much more computationally intensive for hands with fewer than four cards, and so in this case we instead use estimated *a-priori* probabilities of hand types as weights. These probabilities are then used to compute a weighted sum in the same way as in a four-card hand. Note, however, that by this measure hands with fewer cards will be inadvertently favored, because fewer cards will tend to mean more possible hand-types. To counter this, we apply weights α, β, and γ to one, two, and three-card hand heuristic values, respectively. For now, we fix these values at $\alpha = 0.2$, $\beta = 0.4$, and $\gamma = 0.6$, with tuning experiments described below.

With this heuristic, various selection strategies exist. *UCT* [6] is a standard measure balancing exploration and exploitation with no domain-specific heuristic. *Best Move* always chooses the single unexplored node with the highest heuristic value. *Prune + UCT* prunes nodes below a heuristic score threshold and then applies standard UCT.

In simulation, *Random* is the standard MCTS strategy of choosing random moves without a heuristic. *Prune + Random* chooses moves at random from a tree pruned via the heuristic. *Best Move* chooses the single move with the highest heuristic value.

7.2 Experiments and Results

Table 1 shows results for various experiments. We begin by considering the practical cost of calculating the heuristic itself, since time spent on heuristic calculations means fewer iterations of the core MCTS process. Row (1) reflects standard MCTS, with UCT selection and Random simulation. Rows (2) – (4) also use these standard strategies, but with the "+ Calc." notation indicating that the heuristic calculations are *performed* but not actually *applied*. Note a total cost of 13 points (comparing rows (1) and (4)) in the American scoring system when the heuristic is calculated in both selection and simulation, with most of the cost coming from simulation.

In simulation, ignoring for now the "Tuned" column, note that Prune + Random's score of 95 (row (5)) shows improvement over the 92 of standard MCTS (row (1)) and the 80 of the added heuristic calculation cost (row (3)). Best Move simulation (row (6)) improved more strongly to an untuned score of 112. It seems intuitive that Best Move simulation is more effective than Prune + Random, since Best Move plays a simulated game according to the best choices that the heuristic is capable of suggesting. In contrast, Prune + Random gives the heuristic less control, only determining a set of higher-scoring moves from which a random selection is made.

Table 1. Mean scores over 2,000 games for various selection and simulation strategies

Row	Selection	Simulation	Untuned	Tuned
(1)	UCT	Random	92	
(2)	UCT + Calc	Random	90	
(3)	UCT	Random + Calc	80	
(4)	UCT + Calc	Random + Calc	79	
(5)	UCT	Prune + Random	95	
(6)	UCT	Best Move	112	118
(7)	Best Move	Random	72	
(8)	Prune + UCT	Random	91	94
(9)	Prune + UCT	Best Move	113	123

Next consider the selection strategy results, again ignoring for now the "Tuned" column. Prune + UCT seems unhelpful when comparing rows (1) vs. (8), and (6) vs. (9) (untuned). The final set of experiments will consider this further. Best Move selection, in contrast, appears not merely unhelpful but *harmful*. With a score of 72 (row (7)), it scores even worse than row (2) in which the calculations are performed but not applied. This is not surprising, since such a drastic approach severely limits the number of nodes available for exploration. That is, while Best Move *simulation* is a useful limitation in contrast to Random simulation, the more principled exploration of *selection* with *UCT* should not be so severely restricted by a Best Move approach.

Finally, consider further tuning of α, β, and γ values for weighting one-, two-, and three-card hands, respectively. After experiments on many combinations of settings, it was found that $\alpha = 0.1$, $\beta = 0.3$, $\gamma = 0.85$ gave the best performance on the American scoring system, with other high-scoring settings converging on those values. Results for this setting are shown in the "Tuned" column of Table 1. This newly-tuned heuristic sheds new light on Prune + UCT selection, which seemed ineffective in the untuned results. Row (8) shows that Prune + UCT selection with tuned parameter settings attains a 94, compared to the 91 with the untuned settings, and the 92 (row (1)) of standard MCTS. Similarly, Best Move simulation now scores 118 (row (6)), showing further improvement over the untuned 112. These experiments demonstrate that both Prune + UCT selection and Best Move simulation can be improved and are worthwhile after tuning the heuristic, with a final top score of 123 when both strategies are applied.

8   Conclusion

The inaugural EAAI NSG Challenge was reported to be a very positive experience by both students and faculty. Informal evaluation indicates that more than half of entries perform well beyond human-level play, and most were densely clustered at the top of the distribution, lending confidence to a conjecture that optimal play is not far beyond the performance observed.

In the future, it would be interesting to perform more significance testing across implementations in order to demonstrate the relative value of different design components, e.g., the parallelization of BeeMo. Testing comparable elements of designs would guide a hybridization of approaches, e.g., testing a single search algorithm with each of our various static evaluation functions. We conjecture that an ensemble or hybrid approach would yield performance improvements.

References

1. Arrington, R., Langley, C., Bogaerts, S.: Using domain knowledge to improve monte-carlo tree search performance in parameterized poker squares. In: Proceedings of the 30th National Conference on Artificial Intelligence (AAAI 2016), pp. 4065–4070. AAAI Press, Menlo Park (2016)
2. Auer, P., Cesa-Bianchi, N., Fischer, P.: Finite-time analysis of the multiarmed bandit problem. Mach. Learn. **47**(2–3), 235–256 (2002). http://dx.doi.org/10.1023/A:1013689704352
3. Browne, C., Powley, E., Whitehouse, D., Lucas, S., Cowling, P.I., Rohlfshagen, P., Tavener, S., Perez, D., Samothrakis, S., Colton, S.: A survey of Monte Carlo tree search methods. IEEE Trans. Comput. Intell. AI Games **4**(1), 1–49 (2012). http://www.cameronius.com/cv/mcts-survey-master.pdf
4. Castro-Wunsch, K., Maga, W., Anton, C.: Beemo, a Monte Carlo simulation agent for playing parameterized poker squares. In: Proceedings of the 30th National Conference on Artificial Intelligence (AAAI 2016), pp. 4071–4074. AAAI Press, Menlo Park (2016)
5. Furtak, T., Buro, M.: Recursive Monte Carlo search for imperfect information games. In: 2013 IEEE Conference on Computational Inteligence in Games (CIG), Niagara Falls, ON, Canada, 11–13 August 2013, pp. 1–8 (2013). http://dx.doi.org/10.1109/CIG.2013.6633646
6. Kocsis, L., Szepesvári, C., Willemson, J.: Improved monte-carlo search. Univ. Tartu, Estonia, Technical report 1 (2006)
7. Morehead, A.H., Mott-Smith, G.: The Complete Book of Solitaire & Patience Games, 1st edn. Grosset & Dunlap, New York (1949)
8. Neller, T.W., Messinger, C.M., Zuozhi, Y.: Learning and using hand abstraction values for parameterized poker squares. In: Proceedings of the 30th National Conference on Artificial Intelligence (AAAI 2016), pp. 4095–4100. AAAI Press, Menlo Park (2016)
9. Parlett, D.: The Penguin Book of Card Games. Penguin Books, updated edn. (2008)

Monte Carlo Tree Search with Robust Exploration

Takahisa Imagawa[1,2(✉)] and Tomoyuki Kaneko[1]

[1] Graduate School of Arts and Sciences, The University of Tokyo, Tokyo, Japan
{imagawa,kaneko}@graco.c.u-tokyo.ac.jp
[2] Research Fellow of Japan Society for the Promotion of Science, Tokyo, Japan

Abstract. This paper presents a new Monte-Carlo tree search method that focuses on identifying the best move. UCT which minimizes the cumulative regret, has achieved remarkable success in Go and other games. However, recent studies on simple regret reveal that there are better exploration strategies. To further improve the performance, a leaf to be explored is determined not only by the mean but also by the whole reward distribution. We adopted a hybrid approach to obtain reliable distributions. A negamax-style backup of reward distributions is used in the shallower half of a search tree, and UCT is adopted in the rest of the tree. Experiments on synthetic trees show that this presented method outperformed UCT and similar methods, except for trees having uniform width and depth.

1 Introduction

Monte Carlo tree search (MCTS) algorithms including UCT [5] have achieved remarkable success, especially in the game of Go [10].

UCT is an algorithm based on the minimization of cumulative regret [1,13], which is suitable for estimating the expected score at each node. However, in game-playing algorithms, it is more important to identify the best move at the root, than to identify its score. Both goals are closely related but still different, as MTD(f) [16] exploits this difference in the context of $\alpha\beta$ search. Recent studies have shown that the performance of MCTS is improved by focusing on simple regret instead of on cumulative regret [6,14,15,19]. However, it is also known to be difficult to directly minimize the simple regret in tree search algorithms.

This paper presents an alternative Monte-Carlo tree search method that focuses on the confidence when choosing the best move. Our work is based on the careful combination of two ideas, each of which can be found in existing work: (1) negamax-style backup of the distribution of rewards at each interior node [4,18] in a main search tree, and (2) hybrid MCTS on top of UCT [15,19]. By using reward distributions obtained with a negamax-style backup, we can estimate the probability that the current move will be superseded by another move by a deeper search [4]. By using these distributions, we can identify the best leaf that most influences the confidence at the root. The negamax-style backup

© Springer International Publishing AG 2016
A. Plaat et al. (Eds.): CG 2016, LNCS 10068, pp. 34–46, 2016.
DOI: 10.1007/978-3-319-50935-8_4

also contributes to the convergence [18]. We adopted UCT on an extended tree in order to obtain the distribution at each leaf in the main search tree.

The experiments on incremental random trees show that the presented method outperforms UCT, except in trees with a uniform width and depth.

2 Background and Related Work

This section briefly reviews related work on best-first search methods including Monte-Carlo tree search and negamax-style backup of reward distributions.

Monte Carlo tree search (MCTS) [5] is a kind of best-first algorithm that iteratively expands and evaluates a game tree by using a random simulation. In this section, we consider a general framework of best-first search algorithms where each iteration consists of the following four steps.

1. leaf selection: a leaf with the highest priority is selected.
2. expansion: if necessary, the leaf is expanded, and a leaf is selected again among newly created leaves.
3. evaluation: the leaf is evaluated or the evaluation is elaborated (e.g., by random simulation in UCT).
4. backpropagation: the evaluated value is shared throughout the tree.

We followed the convention in which MCTS starts with a tree having only its root and the immediate successor nodes. Then a leaf is expanded when we visit the leaf for the first time in step 2 [3,5,8]. Sometimes, a search tree is fixed to simplify analysis [18,19]. This is necessary in typical game programs in order to handle expansion of the tree during the search process. The other steps—leaf selection, evaluation, and backpropagation—characterize the search algorithms as discussed in the Subsects. 2.1 to 2.3. In this paper, we use move a or the position after move a interchangeably for simplicity, because a position after move a is defined without ambiguity in deterministic games.

2.1 Monte Carlo Tree Search and UCT

UCT [13] has been applied to many games including Go and has achieved remarkable success. For the evaluation of a leaf, it conducts random play (called simulation, or roll-out) starting at the position corresponding to the leaf and observes its outcome as a *reward*. In this paper, we assume reward r to be a win (1), loss (0), or draw (0.5), following the usual convention. Focusing on wins/losses/draws instead of raw game scores is known to be effective in Go [3,8]. Note that reward r is replaced by $1 - r$ for nodes where the opponent player moves. The observed reward is shared among the nodes between the leaf and the root in the backpropagation step, and the average of the rewards $\overline{X}_{i,t_i} = \sum_{t'}^{t_i} r_{t'}/t_i$ is maintained for each node i, where t_i is the number of visits to the node.

In the selection step, the algorithm descends from the root to a leaf by recursively selecting the most urgent child at each node. The urgency of a node among its siblings is determined by UCB defined by the following equation:

$$\text{UCB} = \overline{X}_{i,t_i} + \sqrt{2\ln t/t_i}, \tag{1}$$

where t is the number of times the parent of node i is visited up to now. UCT models a move in a game as an arm in a multi-armed bandit problem [1], assuming that the reward is stochastically determined by a distribution with mean μ_i when arm i is pulled. In typical game playing programs, we need to handle terminal or solved positions where the reward is fixed [20]. We need to ignore losing moves in the selection step by propagating win/loss information that is found to ancestors.

2.2 Improvements in UCT

UCT works so that the cumulative regret of the root is minimized [1,13]. Cumulative regret is the summation of the difference between the best choice, which is unknown to the agent, and his or her actual choice over time, $\sum_t^T (r^* - r_t)$, where r^* is the mean reward of the best arm and r_t is the observed reward at time t. Therefore, it is suitable for the estimation of the expected reward at a root. Simple regret is an alternative criterion for the accuracy of the final choice, $r^* - r_T$, where r_T is the mean reward of the agent's final choice after time T [6]. Informally, if one does more exploration of sub-optimal moves, simple (cumulative) regret decreases (increases).

Recent studies suggest that a hybrid approach is effective. This is a primary strategy for a root (or shallower part of a tree) to reduce simple regret at the root, and a sub-strategy to reduce cumulative regret in the rest of the tree. For a primary strategy, the approximated value of information (VOI) is reported to be effective in MCTS SR+CR [19], while SHOT [7] is used in H-MCTS [15]. H-MCTS has been tested on various domains; however, it inherits the limitation of SHOT in which the number of simulations must be fixed in advance. Our approach adopts alternative primary strategies and achieves an anytime algorithm. Additionally, Liu and Tsuruoka presented an adjustment in confidence bounds to reduce simple regret [14].

2.3 Minimax Backup of Reward Distribution

Usually, only the average of observed rewards is maintained at each node in MCTS. However, if a histogram of rewards is maintained in addition to the average, more information about positions can be extracted from the histogram[1] [11,12]. Moreover, reward distribution can be propagated in negamax style [4,18].

Bayes-UCT [18] is a Bayesian extension to UCT that selects a node having the maximum Bayes-UCT value among the siblings:

$$\text{Bayes-UCT1} := \hat{\mu}_i + \sqrt{2 \ln t / T_i(t)}, \quad \text{Bayes-UCT2} := \hat{\mu}_i + \sqrt{2 \ln t}\, \sigma_i, \quad (2)$$

where $\hat{\mu}_i$ is the estimated mean of child i's reward distribution obtained by negamax backup, i.e., $\hat{\mu}_i = \int_x (1-x) p_i(x)$, where $p_i(x)$ is the probability that node i

---

[1] http://www.althofer.de/crazy-shadows.html.

Table 1. Comparison of similar work and our work. The top half of the table summarizes existing methods. The column "minimax backup" indicates how the distribution of each node is presented, where "-" means the minimax backup of reward distributions is not adopted. The column "primary strategy" gives the main strategy of choosing a leaf to be expanded or that for a playout. The column "sub-strategy" lists a sub-strategy for the deeper part of a tree if a hybrid approach is adopted, or "-" otherwise. The bottom half of the table summarizes our approaches discussed in this paper, which respectively adopt discrete and UCT for minimax backup and hybrid.

Existing method	minimax backup	primary strategy	sub-strategy
Baum and Smith [4]	discrete	QSS	-
BayesUCT [18]	Beta distribution	UCB (Bayes)	-
H-MCTS [15]	-	SHOT [7]	UCT
MCTS SR+CR [19]	-	ϵ-greedy, UCB$_{\sqrt{(\cdot)}}$, VOI	UCT
Yokoyama and Kitsuregawa [21]	discrete [4]	QSS [4], UCT	$\alpha\beta$ search
Work in this paper			
HB+E^{Expected}	discrete [4]	E^{Expected}	UCT
HB+E^{Robust}		E^{Robust}	
HB+E^{Terminal}		E^{Terminal}=QSS [4]	
HB+BayesUCT1		$\hat{\mu}_i + \sqrt{2\ln t/t_i}$ [18]	
HB+BayesUCT2		$\hat{\mu}_i + \sqrt{2\ln t}\sigma_i$ [18]	

has the game theoretical value x for player to move, and σ_i is the standard deviation of the distribution. Note that reward $1-x$ in a node corresponds to reward x in a parent node because the player whose turn it is to move changes with each move. Here, the observed average X_i in UCT (Eq. (1)) is replaced by $\hat{\mu}_i$, and it is shown that $\hat{\mu}_i$ converges more rapidly to the game theoretical reward of node i. There are many differences between this approach and our work, including exploration strategies and the adoption (or not) of a prior distribution or continuous probability distribution. In this work, we used $\hat{\mu}_i = \sum_{x \in \{0, 0.5, 1\}}(1 - x)p_i(x)$ instead.

Before the introduction of MCTS, Baum and Smith presented a best-first search method that utilizes the reward distribution at each node [4].

Bayes-UCT as well as Baum and Smith's method assumes the existence of an external function to assign a probability distribution to each leaf, as a prior or special kind of evaluation function. In this work, the assumption is not necessary due to the use of UCT to yield the distribution. We also present improved strategies for exploration. The upper half of Table 1 summarizes the existing methods.

3 Exploration with Refinement of Confidence

We present a new hybrid MCTS algorithm that iteratively refines the confidence of the choice at the root. Our algorithm maintains the main tree for our primary

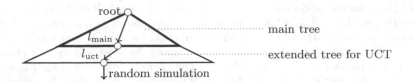

Fig. 1. Two parts of a search tree maintained with our algorithm

1. leaf selection: the most valuable leaf in the main tree is selected, with respect to the exploration strategy defined in Sect. 3.2.
2. evaluation: evaluation of the leaf l_{main} is elaborated by *budget* times of internal playouts in UCT with root l_{main}:
   (a) leaf selection: the most valuable leaf l_{uct} is identified by recursively descending successor node having the highest UCB1 value from l_{main}.
   (b) expansion: if the same condition in step 2 in Sect. 2 is satisfied, the leaf l_{uct} is expanded, and a new l_{uct} is then selected among newly created leaves.
   (c) evaluation: the evaluation of the leaf is elaborated by a random simulation that starts from the leaf.
   (d) backpropagation: the reward is stored in each node between l_{main} and l_{uct}. In addition to the usual back up of the reward, we maintain a histogram of the rewards (i.e., the frequencies of $\{0, 0.5, 1\}$) in each node.
3. expansion: after evaluation, if there appear such nodes in the UCT tree that meet the conditions described in Sect. 3.3, they are promoted into the main tree.
4. backpropagation: the distribution of the rewards is updated for each node between l_{main} and the root, by using Eq. (4).

Fig. 2. Outline of our algorithm

strategy introduced in the next subsections, as well as the extended tree for our sub-strategy, UCT, as depicted in Fig. 1. The algorithm iteratively extends the whole tree and refines evaluations in a best-first manner as listed in Fig. 2. Steps 1 through 4 are for the primary strategy, and steps 2(a) through 2(d) are for the sub-strategy, UCT (see Sect. 3.1). We first select leaf l_{main} in the main tree by using a strategy introduced in Sect. 3.2. Then, it runs playouts according to UCT *budget* times, where the budget is usually one. A newly created leaf is first added to the UCT tree and will be incorporated into the main tree when they meet the conditions described in Sect. 3.3.

3.1   Hybrid Backup of Reward Distribution

For each node in a search tree, an array of size 3 is assigned to present the reward distribution of the node. We introduce different backup procedures for the main tree and extended tree and call the scheme hybrid backup (HB). In each node in the extended tree, we maintain a histogram that holds the frequency of each reward value (i.e., $\{0, 0.5, 1\}$) and adapt it for the reward distribution of the node. When a playout is completed, the corresponding frequency count in the histogram in each node involved in the playout is updated by one.

For nodes in the main tree, a negamax-style backup is adopted. Let $p_i(x)$ be the probability that the game theoretical value of node i is x, and $\underline{c}^{(i)}(x)$ ($\overline{c}^{(i)}(x)$) be the cumulative distribution function, CDF, for probability $p_i(x)$ being less (more) than or equal to x:

$$\underline{c}^{(i)}(x) := \sum_{k:k \leq x} p_i(k), \text{ and } \overline{c}^{(i)}(x) := \sum_{k:k \geq x} p_i(k). \tag{3}$$

Inversely, probability $p_i(x)$ is easily computed by function $\underline{c}^{(i)}(x)$ or $\overline{c}^{(i)}(x)$. We introduce the negamax backup of probability distributions, following Baum and Smiths method [4]. The distribution of internal node n is defined based on those of the successor nodes assuming that there is no correlation between sibling nodes:

$$\underline{c}^{(n)}(1 - x) = \prod_{c \in \text{successor}(n)} \overline{c}^{(c)}(x). \tag{4}$$

The CDF $\underline{c}^{(i)}(x)$ in each node in the main tree is updated by using Eq. (4), so that it represents the negamax CDF of distributions of its successors. Recall that we limit the reward in $\{0, 0.5, 1\}$ in this work. Therefore, p_i or $\underline{c}^{(i)}(\cdot)$ can be stored in an array of size three. Also, $\sum_x p_i(x) = 1$ holds for any node i.

The intuition behind this design is that the estimated probability distribution is not accurate without a carefully designed prior distribution when the number of samples remains small. Therefore, we count the frequencies of reward values in the deeper part of the tree to average the results. If the number of samples is sufficient, the estimated distribution is accurate. Consequently, the negamax backup of probability distributions is adopted in the shallower part of the tree to achieve better convergence.

3.2   Exploration Strategy

Here, we introduce the primary strategy to select leaf l_{main} in the main tree to be explored next in step 1 in Fig. 2. Let m_0 be the best move at the root, estimated so far by searching. We define the uncertainty U as the difference between the estimated mean reward of root R and that of m_0:

$$U := \hat{\mu}'_R - \hat{\mu}'_{m_0}, \tag{5}$$

where each of $\hat{\mu}'_R$ ($= 1 - \hat{\mu}_R$) and $\hat{\mu}'_{m0}$ ($= \hat{\mu}_{m0}$) is the mean of the distribution at corresponding node (with respect to the root player). We can focus on the identification of the best move by minimizing U rather than by minimizing the variance of $\hat{\mu}_R$. For example, if U is zero, we can be confident that the best move is m_0 regardless of the value of the leaves, under the given distributions. Otherwise, there would be another move m_i that potentially has a better value than m_0.

Our goal is to select leaf l with the highest priority in the main tree to continue the exploration. Let U_l be the value of U after the exploration of leaf l, which is not known until the exploration is completed. When U_l is much smaller than U ($U_l \ll U$), it means that the best move become clearly distinguished from other moves. When U_l is much larger than U ($U_l \gg U$), it means that the previous estimation of U was inaccurate and needed to be updated. Therefore, in the both cases, such l has a high priority for exploration, as discussed in the literature [4].

Below we discuss four strategies to select l (strategy four has two variants).

HB + E^{Terminal}. One reasonable strategy is to select l that has the maximum absolute difference $|U_l - U|$, averaging over all possible U_l values with its probability. Let us assume that the exploration of leaf l reveals that l is terminal or solved with a game-theoretical value r according to its current distribution. Let $\hat{U}_l^{=r}$ be the value U_l when leaf l is found to be terminal with value r. Further assuming that the distributions of other leaves are not changed during the exploration of l, we can directly calculate $\hat{U}_l^{=r}$. Then, in strategy HB+E^{Terminal}, we select l that has the maximum absolute difference $|U_l^{=r} - U|$ averaging over all possible $U_l^{=r}$ values with its probability:

$$\arg\max_l \sum_{r \in \{0, 0.5, 1\}} p_l(r)|\hat{U}_l^{=r} - U| \tag{6}$$

This strategy is equivalent to QSS [4], though their work does not involve MCTS.

HB + E^{Expected}. In many games, terminal nodes are relatively rarer than nonterminal nodes. Following this observation, we introduce a model in which leaf l is assumed to be an unsolved node after exploration with an additional playout result r with probability $p_l(r)$. This assumption is natural when we adopt UCT as a sub-strategy. Let $\hat{U}_l^{+r}$ be the value of U_l when the distribution of leaf l is changed by observing an additional result r. Then, we select l that has the maximum absolute difference $|U_l^{+r} - U|$, averaging all over possible U_l^{+r} values with its probability:

$$\arg\max_l \sum_{r \in \{0, 0.5, 1\}} p_l(r)|\hat{U}_l^{+r} - U| \tag{7}$$

HB + E^{Robust}. This is our main strategy that identifies the worst playout result on any leaf l that maximizes U_l. Recall that a U_l larger than the current U suggests an error in the current estimation. To extend this idea further, HB+E^{Robust} explores l that can achieve the maximum U_l considering all U_l^{+r}:

$$\arg\max_l \max_{r \in \{0, 0.5, 1\}} U_l^{+r}. \tag{8}$$

A distribution obtained by the negamax procedure tends to be unstable in that a single playout may substantially modify the distribution. This strategy is expected to remedy the instability by exploring such nodes first.

Property 1. Value U_l^{+r} is maximized when r is 1 (0) for a leaf l that is (is not) the descendant of the current best move m_0 at the root. Note that reward r here is for a player to move at the root. When a player to move at leaf l differs from that at the root, reward r at the root, corresponds to $1 - r$ at leaf l.

HB+BayesUCT. All strategies introduced so far are aimed at minimizing the uncertainty U. Alternatively, we can adopt BayesUCT [18]. HB+BayesUCT descends from the root to a leaf, choosing the node having the largest Bayes-UCB value shown in Eq. (2). Here, $\hat{\mu}_i$ is the mean of probability $p(r)$ for $r \in \{0, 0.5, 1\}$.

The lower half of Table 1 summarizes our strategies.

3.3   Implementation Details

Nodes in the extended tree should be promoted to the main tree in step 3 in each iteration in Fig. 2, when the sub-trees under the nodes are sufficiently searched. In our experiments, all of leaf l_{main}'s children are promoted at the same time, when the number of visits to l_{main} reaches at least 20 and when the minimum number of visits to each of them reaches at least 2. The condition on the number of visits is crucial, especially in strategies HB+E^{Terminal} and HB+E^{Expected}. In these strategies, such a node has the least priority and is rarely selected for exploration if it has a single reward of positive frequency. If the playout result of node l up to this point is always a win, for example the same result is assumed to be observed in the next playout in E^{Terminal} and E^{Expected}, then it yields that $U_l = U$. Here we note that HB+E^{Robust} is free from this problem.

In strategies HB+E^{Terminal}, HB+E^{Expected} and HB+E^{Robust}, the computation of the priority of each leaf can be accelerated by first identifying the influence of each leaf on the root [4]. We followed this technique in the current work. Still, it requires computation proportional to the number of nodes in the main tree. Note that this computational cost is usually concealed because the number of nodes in the main tree is much less than that in the extended tree.

Also, the balance in the computational costs in a primary strategy and in UCT can be adjusted by the budget, which is the number of internal playouts performed in step 2. When the budget is more than 1, we need to estimate U_l after multiple playouts. In HB+E^{Robust}, such U_l is estimated without additional computational costs because reward r giving the maximum $\hat{U}_l^{+r}$ remains the same, regardless of the budget, for each leaf l by Property 1 (see 3.2). Additionally, in HB+E^{Terminal}, we assumed the same U_l for multiple playouts. However, in HB+E^{Expected}, U_l must be computed with additional costs.

We handled solved nodes using the method by Winands et al. [20]. Note that the reward distribution of a solved node automatically converges when a negamax-style backup is adopted. However, we still need to maintain solved nodes for UCT in the extended tree. Also, in HB+BayesUCT, solved nodes of a draw reward may be chosen in Eq. (2). Therefore, such nodes should be excluded from the candidates for exploration because the exploration no longer contributes to updating the probability distribution. Further it is noted that in UCT, solved nodes of a draw reward should be kept as candidates for exploration so as to stabilize the reward average.

4   Experimental Results

We conducted experiments on incremental random trees in order to compare the performance of various algorithms. A random value in a uniform distribution was assigned to each edge. The game score at a leaf was the summation of edge values from the root, and the reward of the leaf with respect to the root player was 1 for a positive score, 0.5 for score zero, and 0 for a negative score. All trees were generated with uniform width and depth, but some sub-trees were pruned in advance to introduce variations in width and depth. In the pruning procedure, each internal node in a tree is set to be terminal with probability P, and the sub-tree under the node is pruned. Also, exactly one edge at each node is assigned value zero instead of a random value so that the score of the principal variation is zero, for simplicity of analysis [9]. However, it is known that the performance of UCT is sensitive to the rewards of moves at the root [2,12]. We introduced the bias parameter Bi that is added to the game scores of all leaves, in order to introduce diversity in the game score for the principal variation. Because each edge value is an integer, the reward of each leaf cannot be a draw when the bias is 0.5.

4.1   Failure Rates

We compared six algorithms: five variations of the proposed method with hybrid backup, and the usual UCT for reference. Algorithms HB+E^{Terminal}, HB+E^{Expected}, HB+E^{Robust}, HB+BayesUCT1, and HB+BayesUCT2 were introduced in Sect. 3. In this experiment, the budget in our algorithms was fixed in 1, and all algorithms incorporated MCTS Solver for handling solved nodes [20]. At the beginning of the search, we initialized the current best move randomly, because all moves have an equal mean of reward distribution. The current best move was replaced if and only if there appeared a better move with respect to the mean of its reward distribution.

Although we generated game trees in advance, each search algorithm starts with only its root with the immediate successor nodes and then gradually incorporates new leaves as explained in Sect. 3. We tested two configurations of branching factor and depth; (4, 12) and (8, 8). In addition, its terminal probability P was 0, 0.1, or 0.2. For each configuration of trees, we generated 400 instances and ran each algorithm 200 times. We measured the effectiveness of each algorithm through the failure rate, following the method described by Kocsis and Szepesvári [13]. The failure rate is the rate in which the algorithm fails to choose the optimal move at the root.

The results are summarized in Table 2. The proposed method HB+E^{Robust} achieved the best results among all methods in trees where terminal probability P was not zero, while UCT achieved the best results when P was zero. These results are consistent with previous reports that found the performance of UCT degrades when a tree has a non-uniform width or has traps each of which is a losing move [17,18]. The performance of both HB+E^{Robust} and UCT improved when bias was added to the trees. The performance of BayesUCT was not as good as expected in these configurations. Although a detailed analysis of the reasons for this is beyond the scope of this paper, the differences in discrete histograms or Beta distributions in the representation of reward distributions may affect the performance. It might also depend whether a game tree is fixed or iteratively expanded during the search.

In Fig. 3, we can see how the failure rate decreases as the number of playouts increases. We can observe that the failure rate of HB+E^{Robust} decreases faster than UCT and the other methods if the terminal probability is positive.

Table 2. Table of failure rates when there were 4000 playouts, where B is branching factor, D is maximum depth, P is terminal probability, and Bi is bias. In each setting, the lowest failure rate observed is indicated in bold.

B - D	P	Bi	Hybrid Backup (HB)					UCT
			E^{Terminal}	E^{Expected}	E^{Robust}	BayesUCT1	BayesUCT2	
4-12	0.0	0	0.079025	0.078487	0.078575	0.037750	0.129050	**0.013088**
		0.5	0.060987	0.058975	0.029712	0.057512	0.085550	**0.016987**
	0.1	0	0.001275	0.001212	**0.000188**	0.005525	0.017175	0.040137
		0.5	0.000163	0.000238	**0.000000**	0.001225	0.000988	0.000213
	0.2	0	**0.000000**	**0.000000**	**0.000000**	0.000650	0.000450	0.002288
		0.5	**0.000000**	**0.000000**	**0.000000**	**0.000000**	**0.000000**	**0.000000**
	0.0	1	0.050350	0.046487	0.025087	0.066387	0.145387	**0.023013**
	0.1	1	0.001213	0.001225	**0.000325**	0.034000	0.028837	0.007738
	0.2	1	**0.000000**	**0.000000**	**0.000000**	0.001088	0.002325	0.000025
	0.0	2	0.008500	0.008138	0.001512	0.003912	0.067475	**0.000000**
	0.1	2	0.000113	0.000100	**0.000000**	0.001438	0.007950	0.000013
	0.2	2	**0.000000**	**0.000000**	**0.000000**	**0.000000**	0.000450	**0.000000**
8-8	0.0	0	0.264350	0.251387	0.301200	0.777625	0.174887	**0.016825**
	0.1	0	0.090300	0.074125	**0.046825**	0.093362	0.068025	0.098437
	0.2	0	0.007125	0.004425	**0.001187**	0.036912	0.014563	0.067225

Table 3. Average milliseconds consumed by single playout.

	budget	P = 0.0	P = 0.1	P = 0.2		budget	P = 0.0	P = 0.1	P = 0.2
HB+E^{Robust}	1	0.151095	0.079921	0.041580	UCT	1	0.012968	0.008496	0.004249
	10	0.021505	0.015718	0.011130					
	20	0.016167	0.012834	0.008930					

4.2   Acceleration by Increasing Budget

We measured the computational efficiency of HB+E^{Robust}, which was the most effective algorithm in the previous experiments. The computational cost of the primary strategy in HB+E^{Robust} is more expensive than that of UCT. Therefore, the computational efficiency per playout is improved by increasing the number of internal playouts and the budget at the expense of exploration accuracy.

We measured the average consumed time for a playout by dividing the total time consumed by the number of playouts. We used trees with branching factor 4 and depth 12 and performed 4000 playouts for each tree, which means that the main tree is explored 4000/budget times. In our hybrid algorithms, UCT sometimes identifies that the root of the current exploration, which is a leaf in the main tree, is solved. In such cases, exploration on the node is stopped, and the distributions of the main tree are updated, even before the number of playouts reaches a given budget. We used a computer equipped with an AMD Opteron Processor 6274, 2.2 GHz, running Linux for this experiment.

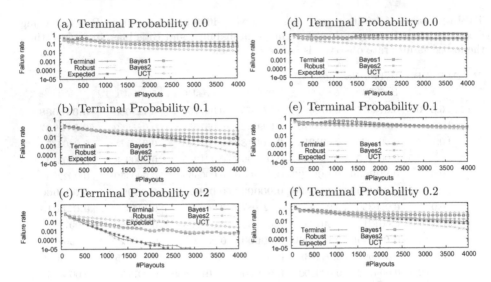

Fig. 3. Failure rates: (branching factor, depth) is $(4, 12)$ on left, and $(8, 8)$ on right.

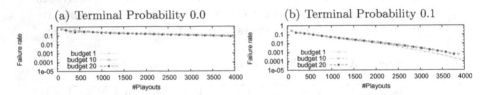

Fig. 4. Failure rates of HB+E^{Robust} for budgets, 1, 10, and 20.

The failure rate is slightly increased by increasing the budget, although the difference is limited, as shown in Fig. 4. Table 3 lists the average time consumed per playout in HB+E^{Robust} and in UCT. We can see that the efficiency improved by increasing the budget. Though UCT is still faster than HB+E^{Robust} with a budget of 20, we argue that the difference is almost negligible in typical situations where a random simulation for each playout consumes about 1 ms.

5   Conclusion

This paper presented a new anytime Monte-Carlo tree search method that iteratively refines the confidence on the best move. It is estimated by the reward distribution of each move at the root, where the distributions of interior nodes are obtained by a negamax-style backup in the main game tree and by UCT in the extended tree. In each iteration, the leaf that most contributes to the confidence is explored further by UCT. The experiments on synthetic trees showed that the presented method outperformed UCT and similar methods, except for trees having uniform width and depth. Among several strategies, the experimental results suggest that a strategy expecting the worst playout outcome performed the best.

Acknowledgement. This work was partially supported by Grant-in-Aid for JSPS Fellows 16J07455.

References

1. Auer, P., Cesa-Bianchi, N., Fischer, P.: Finite-time analysis of the multiarmed bandit problem. Mach. Learn. **47**(2–3), 235–256 (2002)
2. Baudiš, P.: Balancing MCTS by dynamically adjusting the komi value. ICGA J. Int. Comput. Games Assoc. **34**(3), 131 (2011)
3. Baudiš, P., Gailly, J.: PACHI: state of the art open source go program. In: Herik, H.J., Plaat, A. (eds.) ACG 2011. LNCS, vol. 7168, pp. 24–38. Springer, Heidelberg (2012). doi:10.1007/978-3-642-31866-5_3
4. Baum, E.B., Smith, W.D.: A bayesian approach to relevance in game playing. Artif. Intell. **97**(1), 195–242 (1997)
5. Browne, C., Powley, E.J., Whitehouse, D., Lucas, S.M., Cowling, P.I., Rohlfshagen, P., Tavener, S., Perez, D., Samothrakis, S., Colton, S.: A survey of Monte Carlo tree search methods. IEEE Trans. Comput. Intellig. AI Games **4**(1), 1–43 (2012)
6. Bubeck, S., Munos, R., Stoltz, G.: Pure exploration in finitely-armed and continuous-armed bandits. Theor. Comput. Sci. **412**(19), 1832–1852 (2011). Algorithmic Learning Theory (ALT 2009)
7. Cazenave, T.: Sequential halving applied to trees. IEEE Trans. Comput. Intellig. AI Games **7**(1), 102–105 (2015)
8. Enzenberger, M., Muller, M., Arneson, B., Segal, R.: Fuego-an open-source framework for board games and go engine based on Monte Carlo tree search. IEEE Trans. Comput. Intellig. AI Games **2**(4), 259–270 (2010)
9. Furtak, T., Buro, M.: Minimum proof graphs and fastest-cut-first search heuristics. In: IJCAI, pp. 492–498 (2009)
10. Gelly, S., Kocsis, L., Schoenauer, M., Sebag, M., Silver, D., Szepesvári, C., Teytaud, O.: The grand challenge of computer go: Monte Carlo tree search and extensions. Commun. ACM **55**(3), 106–113 (2012)
11. Graf, T., Schaefers, L., Platzner, M.: On semeai detection in Monte-Carlo go. In: Herik, H.J., Iida, H., Plaat, A. (eds.) CG 2013. LNCS, vol. 8427, pp. 14–25. Springer, Heidelberg (2014). doi:10.1007/978-3-319-09165-5_2
12. Imagawa, T., Kaneko, T.: Enhancements in Monte Carlo tree search algorithms for biased game trees. In: IEEE Computational Intelligence and Games (CIG), pp. 43–50 (2015)
13. Kocsis, L., Szepesvári, C.: Bandit based Monte-Carlo planning. In: Fürnkranz, J., Scheffer, T., Spiliopoulou, M. (eds.) ECML 2006. LNCS (LNAI), vol. 4212, pp. 282–293. Springer, Heidelberg (2006). doi:10.1007/11871842_29
14. Liu, Y.C., Tsuruoka, Y.: Regulation of exploration for simple regret minimization in Monte-Carlo tree search. In: 2015 IEEE Conference on Computational Intelligence and Games (CIG), pp. 35–42, August 2015
15. Pepels, T., Cazenave, T., Winands, M.H.M., Lanctot, M.: Minimizing simple and cumulative regret in Monte-Carlo tree search. In: Cazenave, T., Winands, M.H.M., Björnsson, Y. (eds.) CGW 2014. CCIS, vol. 504, pp. 1–15. Springer, Heidelberg (2014). doi:10.1007/978-3-319-14923-3_1
16. Plaat, A., Schaeffer, J., Pijls, W., de Bruin, A.: Best-first fixed depth minimax algorithms. Artif. Intell. **87**, 255–293 (1996)
17. Ramanujan, R., Sabharwal, A., Selman, B.: On adversarial search spaces and sampling-based planning. In: ICAPS, pp. 242–245 (2010)

18. Tesauro, G., Rajan, V., Segal, R.: Bayesian inference in Monte-Carlo tree search. In: the 26th Conference on Uncertainty in Artificial Intelligence (UAI 2010) (2010)
19. Tolpin, D., Shimony, S.E.: MCTS based on simple regret. In: AAAI (2012)
20. Winands, M.H.M., Björnsson, Y., Saito, J.-T.: Monte-Carlo tree search solver. In: Herik, H.J., Xu, X., Ma, Z., Winands, M.H.M. (eds.) CG 2008. LNCS, vol. 5131, pp. 25–36. Springer, Heidelberg (2008). doi:10.1007/978-3-540-87608-3_3
21. Yokoyama, D., Kitsuregawa, M.: A randomized game-tree search algorithm for shogi based on Bayesian approach. In: Pham, D.-N., Park, S.-B. (eds.) PRICAI 2014. LNCS (LNAI), vol. 8862, pp. 937–944. Springer, Heidelberg (2014). doi:10.1007/978-3-319-13560-1_81

Pruning Playouts in Monte-Carlo Tree Search for the Game of Havannah

Joris Duguépéroux, Ahmad Mazyad, Fabien Teytaud, and Julien Dehos[✉]

LISIC, ULCO, Université du Littoral Côte d'Opale, Calais, France
dehos@lisic.univ-littoral.fr

Abstract. Monte-Carlo Tree Search (MCTS) is a popular technique for playing multi-player games. In this paper, we propose a new method to bias the playout policy of MCTS. The idea is to prune the decisions which seem "bad" (according to the previous iterations of the algorithm) before computing each playout. Thus, the method evaluates the estimated "good" moves more precisely. We have tested our improvement for the game of Havannah and compared it to several classic improvements. Our method outperforms the classic version of MCTS (with the RAVE improvement) and the different playout policies of MCTS that we have experimented.

1 Introduction

Monte-Carlo Tree Search (MCTS) algorithms are recent algorithms for decision making problems [6,7]. They are competitively used in discrete, observable and uncertain environments with a finite horizon and when the number of possible states is large. MCTS algorithms evaluate a state of the problem using a Monte-Carlo simulation (roughly, by performing numerous playouts starting from this state). Therefore, they require no evaluation function, which makes them quite generic and usable on a large number of applications. Many games are naturally suited for these algorithms so games are classically used for comparing such algorithms.

In this paper, we propose a method to improve the Monte-Carlo simulation (playouts) by pruning some of the possible moves. The idea is to ignore the decisions which seem "bad" when computing a playout, and thus to consider the "good" moves more precisely. We choose the moves to be pruned thanks to statistics established during previous playouts.

We experiment our improvement, called "Playout Pruning with Rave" (PPR) on the game of Havannah. Classic MCTS algorithms already provide good results with this game but our experiments show that PPR performs better. We also compare PPR to four well-known MCTS improvements (PoolRave, LGRF1, MAST and NAST2).

The remaining of this paper presents the game of Havannah in Sect. 2 and the Monte-Carlo Tree Search algorithms in Sect. 3. Our new improvement is described in Sect. 4. We present our results in Sect. 5. Finally, we conclude in Sect. 6.

© Springer International Publishing AG 2016
A. Plaat et al. (Eds.): CG 2016, LNCS 10068, pp. 47–57, 2016.
DOI: 10.1007/978-3-319-50935-8_5

2   Game of Havannah

The game of Havannah is a 2-player board game created by Christian Freeling in 1979 and updated in 1992 [26]. It belongs to the family of connection games with hexagonal cells. It is played on a hexagonal board, meaning 6 corners and 6 edges (corner stones do not belong to edges). At each turn a player has to play a stone in an empty cell. The goal is to realize one of these three shapes (i) a ring, which is a loop around one or more cells (empty or occupied by any stones) (ii) a bridge, which is a continuous string of stones connecting two corners (iii) a fork, which is a continuous string of stones connecting three edges. If there is no empty cell left and if no player wins then it is a draw (see Fig. 1). Previous studies related to the Monte-Carlo Tree Search algorithm applied to the game of Havannah can be found in [10, 20, 30].

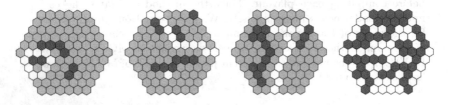

Fig. 1. The three winning shapes of Havannah (wins for the white player): a ring (left), a bridge (middle left) and a fork (middle right), and a draw (right).

3   Monte-Carlo Tree Search Algorithms

The Monte-Carlo Tree Search (MCTS) algorithm is currently a state-of-the-art algorithm for many decision making problems [3, 9, 16, 31], and is particularly relevant in games [1, 5, 12, 14, 15, 19, 21, 22, 29, 30]. The general principle of MCTS is to iteratively build a tree and perform playouts to bias the decision making process toward the best decisions [6, 7, 18]. Starting with the current state s_0 of a problem, the MCTS algorithm incrementally builds a subtree of the future states. Here, the goal is to get an unbalanced subtree, where the branches with (estimated) good states are more developed. The subtree is built in four steps: *selection, expansion, simulation* and *backpropagation* (see Fig. 2).

The *selection* step is to choose an existing node among available nodes in the subtree. The most common implementation of MCTS is the Upper Confidence Tree (UCT) [18] which uses a bandit formula for choosing a node. A possible bandit formula is defined as follows:

$$s_1 \leftarrow \underset{j \in \mathcal{C}_{s_1}}{\arg \max} \left[\frac{w_j}{n_j} + K \sqrt{\frac{\ln(n_{s_1})}{n_j}} \right],$$

where $\mathcal{C}_{s_1}$ is the set of child nodes of the node s_1, w_j is the number of wins for the node j (more precisely, the sum of the final rewards for j), n_j is the number

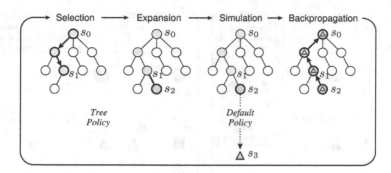

Fig. 2. The MCTS algorithm iteratively builds a subtree of the possible future states (circles). This figure (from [4]) illustrates one iteration of the algorithm. Starting from the root node s_0 (current state of the problem), a node s_1 is selected and a new node s_2 is created. A playout is performed (until a final state s_3 is reached) and the subtree is updated.

of playouts for the node j and n_{s_1} is the number of playouts for the node s_1 ($n_{s_1} = \sum_j n_j$). K is called the exploration parameter and is used to tune the trade-off between exploitation and exploration.

Once a leaf node s_1 is selected, the *expansion* step creates a new child node s_2. This new node corresponds to a decision of s_1 which has not been considered yet. Then, the *simulation* step is to perform a playout (a random game) until a final state s_3 is reached. This final state gives a reward (for example, in games, the reward corresponds to a win, a loss or a draw). The last step (*backpropagation*) is to use the reward to update the statistics (number of wins and number of playouts) in all the nodes encountered during the *selection* step.

3.1 Rapid Action Value Estimate

One of the most common improvements of the MCTS algorithm is the Rapid Action Value Estimate (RAVE) [12]. The idea is to share some statistics about moves between nodes: if a move is good in a certain state, then it may be good in other ones.

More precisely, let s be a node and m_i the possible moves from s, leading to the child nodes s'_i. For the classic MCTS algorithm, we already store, in s, the number of winning playouts w_s and the total number of playouts n_s (after s was selected). For the RAVE improvement, we also store, in s and for each move m_i, the number of winning playouts w'_{s,s'_i} and the total number of playouts n'_{s,s'_i} obtained by choosing the move m_i. These "RAVE statistics" are updated during the backpropagation step and indicate the estimated quality of the moves already considered in the subtree (see Fig. 3).

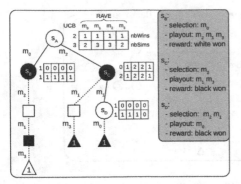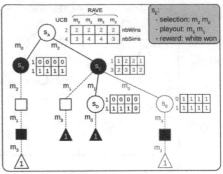

Fig. 3. Illustration of the RAVE process. In each node, an array stores the RAVE statistics of all possible moves (left); this array is updated when a corresponding move is played (right). In this example, a new node (S_E) is created and all the moves chosen in the *selection* step (m_2, m_0) and in the *simulation* step (m_3, m_1) are updated in the RAVE statistics of the selected nodes (S_A, S_C, S_E) during the *backpropagation* step.

Thus, the selection step can be biased by adding a RAVE score in the bandit formula defined previously:

$$s_1 \leftarrow \arg\max_{j \in \mathcal{C}_{s_1}} \left[(1 - \beta) \, \frac{w_j}{n_j} + \beta \, \frac{w'_{s_1,j}}{n'_{s_1,j}} + K \, \sqrt{\frac{\ln(n_{s_1})}{n_j}} \right],$$

where β is a parameter approaching 0 as n_j tends to infinity (for instance, $\beta = \sqrt{\frac{R}{R+3n_j}}$ where R is a parameter [13]).

3.2 Playout Improvements

PoolRave is an extension of RAVE [17,25]. The idea is to use the RAVE statistics to bias the simulation step (unlike the RAVE improvement which biases the selection step). More precisely, when a playout is performed, the PoolRave improvement firstly builds a pool of possible moves by selecting the N best moves according to the RAVE statistics. Then, in the simulation step, the moves are chosen randomly in the pool with probability p, otherwise (with probability $1-p$) a random possible move is played, as in the classic MCTS algorithm.

The Last-Good-Reply improvement [2,8] is based on the principle of learning how to respond to a move. In each node, LGR stores move replies which lead to a win in previous playouts. More precisely, during a playout, if the node has a reply for the last move of the opponent, this reply is played, otherwise a new reply is created using a random possible move. At the end of the playout, if the playout leads to a win, the corresponding replies are stored in the node. If the playout leads to a loss, the corresponding replies are removed from the node (*forgetting* step). This algorithm is called LGRF1. Other algorithms have been proposed using the same idea but LGRF1 is the most efficient one with connection games [27].

The principle of the Move-Average Sampling Technique (MAST) [11] is to store move statistics globally and to use these statistics to bias the playouts. This is similar to the PoolRave improvement, except that here, the statistics are independent of the position of the move in the tree.

The N-gram Average Sampling Technique (NAST) is a generalization of MAST [23,28]. The idea is to look at sequences of N moves instead of one move only. This improvement can be costly according to N but it is already efficient with $N = 2$ (NAST2) for the game of Havannah [27].

4   Pruning in the Simulation Step

We propose a new improvement of the MCTS algorithm, called "Playout Pruning with Rave" (PPR). The idea is to prune bad moves in the simulation step in order to focus the simulation on good playouts (see Fig. 4, left). More precisely, before the playout, we compute a list of good moves by pruning the moves which have a winning rate lower than a given threshold $T_{w'}$. The winning rate of a node j is computed using the RAVE statistics of a node s_{PPR}, with $\frac{w'_{s_{\text{PPR}},j}}{n'_{s_{\text{PPR}},j}}$.

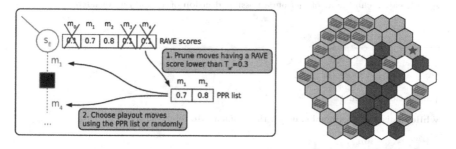

Fig. 4. During a playout (left), the PPR process discards all moves with a RAVE winning rate lower than a given threshold, then plays a move among this pruned list (or a random move, according to a given probability). For example (right), after 100 k MCTS iterations for black, PPR prunes the scratched cells and finally plays the starred cell, which seems relevant: the three scratched cells on the right cannot be used by black to form a winning shape; at the top left of the board several white cells prevent black from accessing the scratched cells easily; the three remaining scratched cells are seen by PPR as functionally equivalent to other possible cells of the board.

The node s_{PPR}, giving the RAVE statistics, has to be chosen carefully. Indeed, the node s_2, selected during the selection step of the MCTS algorithm, may still have very few playouts, hence inaccurate RAVE statistics. To solve this problem, we traverse the MCTS tree bottom-up, starting from s_2, until we reach a node with a minimum ratio T_n, representing the current number of playouts for s_{PPR} over the total number of playouts performed.

After the PPR list is computed, the simulation step is performed. The idea is to use the moves in the PPR list, which are believed to be good, but we also have to choose other moves to explore other possible playouts. To this end, during the simulation step, each move is chosen in the PPR list with a probability p, or among the possible moves with a probability $1 - p$. In the latter case, we have observed that considering only a part of all the possible moves gives better results; this can be seen as a default pruning with, in return, an additional bias (see Algorithm 1).

Algorithm 1. Monte-Carlo Tree Search with RAVE and PPR

{initialization}
$s_0 \leftarrow$ create root node from the current state of the problem

while there is some time left **do**

  {selection}
  $s_1 \leftarrow s_0$
  while all possible decisions of s_1 have been considered **do**
    $C_{s_1} \leftarrow$ child nodes of s_1
    $\beta \leftarrow \sqrt{\frac{R}{R + 3n_j}}$
    $s_1 \leftarrow \underset{j \in C_{s_1}}{\arg\max} \left[(1 - \beta)\frac{w_j}{n_j} + \beta \frac{w'_{s_1,j}}{n'_{s_1,j}} + K \sqrt{\frac{\ln(n_{s_1})}{n_j}} \right]$

  {expansion}
  $s_2 \leftarrow$ create a child node of s_1 from a possible decision of s_1 not yet considered

  {pruning}
  $s_{\text{PPR}} \leftarrow s_2$
  while $n_{s_{\text{PPR}}} < T_n$ **do**
    $s_{\text{PPR}} \leftarrow$ parent node of s_{PPR}
  $\text{PPR} \leftarrow \{ j \mid \frac{w'_{s_{\text{PPR}} \cdot j}}{n'_{s_{\text{PPR}} \cdot j}} > T_{w'} \}$

  {simulation/playout}
  $s_3 \leftarrow s_2$
  while s_3 is not a terminal state for the problem **do**
    $\xi \leftarrow$ random()
    if $\xi \leq p$ **then**
      $s_3 \leftarrow$ randomly choose next state in PPR
    else
      $s_3 \leftarrow$ randomly choose next state in the $(1 - \xi)$ last part of the possible moves

  {backpropagation}
  $s_4 \leftarrow s_2$
  while $s_4 \neq s_0$ **do**
    $w_{s_4} \leftarrow w_{s_4} +$ reward of the terminal state s_3 for the player of s_4
    $n_{s_4} \leftarrow n_{s_4} + 1$
    for all nodes j belonging to the path $s_0 s_3$ **do**
      $w'_{s_4,j} \leftarrow w'_{s_4,j} +$ reward of the terminal state s_3 for the player of j
      $n'_{s_4,j} \leftarrow n'_{s_4,j} + 1$
    $s_4 \leftarrow$ parent node of s_4

return best child of s_0

The PPR improvement can be seen as a dynamic version of the PoolRave improvement presented in the previous section: instead of selecting the N best moves in a pool, we discard the moves which have a winning rate lower than $T_{w'}$.

PoolRave uses a static pool size, which implies that good moves may be discarded (if the pool size is small in front of the number of good moves) or that bad moves may be chosen (if the pool size is large in front of the number of good moves). PPR automatically deals with this problem since the size of the PPR list is naturally dynamic: the list is small if there are only few good moves, and large if there are many good moves.

5   Experiments

We have experimented with the proposed MCTS improvement (PPR) for the game of Havannah. Since RAVE is now considered as a classic MCTS baseline, we have compared PPR against RAVE (using the parameters $R = 130$ and $K = 0$). To have adequate statistical properties, we have played 600 games for each experiment. Since the first player has an advantage in the game of Havannah, we played, for each experiment, half the games with the first algorithm as the first player and the other half with the second algorithm as the first player.

   Below we report on the influence of the PPR parmeters (Sect. 5.1), scalability of the playout pruning (Sect. 5.2), and the comparison between PPR and other playout improvements (Sect. 5.3).

5.1   Influence of the PPR Parameters

To study the influence of the three parameters of the PPR improvement (T_n, $T_{w'}$, P), we have compared PPR against RAVE using 1 k MCTS iterations and a board size of 6. For each parameter, we have experimented with various values while the other parameters were set to default values (see Fig. 5).

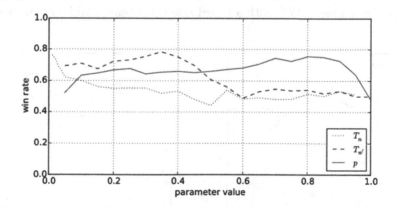

Fig. 5. Influence of the PPR parameters in the game of Havannah (PPR vs RAVE, 1 k MCTS iterations, board size 6). Each parameter is studied while the other ones are set to default values: $T_n = 1\%$, $T_{w'} = 25\%$ and $p = 80\%$, where T_n is the minimum ratio of playouts for the node s_{PPR}, $T_{w'}$ is the win rate threshold for pruning bad moves and p is the probability for using the PPR list.

PPR has better win rates against RAVE when T_n (the minimum ratio of playouts for the node s_{PPR} over the total number of playouts) is lower than 10%. A low value for T_n means that we take a node s_{PPR} close to the node s_2 which has launched the playout; thus the PPR list is built using RAVE statistics that are meaningful for the playout but quite unreliable. When T_n is too large, no node has sufficient playouts so the PPR list is empty and PPR is equivalent to RAVE (win rate of 50%).

The best values for the pruning threshold $T_{w'}$ (win rate in the RAVE statistics of s_{PPR}) stand between 20% and 40%. The moves with a winning rate lower than this threshold are pruned when building the PPR list. Therefore, if $T_{w'}$ is too high, all moves are pruned (i.e., the PPR list is empty) and the algorithm is equivalent to RAVE (win rate of 50%). In addition, if $T_{w'}$ is too low, then the PPR list also contains bad moves (low winning rate) which lowers the efficiency of PPR.

Finally, the best values for the parameter p (probability for using the PPR list instead of a random sampling, to choose a move) stand between 60% and 80% in our experiments. A low value implies that the PPR list is rarely used, making PPR almost equivalent to RAVE. With a very high value, the PPR list is frequently used, so PPR does not explore other moves, hence a highly biased playout computation.

5.2   Scalability of the Playout Pruning

Like classic improvements of the simulation step (for instance, PoolRave and LGRF1), PPR is useful for small numbers of playouts and large board sizes (see Fig. 6).

In our experiments, PPR wins almost 80% of the games against RAVE with 1 k MCTS iterations, and almost 70% with 10 k iterations. PPR wins 60% or less of the games against RAVE with a board size lower than 5 and 80% or more of

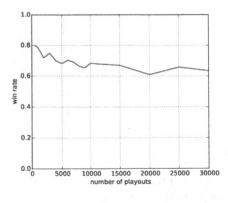
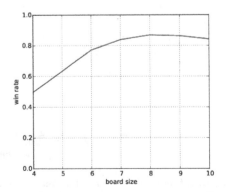

Fig. 6. Influence of the number of MCTS iterations (left, with board size 6) and board size (right, with 1 k MCTS iterations) in the game of Havannah (PPR vs RAVE, $T_n = 1\%$, $T_{w'} = 25\%$ and $p = 80\%$).

the games with a board size larger than 7. This is not very surprising because RAVE is already very efficient when the board size is small, so adding pruning is useless in this case. However, large boards have many more "dead areas" (i.e., irrelevant cells) that PPR can detect and prune (see Fig. 4, right).

5.3 PPR Vs Other Playout Improvements

We have compared PPR against several MCTS improvements (RAVE, PoolRave, LGRF1, MAST, NAST2) for several board sizes and numbers of MCTS iterations (see Table 1). Since RAVE is now considered as the classic MCTS baseline, we have implemented all playout improvements (PPR, PoolRave, LGRF1, MAST, NAST2) based on the RAVE algorithm.

Our results indicate that PPR outperforms the previous algorithms for the game of Havannah. For a board size of 6, PPR wins more than 70% of the games with 1 k MCTS iterations and more than 60% of the games with 10 k or 30 k iterations. For a board size of 10, PPR is even better (more than 70%).

Table 1. PPR vs other MCTS improvements. We have performed 200 games for the experiments with size = 10 and playouts = 30, 000; 600 games for the other experiments.

size	playouts	player	win rate	std dev	size	playouts	player	win rate	std dev
		Rave	74.4%	±1.78			Rave	86.33%	±1.40
		PoolRave	70.17%	±1.87			PoolRave	72.16%	±1.82
	1,000	LGRF1	71.67%	±1.84		1,000	LGRF1	79.00%	±1.66
		MAST	74.0%	±1.79			MAST	83.66%	±1.50
		NAST2	85.0%	±1.46			NAST2	85.50%	±1.43
		Rave	63.67%	±1.96			Rave	79.16%	±1.65
		PoolRave	67.0%	±1.92			PoolRave	89.00%	±1.27
6	10,000	LGRF1	63.17%	±1.97	10	10,000	LGRF1	83.83%	±1.50
		MAST	64.5%	±1.95			MAST	79.00%	±1.66
		NAST2	76.5%	±1.73			NAST2	85.16%	±1.45
		Rave	66.33%	±1.92			Rave	75.85%	±2.13
		PoolRave	73.66%	±1.79			PoolRave	91.01%	±1.42
	30,000	LGRF1	65.66%	±1.93		30,000	LGRF1	79.69%	±2.01
		MAST	65.5%	±1.94			MAST	82.04%	±1.91
		NAST2	60.5%	±1.99			NAST2	84.08%	±1.82

6 Conclusion

In this paper, we have proposed a new improvement (called PPR) of the MCTS algorithm, based on the RAVE improvement. The idea is to prune the moves which seem "bad" according to previous playouts during the simulation step. We have compared PPR to previous MCTS improvements (RAVE, PoolRave,

LGRF1, MAST, NAST2) for the game of Havannah. In our experiments, PPR is the most efficient algorithm, reaching win rates of at least 60 %.

In future work, it would be interesting to compare PPR with other MCTS improvements such as Contextual Monte-Carlo [24] or with stronger bots [10]. We would also try PPR for other games or decision making problems to determine if the benefit of PPR is limited to the game of Havannah or if it is more general.

Acknowledgements. Experiments presented in this paper were carried out using the CALCULCO computing platform, supported by SCOSI/ULCO (Service Commun du Système d'Information de l'Université du Littoral Côte d'Opale).

References

1. Arneson, B., Hayward, R., Henderson, P.: Monte-Carlo tree search in hex. IEEE Trans. Comput. Intell. AI Games **2**(4), 251–258 (2010)
2. Baier, H., Drake, P.: The power of forgetting: improving the last-good-reply policy in Monte-Carlo go. IEEE Trans. Comput. Intell. AI Games **2**(4), 303–309 (2010)
3. Bertsimas, D., Griffith, J., Gupta, V., Kochenderfer, M.J., Mišić, V., Moss, R.: A comparison of Monte-Carlo tree search and mathematical optimization for large scale dynamic resource allocation (2014). arXiv:1405.5498
4. Browne, C., Powley, E., Whitehouse, D., Lucas, S., Cowling, P., Rohlfshagen, P., Tavener, S., Perez, D., Samothrakis, S., Colton, S.: A survey of Monte-Carlo tree search methods. IEEE Trans. Comput. Intell. AI Games **4**(1), 1–43 (2012)
5. Cazenave, T.: Monte-Carlo kakuro. In: Herik, H.J., Spronck, P. (eds.) ACG 2009. LNCS, vol. 6048, pp. 45–54. Springer, Heidelberg (2010). doi:10.1007/978-3-642-12993-3_5
6. Chaslot, G., Saito, J., Bouzy, B., Uiterwijk, J., Herik, H.: Monte-Carlo strategies for computer go. In: Proceedings of the 18th BeNeLux Conference on Artificial Intelligence, pp. 83–91, Namur, Belgium (2006)
7. Coulom, R.: Efficient selectivity and backup operators in Monte-Carlo tree search. In: Herik, H.J., Ciancarini, P., Donkers, H.H.L.M.J. (eds.) CG 2006. LNCS, vol. 4630, pp. 72–83. Springer, Heidelberg (2007). doi:10.1007/978-3-540-75538-8_7
8. Drake, P.: The last-good-reply policy for Monte-Carlo go. Int. Comput. Games Assoc. J. **32**(4), 221–227 (2009)
9. Edelkamp, S., Tang, Z.: Monte-Carlo tree search for the multiple sequence alignment problem. In: Eighth Annual Symposium on Combinatorial Search (2015)
10. Ewalds, T.: Playing and Solving Havannah. Master's thesis, University of Alberta (2012)
11. Finnsson, H., Björnsson, Y.: Simulation-based approach to general game playing. In: Proceedings of the 23rd National Conference on Artificial Intelligence, AAAI 2008, vol. 1, pp. 259–264. AAAI Press (2008)
12. Gelly, S., Silver, D.: Combining online and offline knowledge in UCT. In: Proceedings of the 24th International Conference on Machine Learning, pp. 273–280. ACM (2007)
13. Gelly, S., Silver, D.: Monte-Carlo tree search and rapid action value estimation in computer go. Artif. Intell. **175**(11), 1856–1875 (2011)
14. Guo, X., Singh, S., Lee, H., Lewis, R.L., Wang, X.: Deep learning for real-time atari game play using offline Monte-Carlo tree search planning. In: Advances in Neural Information Processing Systems, pp. 3338–3346 (2014)

15. Heinrich, J., Silver, D.: Self-play Monte-Carlo tree search in computer poker. In: Workshops at the Twenty-Eighth AAAI Conference on Artificial Intelligence (2014)
16. Herik, H.J., Kuipers, J., Vermaseren, J.A.M., Plaat, A.: Investigations with Monte Carlo tree search for finding better multivariate horner schemes. In: Filipe, J., Fred, A. (eds.) ICAART 2013. CCIS, vol. 449, pp. 3–20. Springer, Heidelberg (2014). doi:10.1007/978-3-662-44440-5_1
17. Hoock, J., Lee, C., Rimmel, A., Teytaud, F., Wang, M., Teytaud, O.: Intelligent agents for the game of go. IEEE Comput. Intell. Mag. 5(4), 28–42 (2010)
18. Kocsis, L., Szepesvári, C.: Bandit based Monte-Carlo planning. In: Fürnkranz, J., Scheffer, T., Spiliopoulou, M. (eds.) ECML 2006. LNCS (LNAI), vol. 4212, pp. 282–293. Springer, Heidelberg (2006). doi:10.1007/11871842_29
19. Lanctot, M., Saffidine, A., Veness, J., Archibald, C., Winands, M.: Monte Carlo*-minimax search. In: Proceedings of the Twenty-Third International Joint Conference on Artificial Intelligence, pp. 580–586. AAAI Press (2013)
20. Lorentz, R.: Improving Monte-Carlo tree search in Havannah. In: Computers and Games 2010, pp. 105–115 (2010)
21. Lorentz, R.J.: Amazons discover Monte-Carlo. In: Herik, H.J., Xu, X., Ma, Z., Winands, M.H.M. (eds.) CG 2008. LNCS, vol. 5131, pp. 13–24. Springer, Heidelberg (2008). doi:10.1007/978-3-540-87608-3_2
22. Mazyad, A., Teytaud, F., Fonlupt, C.: Monte-Carlo Tree Search for the "mr jack" board game. J. Soft Comput. Artif. Intell. Appl. (IJSCAI) 4(1) (2015)
23. Powley, E.J., Whitehouse, D., Cowling, P.I.: Bandits all the way down: UCB1 as a simulation policy in Monte-Carlo tree search. In: CIG, pp. 81–88. IEEE (2013)
24. Rimmel, A., Teytaud, F.: Multiple overlapping tiles for contextual Monte Carlo tree search. In: Chio, C., Cagnoni, S., Cotta, C., Ebner, M., Ekárt, A., Esparcia-Alcazar, A.I., Goh, C.-K., Merelo, J.J., Neri, F., Preuß, M., Togelius, J., Yannakakis, G.N. (eds.) EvoApplications 2010. LNCS, vol. 6024, pp. 201–210. Springer, Heidelberg (2010). doi:10.1007/978-3-642-12239-2_21
25. Rimmel, A., Teytaud, F., Teytaud, O.: Biasing Monte-Carlo simulations through RAVE values. In: Herik, H.J., Iida, H., Plaat, A. (eds.) CG 2010. LNCS, vol. 6515, pp. 59–68. Springer, Heidelberg (2011). doi:10.1007/978-3-642-17928-0_6
26. Schmittberger, R.: New Rules for Classic Games. Wiley, New York (1992)
27. Stankiewicz, J.A., Winands, M.H.M., Uiterwijk, J.W.H.M.: Monte-Carlo tree search enhancements for havannah. In: Herik, H.J., Plaat, A. (eds.) ACG 2011. LNCS, vol. 7168, pp. 60–71. Springer, Heidelberg (2012). doi:10.1007/978-3-642-31866-5_6
28. Tak, M.J., Winands, M.H., Björnsson, Y.: N-grams and the last-good-reply policy applied in general game playing. IEEE Trans. Comput. Intell. AI Games 4(2), 73–83 (2012)
29. Taralla, D.: Learning Artificial Intelligence in Large-Scale Video Games. Ph.D. thesis, University of Liège (2015)
30. Teytaud, F., Teytaud, O.: Creating an upper-confidence-tree program for havannah. In: Herik, H.J., Spronck, P. (eds.) ACG 2009. LNCS, vol. 6048, pp. 65–74. Springer, Heidelberg (2010). doi:10.1007/978-3-642-12993-3_7
31. Wilisowski, Ł., Dreżewski, R.: The application of co-evolutionary genetic programming and TD(1) reinforcement learning in large-scale strategy game VCMI. In: Jezic, G., Howlett, R.J., Jain, L.C. (eds.) Agent and Multi-Agent Systems: Technologies and Applications. SIST, vol. 38, pp. 81–93. Springer, Heidelberg (2015). doi:10.1007/978-3-319-19728-9_7

Fast Seed-Learning Algorithms for Games

Jialin Liu[1]([✉]), Olivier Teytaud[1], and Tristan Cazenave[2]

[1] TAO, Inria, University of Paris-Sud, UMR CNRS 8623, Gif-sur-yvette, France
jialin.liu.cn@gmail.com
[2] LAMSADE, Université Paris-Dauphine, Paris, France

Abstract. Recently, a methodology has been proposed for boosting the computational intelligence of randomized game-playing programs. We propose faster variants of these algorithms, namely rectangular algorithms (fully parallel) and bandit algorithms (faster in a sequential setup). We check the performance on several board games and card games. In addition, in the case of Go, we check the methodology when the opponent is completely distinct to the one used in the training.

1 Introduction: Portfolios of Random Seeds

Artificial intelligence (AI) has been invaded by ensemble methods [2,13]. In games, some recent papers propose to do so, and in particular to combine variants of a single program, thanks to tricks on random seeds.

The Impact of Random Seeds. We assume that an AI is given. This AI is supposed to be stochastic; even with the same flow of information, it will not always play the same sequence of moves. This is for example the case for Monte Carlo Tree Search [5,10]. Given such an AI, we can check its performance against a baseline program (possibly itself) as we vary the random seed, i.e., we can generate K different random seeds, and for each of these seeds play K_t games against the baseline. We can then plot the success rates, sort, and compare the differences to the standard deviations. Results are presented in Fig. 1 and show for several games that the seed has a significant impact. The methodologies presented in this paper are based on this phenomenon.

Related Work. Several works were dedicated to combining several AIs in the past. [11] combines several different AIs. Nash methods have been used in [7] for combining several opening books.

The work in [12] constructed several AIs from a single stochastic one and combined them by the BestSeed and Nash methods, detailed in Sect. 2. The application of the methodologies above to Go has already been investigated in [12]. These results were tested in cross-validation. We extend these results in Go to the case with transfer (i.e. we check the impact in terms of the success rate against other opponents, not related to the ones in learning) and we provide quadratically faster algorithms. We also perform experiments on additional games (Atari-Go, Breakthrough, Domineering, and several games from the GameTestBed platform).

© Springer International Publishing AG 2016
A. Plaat et al. (Eds.): CG 2016, LNCS 10068, pp. 58–70, 2016.
DOI: 10.1007/978-3-319-50935-8_6

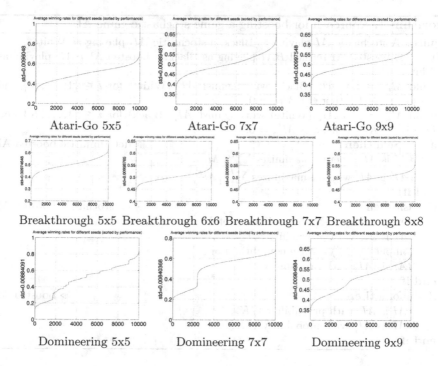

Atari-Go 5x5 Atari-Go 7x7 Atari-Go 9x9

Breakthrough 5x5 Breakthrough 6x6 Breakthrough 7x7 Breakthrough 8x8

Domineering 5x5 Domineering 7x7 Domineering 9x9

Fig. 1. Impact of the seed on the success rate. x-axis: index of seed; y-axis: success rate. For the nth value, we consider the nth worst seed for Black and the nth seed for White, and display their average scores against all opponent seeds. The label on the y-axis shows the standard deviation of these averages; we see that there are good seeds, which obtain a success rate far above 50% - by much more than the standard deviation.

2 Known Algorithms for Boosting an AI Using Random Seeds

This section presents an overview of two methods proposed in [12] for building a boosted algorithm from a set of seeds: the Nash-approach and the BestSeed-approach. We propose extensions of these methods and apply them to some new games. Typically, a stochastic computer program uses a random seed. The random seed ω is randomly drawn (using the clock, usually) and then a pseudo-random sequence is generated. Therefore, a stochastic program is in fact a random variable, distributed over deterministic program. Let us define: AI is our game playing artificial intelligence; it is stochastic. $AI(\omega)$ is a deterministic version; ω is a seed, which is randomly drawn in the original AI. We can easily generate plenty of ω and therefore one stochastic AI becomes several deterministic AIs, termed AI_1, AI_2, ... Let us assume that one of the players plays as Black and the other plays as White. We can do the same construction as

---

Algorithm 1. Approach for boosting a game stochastic game AI.

Require: A stochastic AI playing as Black, a stochastic AI' playing as White.
Output: A boosted AI termed BAI playing as Black, a boosted AI BAI' playing as White.

1: Build $M_{i,j} = 1$ if AI_i (Black) wins against AI'_j (White) for $i \in \{1,\ldots,K\}$ and $j \in \{1,\ldots,K_t\}$, otherwise $M_{i,j} = 0$.
2: Build $M'_{i,j} = 1$ if AI'_i (White) wins against AI_j (Black) for $i \in \{1,\ldots,K\}$ and $j \in \{1,\ldots,K_t\}$, otherwise $M'_{i,j} = 0$.
3: **if** BestSeed **then**   ▷ deterministic boosted AI
4:      BAI is AI_i where i maximizes $\sum_{j=1}^{K_t} M_{i,j}$.
5:      BAI' is AI'_i where i maximizes $\sum_{j=1}^{K_t} M'_{i,j}$.
6: **end if**
7: **if** Nash **then**   ▷ stochastic boosted AI
8:      Compute (p,q) a Nash equilibrium of M.
9:      BAI is AI_i with probability p_i
10:     Compute (p',q') a Nash equilibrium of M'.
11:     BAI' is AI'_j with probability p'_i
12: **end if**
13: **if** Uniform **then**   ▷ boosted AI
14:     BAI is AI_i with probability $1/K$.
15:     BAI' is AI'_j with probability $1/K$.
16: **end if**

---

above for the AI playing as Black and for the AI' playing as White. We get AI_1, AI_2,... for Black, and AI'_1, AI'_2, ... for White. From now on, we present the learning algorithm for Black - still, for this, we need the AI' for White as well. The algorithm for enhancing the AI as White is similar. Let us define, for $i \in \{1,\ldots,K\}$ and $j \in \{1,\ldots,K_t\}$, $M_{i,j} = 1$ when AI_i (playing as Black) wins against AI'_j (playing as White). Otherwise, $M_{i,j} = 0$. Also, let us define $M'_{i,j} = 1$ when AI'_i (playing as White) wins against AI_j (playing as Black). Thus, we have $M'_{i,j} = 1 - M_{j,i}$. [12] uses $K = K_t$, hence they use the same squared matrix for Black and for White - up to a transformation $M \mapsto 1 - M'$. The point in the present paper is to show that we can save up time by using $K \neq K_t$. This means that we need two matrices: M (used for the learning for Black) is the matrix of $M_{i,j}$ for $i \in \{1,\ldots,K\}$ and $j \in \{1,\ldots,K_t\}$; and M' (used for the learning for White) is the matrix of $(M')_{i,j}$ for $i \in \{1,\ldots,K\}$ and $j \in \{1,\ldots,K_t\}$. If $K_t \leq K$, M and M' have $K_t \times K_t$ entries in common (up to transformation $(M')_{i,j} = 1 - M_{j,i}$); therefore building M and M' needs simulating $2K \times K_t - K_t^2$ games.

For arbitrary values of K and K', boosted AIs can be created using BestSeed and Nash approaches, summarized in Algorithm 1. The Nash approach provides a stochastic policy, usually stronger than the original policy [12]. This can be done even if the matrix is not squared.

3 Faster Methods

3.1 Rectangular Learning

At first view, the approach in [12] is simple and sound: they need one squared matrix for both Black and White. However, their approach needs the result of K^2 games. With our rectangular approach, if we use K different seeds and K_t opponent seeds, we need $2K \times K_t - K_t^2$ games.

Let us now check the precision of our approach. Our algorithms use averages of rows and averages of columns. Let us define μ_i the average value of the ith row of M, if K_t was infinite - this is the average success rate of AI_i playing as Black against AI playing as White. And let us define $\hat{\mu}_i$ the average value that we get, with our finite value K_t. Hoeffding's bound [9] tells us that with probability $1-\delta$, $|\mu_i - \hat{\mu}_i| \leq \sqrt{-\log(\delta/2)/(2K_t)}$. By Bonferroni correction (i.e. union bound), with probability $1 - \delta$, for all $i \leq K$, $|\mu_i - \hat{\mu}_i| \leq \sqrt{-\log(\delta/(2K))/(2K_t)}$. For a requested precision ϵ, we can do as follows:

- Choose a value of K large enough, so that at least one seed i is optimal within precision $\epsilon/2$.
- Choose K_t such that $\sqrt{-\log(\delta/(2K))/(2K_t)} \leq \epsilon/2$.

We see that K_t slightly more than logarithmic as a function of K is enough for ensuring ϵ arbitrarily small asymptotically in K. On the other hand, we have no bound on K necessary for having at least one seed optimal within precision $\epsilon/2$.

3.2 Bandit Methods

Bandits are a natural method for finding approximate optima quickly. Rather than computing full matrices, we consider the following approach: apply Exp3 [1], both for Black and for White, for sampling in the matrix M (evaluate $M_{i,j}$ only when you need) as a matrix game; Black is the row player and maximizes; White is the column player and minimizes. We use far less evaluations than the size of the matrix.

Finally, we can simply use UCB (separately for Black and White), which can be modified [15] for handling the infinite nature of the set of seeds; we apply this to the game of Go in 9×9 and 19×19.

4 Testbeds

We provide experiments on a list of games. First, we consider MCTS, applied to four board games, namely Domineering, Atari-Go, Breakthrough and Go. Then, we consider the randomized policy in the GameTestBed platform. Domineering is a two-player game with very simple rules: each player in turn puts a tile on empty locations in the board. The game starts with an empty board. The first player who can not play loses the game. Usually, one of the player has vertical 2×1 tiles, and the other has horizontal 1×2 tiles. Domineering can be played on boards of various shapes, most classical cases are rectangles or squares. For squared boards, Domineering is solved until board size 10×10 [3,4]. Domineering was invented by Göran Andersson [6]. Jos Uiterwijk recently proposed a knowledge based method that can solve large rectangular boards without any search [14]. The Breakthrough game, invented by Dan Troyka in 2000, has very simple rules: all pieces can move straight ahead or in diagonal (i.e. three possible target locations). Captures are possible in diagonal only. Players play in turn, and the first player who reaches the opposite first row or captures all opponents pieces has won. There is no draw in Breakthrough - there is always at least one legal move, and pieces can only go forward (straight or diagonal) so that loops can not occur. This game won the 2001 8×8 Game Design Competition. Yasuda Yasutoshi popularized the Atari-Go variant of the game of Go; the key difference is that the first player who makes a capture wins the game. Atari-Go is also known as Ponnuki-Go, One-capture-Go, or Capture-Go. Last but not least, we provide results of experiments on the GameTestBed platform (https://gforge.inria.fr/projects/gametestbed/).

5   Experiments

Besides playing against the original stochastic AI, we consider the following opponent ($K' = 1$ corresponds to the original opponent, whereas $K' >> 1$ is a much stronger opponent):

- Generate K' seeds, randomly, for Black and K' seeds, randomly, for White.
- Consider the worst success rate of our boosted AI playing as White against these K' strategies for Black and consider the worst success rate of our boosted AI playing as Black against these K' strategies for White. Our success rate is the average of these two success rates (Black and White).

This is a strong challenge for K' large; since we consider separately White and Black, we have indeed K'^2 opponent strategies (each of the K' seeds for Black and each of the K' seeds for White) and consider the worst success rate. We will define this opponent as a K'-*exploiter*: it is an approximator of the exploitability property of Nash equilibria. It represents what can be done if our opponent could play the game K' times and select the best outcome. For $K' = 1$, this opponent is playing exactly as the original *AI*: this is the success rate against a randomly drawn seed. A score $\geq 50\%$ against $K' = 1$ means that we have outperformed the original AI, i.e. boosting has succeeded; but it is satisfactory to have also a better success rate, against $K' > 1$, than the original AI.

In order to validate the method, we take care that our algorithm is tested with a proper *cross-validation*: the opponent uses seeds which have never been used during the learning of the portfolio. This is done for all our experiments, BestSeed, Uniform, or Nash. For this reason, there is no bias in our results. In addition, we test our performance, in the case of Go, against another opponent; therefore, this is *transfer* learning, as explained in Sect. 5.

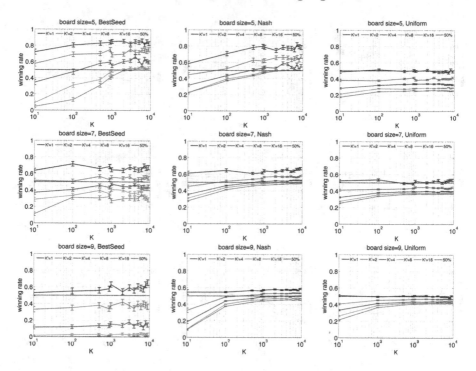

Fig. 2. Results for domineering, with the BestSeed and the Nash approach, against the baseline ($K' = 1$) and the exploiter ($K' > 1$). *x-axis*: K, number of seeds optimized for both players; *y-axis*: success rate. $K_t = 900$ in all experiments. The performance of the uniform version (original algorithm) is also presented for comparison.

Performance of Rectangular Algorithms in Cross-Validation, for Some Board Games. All results are averaged over 100 runs. Results for Domineering, Atari-Go and Breakthrough are presented in Figs. 2, 3, and 4 respectively. Table 3 shows the numerical results when $K = 9000$ and $K_t = 900$.

In short, BestSeed performs well against the original algorithm (corresponding to $K' = 1$), but its performance against the exploiter ($K' > 1$) is very weak. On the other hand, the Nash approach outperforms the original algorithm both in terms of success rate against the baseline ($K' = 1$) in all cases and against the exploiters ($K' > 1$) in most cases (i.e. curves on the middle column in Figs. 2, 3 and 4 are better than those on the right column) - however, for Breakthrough in large size the results were (very) slightly detrimental for $K' > 1$, i.e. the "exploiter" could learn strategies against it.

Performance of the Bandit Method in Cross-Validation In this section, we present results obtained by Exp3 on the GameTestBed platform. We apply 800 iterations of Exp3 with 400 seeds for each player. The arms with frequency greater than 99% of the largest frequency are chosen as possible seeds and we

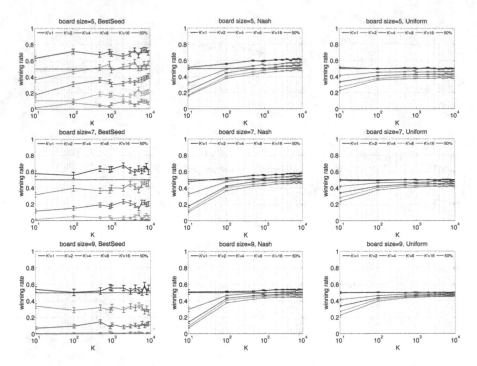

Fig. 3. Results for Atari-Go, with the BestSeed and the Nash approach, against the baseline ($K' = 1$) and the exploiter ($K' > 1$). x-axis: K, number of seeds optimized for both players; y-axis: success rate. $K_t = 900$ in all experiments. The performance of the uniform version (original algorithm) is also presented for comparison.

play them with probability proportional to their frequencies. Each learning is repeated 100 times, and each learnt AI is tested against 400 randomly drawn seeds which have never been used during the learning. Table 1 shows the results against the original algorithm, and against a stronger opponents ($K' = 16$). With the Exp3 method and most frequent arm selection, our boosted algorithm outperforms the original AI and its success rate against the stronger opponent $K' = 16$ is improved. Please note that the presented games are hard to learn: Nim is a simple game but has a brute representation which makes learning hard; and two of the games are phantom games with tricky partially observable states. The policies are the default randomized policies in the freely available code above.

We also tested UCB with progressive widening [15]; the infinite set of arms is handled by considering, after N simulated games, the $\lceil 100N^{\frac{1}{3}} \rceil$ first arms. UCB was parallelized by pulling the arms with the 40 best scores simultaneously. We get the following results (we performed the learning once, the standard deviation refers to the success rate in cross-validation):

Table 1. Success rate for five games of the GameTestBed platform, with the Exp3 method and most frequent arm selection, against the baseline ($K' = 1$) and the stronger exploiter ($K' = 16$). In the game Morra, the AI with given random seed is still stochastic. Hence, the success rate is not greatly improved.

Game	Success rate (%)			
	Baseline		Most frequently chosen	
	$K' = 1$	$K' = 16$	$K' = 1$	$K' = 16$
Phantom 4 in a row	50	0.50 ± 0.00	$\mathbf{69.00 \pm 0.00}$	$\mathbf{8.75 \pm 0.00}$
Nim	50	0.00 ± 0.00	$\mathbf{73.50 \pm 0.00}$	$\mathbf{3.00 \pm 0.00}$
Phantom tic-tac-toe	50	0.50 ± 0.00	$\mathbf{65.50 \pm 0.00}$	$\mathbf{15.25 \pm 0.00}$
Morra	50	47.73 ± 0.22	$\mathbf{52.12 \pm 0.23}$	$\mathbf{48.11 \pm 0.22}$
PigStupid	50	40.78 ± 0.25	$\mathbf{50.04 \pm 0.25}$	$\mathbf{41.30 \pm 0.25}$

- 9×9 Go, MCTS with 400 simulations per move, after 60 000 simulated games, the seed 1125 was selected for Black and the seed 898 was selected for White, success rate 79.8%.
- 19×19 Go, GnuGo *not* MCTS[1], after only 3780 simulated games, the seed 606 was selected for Black and the seed 472 was selected for White, success rate 55.9%. This algorithm is far less stochastic than MCTS.

Table 2. Performance of BestSeed-Gnugo-MCTS against various GnuGo-default programs, compared to the performance of the default Gnugo-MCTS. The results are for GnuGoMCTS playing as Black vs GnuGo-classical playing as White, and the games are completely independent of the learning games (which use only Gnugo-MCTS). Results are averaged over 1000 games. All results in 5×5, komi 6.5, with a learning over 100×100 random seeds.

Opponent	Performance of BestSeed	Performance of the original algorithm with randomized random seed
GnuGo-classical level 1	$\mathbf{1. (\pm 0)}$	$.995 (\pm 0)$
GnuGo-classical level 2	$\mathbf{1. (\pm 0)}$	$.995 (\pm 0)$
GnuGo-classical level 3	$\mathbf{1. (\pm 0)}$	$.99 (\pm 0)$
GnuGo-classical level 4	$\mathbf{1. (\pm 0)}$	$1. (\pm 0)$
GnuGo-classical level 5	$\mathbf{1. (\pm 0)}$	$1. (\pm 0)$
GnuGo-classical level 6	$\mathbf{1. (\pm 0)}$	$1. (\pm 0)$
GnuGo-classical level 7	$\mathbf{.73 (\pm .013)}$	$.061 (\pm .004)$
GnuGo-classical level 8	$\mathbf{.73 (\pm .013)}$	$.106 (\pm .006)$
GnuGo-classical level 9	$\mathbf{.73 (\pm .013)}$	$.095 (\pm .006)$
GnuGo-classical level 10	$\mathbf{.73 (\pm .013)}$	$.07 (\pm .004)$

---

[1] GnuGo does not accept MCTS for 19×19.

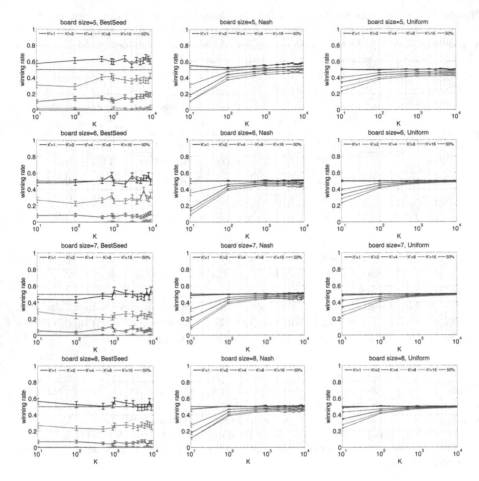

Fig. 4. Results for Breakthrough, with the BestSeed and the Nash approach, against the baseline ($K' = 1$) and the exploiter ($K' > 1$). *x-axis*: K, number of seeds optimized for both players; *y-axis*: success rate. $K_t = 900$ in all experiments. The performance of the uniform version (original algorithm) is also presented for comparison.

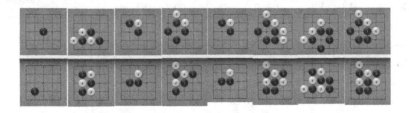

Fig. 5. Comparison between moves played by BestSeed-MCTS (top) and the original MCTS algorithm (bottom) in the same situations. GnugoStrong, used as an evaluator, prefers the moves chosen by BestSeed-MCTS for situations 1, 2, 6, 7, 8; whereas 3, 4 and 5 are equivalent.

Table 3. Success rate for Domineering, Atari-Go and Breakthrough, with the BestSeed and Nash approaches, against the baseline ($K' = 1$) and the exploiter ($K' > 1$). $K = 9000$ and $K_t = 900$. The experiments are repeated 100 times. The standard deviations are shown after $\pm$. $K' = 1$ corresponds to the original algorithm with randomized seed; $K' = 2$ corresponds to the original algorithm but choosing optimally (after checking their performance against its opponent) between 2 possible seeds, i.e. it is guessing, in an omniscient manner, between 2 seeds, each time an opponent is provided. $K' = 4$, $K' = 8$, $K' = 16$ are similar with 4, 8, 16 seeds respectively.

Domineering						
Board	Method	Success rate (%)				
		$K' = 1$	$K' = 2$	$K' = 4$	$K' = 8$	$K' = 16$
5×5	Uniform	49.03 ± 1.30	41.55 ± 0.92	32.53 ± 0.60	28.95 ± 0.45	25.06 ± 0.41
	BestSeed	$\mathbf{82.50 \pm 2.41}$	$\mathbf{75.00 \pm 2.53}$	$\mathbf{59.50 \pm 1.98}$	$\mathbf{53.00 \pm 1.20}$	$\mathbf{50.00 \pm 0.00}$
	Nash	78.50 ± 2.50	67.54 ± 2.39	55.96 ± 1.60	50.00 ± 0.00	$\mathbf{50.00 \pm 0.00}$
7×7	Uniform	53.33 ± 1.41	44.33 ± 0.85	39.58 ± 0.26	37.97 ± 0.17	36.55 ± 0.13
	BestSeed	$\mathbf{67.50 \pm 2.51}$	54.50 ± 2.03	44.50 ± 1.88	41.50 ± 1.90	28.50 ± 2.50
	Nash	66.98 ± 1.39	$\mathbf{58.01 \pm 0.83}$	$\mathbf{52.79 \pm 0.32}$	$\mathbf{50.71 \pm 0.25}$	$\mathbf{48.72 \pm 0.19}$
9×9	Uniform	50.68 ± 0.58	46.68 ± 0.43	44.06 ± 0.26	42.50 ± 0.13	41.56 ± 0.09
	BestSeed	$\mathbf{65.50 \pm 3.40}$	36.50 ± 3.26	14.50 ± 2.50	3.50 ± 1.29	0.50 ± 0.50
	Nash	58.60 ± 0.61	$\mathbf{53.43 \pm 0.46}$	$\mathbf{50.04 \pm 0.37}$	$\mathbf{47.15 \pm 0.28}$	$\mathbf{45.11 \pm 0.26}$
Atari-Go						
Board	Method	Success rate (%)				
		$K' = 1$	$K' = 2$	$K' = 4$	$K' = 8$	$K' = 16$
5×5	Uniform	49.95 ± 0.54	46.72 ± 0.46	43.26 ± 0.37	40.78 ± 0.30	37.85 ± 0.26
	BestSeed	$\mathbf{69.50 \pm 2.76}$	56.50 ± 2.83	41.00 ± 2.89	21.00 ± 2.49	7.00 ± 1.75
	Nash	61.16 ± 0.48	$\mathbf{57.91 \pm 0.50}$	$\mathbf{54.33 \pm 0.40}$	$\mathbf{51.18 \pm 0.39}$	$\mathbf{47.96 \pm 0.26}$
7×7	Uniform	49.76 ± 0.37	47.61 ± 0.30	45.10 ± 0.30	43.02 ± 0.22	41.84 ± 0.18
	BestSeed	$\mathbf{59.50 \pm 3.25}$	45.50 ± 3.28	20.50 ± 2.68	5.00 ± 1.52	1.00 ± 0.71
	Nash	57.79 ± 0.45	$\mathbf{54.66 \pm 0.42}$	$\mathbf{51.40 \pm 0.33}$	$\mathbf{47.97 \pm 0.37}$	$\mathbf{45.99 \pm 0.28}$
9×9	Uniform	50.16 ± 0.25	48.39 ± 0.22	47.01 ± 0.16	$\mathbf{46.04 \pm 0.13}$	$\mathbf{45.11 \pm 0.10}$
	BestSeed	$\mathbf{55.50 \pm 3.49}$	26.00 ± 3.39	12.50 ± 2.19	1.00 ± 0.71	0.00 ± 0.00
	Nash	53.61 ± 0.43	$\mathbf{50.46 \pm 0.37}$	$\mathbf{48.06 \pm 0.24}$	46.02 ± 0.22	44.15 ± 0.21
Breakthrough						
Board	Method	Success rate (%)				
		$K' = 1$	$K' = 2$	$K' = 4$	$K' = 8$	$K' = 16$
5×5	Uniform	50.12 ± 0.45	47.80 ± 0.35	45.42 ± 0.23	43.18 ± 0.20	42.01 ± 0.15
	BestSeed	$\mathbf{60.50 \pm 3.45}$	42.50 ± 3.30	19.00 ± 2.75	4.50 ± 1.45	0.50 ± 0.50
	Nash	57.77 ± 0.54	$\mathbf{54.32 \pm 0.36}$	$\mathbf{50.75 \pm 0.32}$	$\mathbf{48.38 \pm 0.29}$	$\mathbf{45.64 \pm 0.23}$
6×6	Uniform	50.15 ± 0.09	$\mathbf{49.31 \pm 0.07}$	$\mathbf{48.86 \pm 0.05}$	$\mathbf{48.51 \pm 0.04}$	$\mathbf{48.09 \pm 0.04}$
	BestSeed	49.00 ± 3.71	33.00 ± 3.52	11.00 ± 2.09	2.50 ± 1.10	0.00 ± 0.00
	Nash	$\mathbf{50.94 \pm 0.33}$	47.81 ± 0.29	46.73 ± 0.22	45.13 ± 0.16	43.67 ± 0.16
7×7	Uniform	50.08 ± 0.06	$\mathbf{49.51 \pm 0.07}$	$\mathbf{49.03 \pm 0.05}$	$\mathbf{48.70 \pm 0.05}$	$\mathbf{48.36 \pm 0.04}$
	BestSeed	$\mathbf{55.50 \pm 3.19}$	24.50 ± 2.81	6.00 ± 1.64	1.00 ± 0.71	0.00 ± 0.00
	Nash	51.16 ± 0.32	48.40 ± 0.24	46.63 ± 0.18	45.13 ± 0.16	44.12 ± 0.14
8×8	Uniform	50.03 ± 0.07	$\mathbf{49.60 \pm 0.06}$	$\mathbf{49.07 \pm 0.06}$	$\mathbf{48.70 \pm 0.05}$	$\mathbf{48.34 \pm 0.04}$
	BestSeed	49.00 ± 3.50	25.00 ± 2.99	6.50 ± 1.84	0.50 ± 0.50	0.00 ± 0.00
	Nash	$\mathbf{50.91 \pm 0.28}$	48.89 ± 0.22	46.86 ± 0.19	45.65 ± 0.15	44.41 ± 0.16

Performance in Transfer, in the Case of Go. Earlier results [12] and in Sect. 5 are performed in a classical machine learning setting, i.e. with cross-validation; we now check the transfer, i.e. the fact that we boost an AI, we get a better performance also when we test its performance against *another* AI.

Transfer to GnuGo. We applied BestSeed to GnuGo, a well known AI for the game of Go, with Monte Carlo tree search and a budget of 400 simulations. The BestSeed approach was applied with a 100×100 learning matrix, corresponding to seeds $\{1, \ldots, 100\}$ for Black and seeds $\{1, \ldots, 100\}$ for White.

Then, we tested the performance against GnuGo "classical", i.e. the non-MCTS version of GnuGo; this is a really different AI with different playing style. We got positive results as shown in Table 2. Results are presented for Black; for White the BestSeed had a negligible impact.

Transfer. Validation by a MCTS with long thinking time. Figure 5 provides a summary of differences between moves chosen (at least with some probability) by the original algorithm, and the ones chosen in the same situation by the algorithm with optimized seed. These situations are the 8 first differences between games played by the original GnuGo and by the GnuGo with our best seed. We use GnugoStrong, i.e. Gnugo with a larger number of simulations, for checking if Seed 59 leads to better moves. GnugoStrong is precisely defined as << gnugo – monte-carlo –mc-games-per-level 100000 –level 1>>. On these situations (Fig. 5) such that BestSeed differs from the original GnuGo with the same number of simulations, GnugoStrong played 5 games (playing both sides), all leading to the same result in each case.

6   Conclusions

Our results (success rate of the boosted algorithm against the non-boosted baseline) are roughly for BestSeed: 73.5%, 67.5%, 59% for Atari-Go in 5×5, 7×7 and 9×9 respectively; 65.5%, 57.5%, 55.5%, 57% for Breakthrough in 5×5, 6×6, 7×7 and 8×8 respectively; 86%, 71.5%, 65.5% for Domineering in 5×5, 7×7 and 9×9 respectively. On several games in Gametestbed, we got more than 70% success rate against the baseline. We got close to 80% in 9×9 Go. Against $K' = 16$, the results were usually positive, though not always (see Breakthrough) - we believe that this would be solved with larger K, K', as proved in [12]; asymptotically, the Nash method should be optimal against all K'.

Usually, the boosted AIs significantly outperform the baselines, without additional computational cost. This does not require any source code development. The rectangle versions are faster than the original algorithms, and the bandit versions are indeed much faster.

Approximating Nash using the adversarial bandit algorithm, Exp3, does not require computing the whole matrix. The computational cost is decreased to its square root, up to logarithmic factors (see [8]) and with a minor cost in terms of precision. The success rate is significantly improved.

Our work on applying UCB with an infinite set of seeds to Go is preliminary (the parameters of progressive widening are arbitrarily chosen and the UCB parameters are guessed rather than optimized). Nevertheless, the fact that the boosted AI is significantly enhanced validates the effectiveness of our approach.

Further work. The simplest further work consists in optimizing the seeds specifically for time steps. This should provide an easy exploitation of the time structure of the game. A work in progress is the use of Exp3 with infinite set of seeds, handled by progressive widening (as we did for UCB - after N simulated games, only the first $\lceil CN^{\gamma} \rceil$ seeds are considered, with $C \geq 2$ and $\gamma \in (0,1]$). Also, worst-so-far seed might be removed periodically.

References

1. Auer, P., Cesa-Bianchi, N., Freund, Y., Schapire, R.E.: Gambling in a rigged casino: the adversarial multi-armed bandit problem. In: Proceedings of the 36th Annual Symposium on Foundations of Computer Science, pp. 322–331. IEEE Computer Society Press, Los Alamitos (1995)
2. Breiman, L.: Bagging predictors. Mach. Learn. **24**(2), 123–140 (1996). http://www.citeseer.ist.psu.edu/breiman96bagging.html
3. Breuker, D., Uiterwijk, J., van den Herik, H.: Solving 8×8 domineering. Theor. Comput, Sci. **230**(1–2), 195–206 (2000). http://www.sciencedirect.com/science/article/pii/S0304397599000821
4. Bullock, N.: Domineering: solving large combinatorial search spaces. ICGA J. **25**(2), 67–84 (2002)
5. Coulom, R.: Efficient selectivity and backup operators in Monte-Carlo tree search. In: Ciancarini, P., van den Herik, H.J., Donkers, H.H.L.M. (eds.) Proceedings of the 5th International Conference on Computers and Games, pp. 72–83, Italy, Turin (2006)
6. Gardner, M.: Mathematical games. Sci. Am. **230**, 106–108 (1974)
7. Gaudel, R., Hoock, J.B., Pérez, J., Sokolovska, N., Teytaud, O.: A principled method for exploiting opening books. In: International Conference on Computers and Games, pp. 136–144, Kanazawa, Japon (2010). http://hal.inria.fr/inria-00484043
8. Grigoriadis, M.D., Khachiyan, L.G.: A sublinear-time randomized approximation algorithm for matrix games. Oper. Res. Lett. **18**(2), 53–58 (1995)
9. Hoeffding, W.: Probability inequalities for sums of bounded random variables. J. Am. Stat. Assoc. **58**(301), 13–30 (1963)
10. Kocsis, L., Szepesvári, C.: Bandit based Monte-Carlo planning. In: Fürnkranz, J., Scheffer, T., Spiliopoulou, M. (eds.) ECML 2006. LNCS (LNAI), vol. 4212, pp. 282–293. Springer, Heidelberg (2006). doi:10.1007/11871842_29
11. Nagarajan, V., Marcolino, L.S., Tambe, M.: Every team deserves a second chance: identifying when things go wrong (student abstract version). In: 29th Conference on Artificial Intelligence (AAAI 2015), Texas, USA (2015)
12. Saint-Pierre, D.L., Teytaud, O.: Nash and the bandit approach for adversarial portfolios. In: CIG 2014 - Computational Intelligence in Games, pp. 1–7. IEEE, Dortmund, August 2014.https://hal.inria.fr/hal-01077628
13. Shapire, R., Freund, Y., Bartlett, P., Loo, W.: Boosting the margin: a new explanation for the effectiveness of voting methods, pp. 322–330 (1997)

14. Uiterwijk, J.W.H.M.: Perfectly solving domineering boards. In: Cazenave, T., Winands, M.H.M., Iida, H. (eds.) CGW 2013. CCIS, vol. 408, pp. 97–121. Springer, Heidelberg (2014). doi:10.1007/978-3-319-05428-5_8
15. Wang, Y., Audibert, J.Y., Munos, R.: Algorithms for infinitely many-armed bandits. In: Advances in Neural Information Processing Systems, vol. 21 (2008)

Heuristic Function Evaluation Framework

Nera Nešić and Stephan Schiffel[(⊠)]

School of Computer Science, Reykjavik University, Reykjavik, Iceland
{nera13,stephans}@ru.is

Abstract. We present a heuristic function evaluation framework that allows to quickly compare a heuristic function's output to benchmark values that are precomputed for a subset of the state space of the game. Our framework reduces the time to evaluate a heuristic function drastically while also providing some insight into where the heuristic is performing well or below par. We analyze the feasibility of using Monte-Carlo Tree Search to compute benchmark values instead of relying on game theoretic values that are hard to obtain in many cases. We also propose several metrics for comparing heuristic evaluations to benchmark values and discuss the feasibility of using MCTS benchmarks with those metrics.

1 Introduction

Developing heuristics for games or other search problems typically involves a great deal of testing by playing the game repeatedly under realistic time constraints against several different opponents. This process is very time consuming and slows down the development of heuristics. In addition, this form of testing also gives little insight into where the heuristic has deficits.

We propose HEF, a heuristic function evaluation framework that is based on comparing the heuristic values of a sample of the state space to so-called ground truth values. Once the ground truth values for the samples are computed, HEF allows us to quickly evaluate different heuristics. Given sufficient samples and meta-data about those samples, it also allows to analyze in which position in the game the heuristics are accurate or in-accurate. We propose different metrics for this comparison that allow to focus on different aspects of the heuristic, e.g., whether it is more important to find the best move or the exact values of the moves. The source code of HEF is available online[1].

In this paper, we present HEF, as well as several metrics for comparing heuristics to ground truth values. We further analyze to what extent Monte-Carlo Tree Search (MCTS) can be used to compute the ground truth values in absence of game theoretic values. Finally, we show some results we obtained from analysis of a specific heuristic in the General Game Playing [5] domain using HEF.

---

[1] https://github.com/nnesic/HEF.

© Springer International Publishing AG 2016
A. Plaat et al. (Eds.): CG 2016, LNCS 10068, pp. 71–80, 2016.
DOI: 10.1007/978-3-319-50935-8_7

2   Preliminaries

The development of HEF was driven by the need of evaluating heuristic functions for General Game Playing (GGP) [5]. As such, the implementation of the frameworks is aimed at deterministic, finite, perfect information games with an arbitrary number of players. However, the principles we used naturally extend to non-deterministic games or games with imperfect information. Only a few changes in the framework would be required to extend it to such games.

In particular, we assume the following three properties of games.

- **Finiteness:** The game has finitely many reachable states, each player has finitely many legal moves in each state, and the game ends after finitely many steps.
- **Determinacy:** The successor state is fully determined by the actions of the players and the predecessor state.
- **Perfect information:** All players have always sufficient information to infer the current state of the game.

In other words, we think of games as deterministic acyclic Markov decision processes.

We define a heuristic to be a function $h: S \times P \times M \to \mathbb{R}$ associating a real value with every legal move $m \in M$ for player $p \in P$ in state $s \in S$. It means that our assumption is that heuristics provide a value for each move as opposed to evaluating states of the game. In a turn-taking game, the evaluation of a move is the same as the evaluation of the successor state reached by that move. However, in games of simultaneous moves – which are often encountered in GGP – evaluating moves directly is often more convenient.

3   Heuristic Function Evaluation Framework

We propose an evaluation paradigm that examines a heuristic function's performance at a per-state level. This is done by identifying some features that a good heuristic should exhibit in each state (for example, the ability to accurately identify good moves and traps) and defining metrics which specify evaluation criteria for individual features. The heuristic function is then evaluated by comparing its output on a state to some ground-truth value for that state. To ensure a fast and flexible evaluation at development time, we pre-compute benchmarks of state-action pairs and their ground-truth values, and use these values for our metric evaluation. Below we discuss: structure (Sect. 3.1), proposed metrics (Sect. 3.2), and benchmark ground-truth value computation (Sect. 3.3).

3.1   Structure

We implemented our paradigm in the Heuristic Function Evaluation Framework (HEF), which provides all the necessary infrastructure to facilitate working with the paradigm. HEF offers utilities for benchmark generation and management, data access, metric analysis, and data visualization, allowing users to focus only on defining the metrics that fit their study. HEF services are divided into three layers: benchmark management, metric analysis, and visualization.

The first layer stores and provides access to the benchmark datasets. New datasets can be imported from XML files containing benchmark information of states (such as state description, depth at which the state is found in the game, values of all available actions). Generating benchmarks requires two operations: selecting states to include in the benchmark, and computing the ground-truth values for each state.

HEF comes with a default implementation of a benchmark state selector and a Monte-Carlo tree search based ground-truth evaluator, both of which are based on the Game Definition Language (GDL) [7], allowing them to be used seamlessly on many different games, as long as they are encoded in GDL. The default state selector will somewhat randomly choose a specified number of states on each depth level of the game. The ground-truth evaluator then runs the MCTS algorithm on each selected benchmark state for a specified amount of time, outputting the results in the HEF benchmark format.

The second layer provides an analysis pipeline that is used by HEF metrics. This pipeline filters benchmark states according to player, depth, or other specifications, and passes them to the metric one by one. The heuristic function is then evaluated according to criteria specified by the metric, and it is assigned a score, which is then collected, aggregated across all examined states, and exported to the visualization layer. HEF is designed to allow users to easily define and use custom metrics.

The third layer provides a GUI, allowing the user to select metrics, games, and datasets, and to specify aggregation and visualization options. Since the topology of a game can change significantly throughout a game - for instance, the significance of some board properties or strategies can be more relevant in the endgame - all metric data is aggregated by depth level, allowing users to see how the heuristic's performance adapts to the progress of the game.

3.2   Proposed Metrics

We propose a set of basic metrics to be used with HEF, aimed mainly at Minimax and MCTS heuristics. Each metric specifies a *metric score function* that is used to evaluate different features of a heuristic's performance.

Definition 1 *(metric score function). Given an evaluation metric E, we define the metric score function, MS_E, as a function mapping a game state S and a role R according to policy specified by E to some value v.*

In this section we will briefly describe categories of our proposed metrics, and define the most prominent ones. As many of the metrics operate on game-theoretic values of benchmark states, in our definitions of metric score functions we will use $GTmax(S, R, M)$ to indicate the game-theoretical value of move

M for role R in state S, and $GTmax(S, R)$ and $GTmin(S, R)$, respectively, to indicate the maximum and minimum game-theoretical values of moves available to role R in state S.

Game Property Metrics are a set of measurements not bound to the heuristic functions, which instead keep track of how some properties of the game itself are changing at different depth levels. Of these, we find the *maximum score difference* metric particularly useful. This metric measures the ground-truth score difference between the best and the worst moves available to each player in a state, and helps us identify the "critical zones" of a game where a different choice of moves can lead to very different outcomes.

Definition 2 *(maximum score difference metric). For every state S and role R, we define the maximum score difference metric (DIFFMAX) as*

$$MS_{DIFFMAX}(S, R) = GTmax(S, R) - GTmin(S, R)$$

Best-Only Move Accuracy Metrics measure how accurately a heuristic can identify good moves in a state. They include the *K-best* metric, which requires a heuristic to identify at least one optimal move within the K moves it scores the highest, and *strict-best* metric, which also penalizes a heuristic for assigning a high score to bad moves.

Definition 3 *(k-best metric). Given a state S, role R, a heuristic function H, parameter $K \in \mathbb{N}$, and a set of moves for role R $HM_K = \{hm_1...hm_K\}$ containing K highest-scored moves according to H, we define the K-best metric (KBEST) as*

$$MS_{KBEST}(S, R) = \begin{cases} 1 & \textit{if } \exists \ hm - hm \in HM_K \wedge GT(S, R, hm) = GTmax(S, R) \\ 0 & \textit{otherwise} \end{cases}$$

Definition 4 *(strict best metric). Given a state S, role R, a heuristic function H, and a set of moves for role R $HM_K = \{hm_1...hm_n\}$ containing all moves hm_i such that $H(S, R, hm_i) = H(S, R, hm_1)$, where hm_1 is the highest-scored move according to H, we define the strict best metric (STRICT) as*

$$MS_{STRICT}(S, R) = \frac{1}{n} \sum_{i=1}^{n} \begin{cases} 1 & \textit{if } GT(S, R, hm_i) = GTmax(S, R) \\ 0 & \textit{otherwise} \end{cases}$$

We usually use the best-only metrics in conjunction with their random baselines (showing the optimal move selection accuracy that a heuristic which samples moves randomly would achieve) to identify areas of a game where the accuracy score is influenced by the position configuration (e.g., if all moves result in victory, random selection is 100% accurate).

Expected Score Metrics are used in applications where moves are chosen by sampling moves based on their heuristic scores according to some sampling function. As the name suggests, they calculate the expected score of employing the heuristic and sampling function together.

Definition 5 *(expected score metric). Let F be a move sampling function that maps a heuristic value of a move to the probability of choosing that move. Given a role R, a state S and a set $M = \{m_1...m_n\}$ of all moves available to R, and a heuristic function H, we define the expected score metric (EF) for function F as*

$$MS_{EF}(S, R) = \sum_{i=1}^{n} GT(S, R, m_i) \times F(H(S, R, m_i))$$

Move Ordering Metrics measure a heuristic's ability to not only identify the best moves, but also correctly distinguish between the quality of remaining moves. They do so by comparing the ordering of moves according to their heuristic scores to the ordering according to ground-truth values.

Move Categorization Metrics evaluate the heuristic's ability to produce scores that are similar to the ground-truth scores. These metrics are useful for applications which rely on the absolute value of the heuristic, e.g., using a heuristic as a state evaluation function for Minimax.

3.3   Benchmark Ground-Truth Value Computation

The metrics we proposed are intended to work with a benchmark of game-theoretical values for moves. Generating such datasets, however, may not always be feasible. Instead, we investigated the possibility of using Monte-Carlo tree search [2] (MCTS), in particular UCT, for benchmark generation. The algorithm uses random simulations and an exploitation-exploration policy to drive the exploration of the search tree towards most promising areas. MCTS has seen very successful implementations in game playing (e.g., in GGP [3] or Go [4]), where it is used to identify the best move in a state.

However, we can typically not run MCTS to convergence, which means we will not have the game theoretic values for the moves. Instead, we get q, the average score achieved by taking a move over all simulations, and n, number of times the move was included on the simulation path. Furthermore, MCTS focuses its simulations on the best moves. Thus, the average score q of a bad move is likely an unreliable estimate of the move's game theoretic value.

4   Using MCTS as a Benchmark

We investigated the viability of MCTS benchmarks for HEF analysis by comparing the output of our proposed metrics on a dataset with game-theoretic(GT) move values to their output on the MCTS benchmark for the same heuristic function. We focused on the game of Connect Four, which has a sufficient large search space not to be trivial, while still being solvable in relatively little time. Both GT and MCTS datasets are composed of the same set of 498 game states. Values in the GT dataset were computed with an optimized game solver for Connect Four [9]. We compared the performance of two MCTS datasets, MCTS1H and MCTS3H, obtained through running respectively one and three hours of MCTS simulations per state. The number of simulations per state ranges from approximately 1.5 million (at depth 0) to 54 million (at depth 39) for MCTS1H, and 2 million to 151 million simulations for MCTS3H. Below we discuss the depth score differential (Sect. 4.1), the best-only metrics (Sect. 4.2), the expected score metrics (Sect. 4.3), and the move categorization and move ordering metrics (Sect. 4.4).

4.1   Depth Score Differential

In our first attempt of applying the depth score metric to MCTS datasets we used the q value in the benchmark directly for computing the score differential between best and worst moves. We observed that the result vaguely resembled the GT dataset results for the MCTS1H dataset (having identified the area of greatest score difference, although losing the amplitude of the difference), while the MCTS3H dataset preserved less information revealed by the GT dataset. We concluded that the q value is not reliable for this kind of metric, since its value gets diluted through simulations and it can stray far from its GT value for less explored moves. We had more success using n to calculate the differential by taking the logarithm of the ratio of highest to lowest n value in a state. As we see in Fig. 1a, the two MCTS curves follow the GT one closely, and the extra simulations in MCTS3H pay off in terms of capturing the behavior of the metric on a GT dataset. MCTS is driven by the intention to exploit the best available move as much as possible, so it is reasonable that the n value (counting the number of times a moves has been exploited) would be a good indicator of good and bad moves.

4.2   Best-Only Metrics

Best-only metrics rely on identifying a set of best moves in a benchmark state to compare the heuristic's choice of best moves to. In GT datasets the best moves are easily identifiable by their score, but with MCTS datasets identifying best moves becomes more challenging because of the unreliability of q as an estimator of the game-theoretic value. Therefore, we investigated a method of choosing best moves based on the n values: We order the moves according to n, and choose a "breaking point" that distinguishes the good moves where the difference between consecutive moves' n values is the highest.

Overall, we found the strict-best metrics to adapt to MCTS datasets quite well; Fig. 1b shows the benchmark comparison for the strict-best metric and its baseline, and we can see that both MCTS metrics follow closely the trends exhibited by the GT dataset.

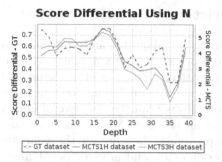
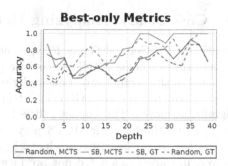

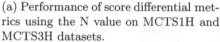

(a) Performance of score differential metrics using the N value on MCTS1H and MCTS3H datasets.

(b) Performance of strict-best (SB) and random baseline metrics on MCTS3H dataset.

Fig. 1. Adapting HEF metrics to MCTS datasets

4.3 Expected Score Metrics

Expected score metrics proved more challenging to adapt to MCTS due to their strong reliance on values of moves. Using q values once again proved inadequate. The choice of sampling function had little impact on the expected score, and the MCTS metric failed to capture the information displayed by the GT metric. We then limited the sampling to the three moves with the highest q value, that is, we only selected among the best three moves based on their score and never selected any of the other moves. While the absolute values of the expected score were much lower in the MCTS dataset compared to the GT one, we observe the same trends and ratios between different sampling functions as we did in the GT dataset. Thus, useability of MCTS datasets for expected score metrics seems limited to cases where we only care about the general trends, but not the exact scores.

4.4 Move Categorization and Move Ordering Metrics

In order for the move categorization metrics to work on MCTS datasets, there needs to exist a mapping from benchmark MCTS values to the GT scores. We used several classifiers offered by Weka [6] to train a model which predicts the GT dataset score based on the q, n, total n, and depth values of a move in a state. The best accuracy of categorizing moves was of 67%, although the performance varied depending on players and depths – with the second player performing as low as 25% accuracy in certain states. With this much inaccuracy in the benchmark itself, we do not believe the move categorization metrics to be viable with MCTS datasets. Likewise, the move ordering metrics rely on the absolute ordering of moves in the benchmark – which, as we saw, is not the case with MCTS – and only achieved an accuracy of 57% in matching GT results.

5   Case Study: Analyzing Heuristics with HEF

Heuristics for General Game Playing need to be adaptable and applicable to many different games. Action heuristic [10], for example, is automatically constructed at the beginning of a match by regression on GDL rules of the game, and used in conjunction with MCTS to steer the random simulations towards more significant moves. The impact of the heuristic was evaluated on several games by pitching the heuristic-MCTS player against the pure MCTS one. In many games the use of heuristic produced in improvement in score for the heuristic player; in some cases it did not produce a difference, and in two cases it made the performance drop.

We used HEF to investigate the behavior of the Action heuristic on various games and to obtain a better insight into the results of the matches. Of particular interest are games of Pentago, where the heuristic player performed the best, winning approximately 73% of 400 test matches against the vanilla player, and Checkers-small, in which the heuristic player lost 90% of matches. To analyze these games, we precomputed benchmarks of 200 states for Pentago and 1100 for Checkers-small, using one hour of MCTS simulations per state. In Fig. 2 we show the score differential, strict-best, and random baseline metrics for the Action heuristic on these two games.

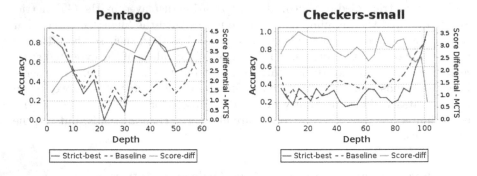

Fig. 2. HEF analysis of Action heuristic

In case of Pentago, we see that strict-best metric overtakes its random baseline strongly in the second half of the game. We also see that the accuracy of the heuristic peaks in sync with the score differential; this is a good thing to observe, as it tells us that the heuristic performs well in the critical areas of the game. Moreover, Pentago is a game with a large branching factor, reaching 38 moves available in some state. As such, the ability of the heuristic to identify good moves and steer the MCTS search in relevant directions has helped the heuristic player achieve much better results.

In the case of Checkers-small, we see that the strict-best metric consistently lags behind its baseline – telling us that the heuristic is actually preferring suboptimal moves. Moreover, we see that the accuracy drops in states at depths

65–85 where the depth differential metric exhibits the highest peak, meaning that at the critical points in the game the heuristic performs on its worst.

This kind of analysis gives us an insight into how the heuristic behaves at different points of the game, and lets us ask targeted questions, expressed in the form of metrics, to investigate various aspects of the heuristic. Having already pre-computed the benchmark, we can change and refine the heuristic and change the metrics as needed, and have the results of our analysis in a matter of minutes.

More case studies and more detailed results can be found in [8].

6   Related Work

In [1], Anantharaman proposes a position-based evaluation scheme for chess heuristics in which he compares the performance of the heuristic coupled with minimax search against the same heuristic and minimax search, but allowing much longer search time in the second case. Anantharaman then proposes several metrics to compare the performance of the heuristic relative to the reference program, and measures the correlation between these metrics and the USCF rating system, concluding that some of the metrics can be used reliably to evaluate heuristic functions, with only one day of computation needed.

Our approach to evaluating the heuristics is similar to Anantharaman's in that we are focusing on evaluating the heuristic's performance on individual states using some user defined metrics. Our emphasis is, however, on producing a paradigm which can recycle computation, while the approach proposed by Anantharaman still requires substantial search time to compute the reference for each specific heuristic. Moreover, we aim for generality of use – we would like our paradigm to be applicable to functions designed to be used with a variety of search algorithms (we can, for example, analyze functions intended for both minimax and MCTS random search guidance) and a large variety of games.

7   Conclusion

We proposed a paradigm for evaluating heuristics in games and we presented a framework that implements it. Our main goal was to provide a fast and focused evaluation method for intermediate stages of heuristic function design. We achieve this by pre-calculating a benchmark dataset containing a set of states that have a value assigned to each action, and using this dataset to answer questions about the heuristic's performance – such as evaluating the accuracy with which it identifies the best move. The Heuristic function Evaluation Framework provides all the infrastructure needed to work with this paradigm, from benchmark generation to data visualization; the users only need to formulate their questions in the form of metrics which verify the heuristics' answers against the benchmark values.

For cases where game-theoretic values are not available, we propose using Monte Carlo Tree Search for generating benchmark datasets. These are less accurate, but easily obtainable. We found that these datasets are usable when we are interested in identifying the best moves in a state, while we do not recommend using them if the correct ordering of moves or estimating the value of a move is of importance. So far, these conclusions are based only on the results in Connect Four. Studying more games is necessary to confirm these findings.

Finally, we presented a case study showing how HEF can provide useful insights into the behavior of heuristics. The conclusions are again not definitive.

Future Work. Currently, we leave the responsibility of deciding the significance of various metrics for given applications to the user of the paradigm. For example, the move categorization metrics are not overly relevant for the heuristics intended to find best moves for MCTS random simulations, so achieving a high score under these metrics does not mean that the heuristic will perform well in the actual MCTS search. In the future, we would like to investigate methods for determining the correlation between scores assigned by a metric to a heuristic and the actual performance of the program on relevant problems.

References

1. Anantharaman, T.: Confidently selecting a search heuristic. ICCA J. **14**(1), 3–16 (1991)
2. Browne, C.B., Powley, E., Whitehouse, D., Lucas, S.M., Cowling, P.I., Rohlfshagen, P., Tavener, S., Perez, D., Samothrakis, S., Colton, S.: A survey of Monte Carlo tree search methods. IEEE Trans. Comput. Intell. AI Games **4**(1), 1–43 (2012)
3. Finnsson, H., Björnsson, Y.: Simulation-based approach to general game playing. In: Proceedings of the 23rd AAAI Conference on Artificial Intelligence. AAAI Press (2008)
4. Gelly, S., Wang, Y., Munos, R., Teytaud, O.: Modification of UCT with patterns in Monte-Carlo Go. Research report RR-6062, INRIA (2006)
5. Genesereth, M.R., Love, N., Pell, B.: General game playing: overview of the AAAI competition. AI Mag. **26**(2), 62–72 (2005)
6. Holmes, G., Donkin, A., Witten, I.H.: Weka: a machine learning workbench. In: Proceedings of the 1994 Second Australian and New Zealand Conference on Intelligent Information Systems, pp. 357–361. IEEE (1994)
7. Love, N., Hinrichs, T., Haley, D., Schkufza, E., Genesereth, M.: General game playing: Game description language specification. Technical report, Stanford University, Recent Version, March 2008. http://games.stanford.edu/
8. Nešić, N.: Introducing heuristic function evaluation framework. Master's thesis, Reykjavik University (2016). http://hdl.handle.net/1946/23743
9. Tromp, J.: John's connect four playground. https://tromp.github.io/c4/c4.html. Accessed 24 Nov 2015
10. Trutman, M., Schiffel, S.: Creating action heuristics for general game playing agents. In: The IJCAI 2015 Workshop on General Game Playing, pp. 39–47 (2015)

Systematic Selection of N-Tuple Networks for 2048

Kazuto Oka and Kiminori Matsuzaki[✉]

Kochi University of Technology, Kami 782–8502, Japan
195061f@gs.kochi-tech.ac.jp, matsuzaki.kiminori@kochi-tech.ac.jp

Abstract. The puzzle game 2048, a single-player stochastic game played on a 4 × 4 grid, is the most popular among similar slide-and-merge games. One of the strongest computer players for 2048 uses temporal difference learning (TD learning) with N-tuple networks, and it matters a great deal how to design N-tuple networks. In this paper, we study the N-tuple networks for the game 2048. In the first set of experiments, we conduct TD learning by selecting 6- and 7-tuples exhaustively, and evaluate the usefulness of those tuples. In the second set of experiments, we conduct TD learning with high-utility tuples, varying the number of tuples. The best player with ten 7-tuples achieves an average score 234,136 and the maximum score 504,660. It is worth noting that this player utilize no game-tree search and plays a move in about 12 μs.

1 Introduction

The puzzle game 2048 [4], a single-player stochastic game played on a 4 × 4 grid, is the most popular among similar slide-and-merge games like Threes and 1024. One of the reasons why the game attracts so many people is that it is very easy to learn but hard to master. The game also attracts researchers in the field of artificial intelligence and computational complexity. The difficulty of the game was discussed from the viewpoint of computational complexity by Abdelkader et al. [2] and Langerman and Uno [6]. As a testbed of artificial intelligence methods, there have been some competitions of computer players for the game 2048 [5,18] and a two-player version of 2048 [1,8].

One of the strongest computer players for 2048 uses temporal difference learning (TD learning for short) with N-tuple networks together with the expectimax algorithm [16]. An N-tuple network consists of a number of N-tuples: each N-tuple covers N cells on the grid and it contributes a number of features each for one distinct occurrence of tiles on the covered cells. Given an N-tuple network, the evaluation function simply calculates the summation of feature weights for all occurring features, where the weights can be obtained through TD learning over a number of self-plays.

In this approach, it matters a great deal how to design (or select) N-tuple networks. The authors of the previous work used hand-designed networks: Wu et al. [16] used a network with four 6-tuples; former work by Szubert and Jaśkowski [14] used a network with two 6-tuples and two 4-tuples. As we can

© Springer International Publishing AG 2016
A. Plaat et al. (Eds.): CG 2016, LNCS 10068, pp. 81–92, 2016.
DOI: 10.1007/978-3-319-50935-8_8

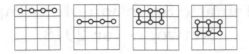

Fig. 1. The N-tuple network (with two 4-tuples and two 6-tuples) by Szubert and Jaśkowski [14]

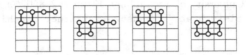

Fig. 2. The N-tuple network (with four 6-tuples) by Wu et al. [16]

easily imagine, the more and the larger tuples we use, the higher score we would obtain. The resources such as memory size or computation time, however, limit the available number and/or size of tuples.

In this paper, we study the N-tuple networks for the game 2048. In the first set of experiments, we conduct TD learning exhaustively for 6- and 7-tuples, and evaluate the usefulness of those tuples. By looking closely at the usefulness of those tuples, we find several interesting facts about them. In the second set of experiments, we conduct TD learning with high-utility tuples, varying the number of tuples. We confirm that the more tuples we use the higher score we obtain up to around 20 tuples where the score peaks for the case of 6-tuples.

The main contributions of the paper are summarized as follows.

- A systematic way of selecting N-tuple networks. The way we select N-tuple networks in this paper does not rely on heuristics or human knowledge of the games.
- Comparing usefulness of N-tuples. We evaluate the usefulness of tuples from exhaustive experiments. The results are consistent with the heuristics of the game.
- The best player with ten 7-tuples achieves the average score 234,136 and the maximum score 504,660. It is worth noting that this player does not utilize game-tree search like expectimax and plays a move in about 12 μs (about 88,000 moves per second).

Rules of 2048. The game 2048 is played on a 4×4 grid. The objective of the original 2048 game is to reach a 2048 tile by moving and merging the tiles on the board according to the rules below. A new tile will be put randomly with number 2 (with probability of 90 %) or 4 (with probability 10 %). In the initial state, two tiles are put randomly (Fig. 3). The player selects a direction (either of up, left, down, and right), and then all the tiles will move in that direction. When two tiles of the same number combine they create a tile with the sum value and the player get the sum as the score. Here, the merges occur from the far side and a newly created tile do not merge again on the same move: moves to

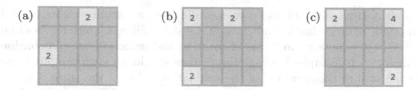

(a) An example of the initial state. Two tiles are put randomly.
(b) After moving up. A new 2-tile appears at the lower-left corner.
(c) After moving right. Two 2-tiles are merged to a 4-tile, and score 4 is given.

Fig. 3. The process of the game 2048

the right from $222_{\sqcup}$, $_{\sqcup}422$ and 2222 result in $_{\sqcup\sqcup}24$, $_{\sqcup\sqcup}44$, and $_{\sqcup\sqcup}44$, respectively. Note that the player cannot select a direction in which no tiles move nor merge. After each move, a new tile appears at an empty cell. If the player cannot move the tiles, the game ends.

Paper Overview. The rest of the paper is organized as follows. Section 2 reviews the idea of applying N-tuple networks and TD learning to the game 2048. In Sect. 3, we analyze the usefulness of 6- and 7-tuples by experiments that selects those tuples exhaustively. Based on the analysis of usefulness of tuples, we select a number of high-utility tuples and conduct experiments in Sect. 4. Section 5 discusses related work and Sect. 6 concludes the paper.

2 N-Tuple Networks and Temporal Difference Learning for 2048

In this section, we review the idea of applying N-tuple networks (in Sect. 2.1) and TD learning to the game 2048 (in Sect. 2.2). The algorithm was given by Szubert and Jaśkowski [14] and it was called TD-AFTERSTATE in their paper.

2.1   Evaluation Function with N-Tuple Networks and Playing Algorithm

An N-tuple network consists of a number of N-tuples where each N-tuple covers N cells on the grid. In this paper, N denotes the number of cells in a tuple, and m the number of tuples in the network. If each cell in the tuple may have one of K values an N-tuple contributes K^N features, that is, we assign a feature weight for each of K^N features. We use $K = 16$, which means the maximum value of a tile is 32768. (We did not know any player that achieved a 65536 tile, at the time we did the experiments. Recently, Yeh et al. [19] reported their success of a 65536 tile.) Note that 6- and 7-tuples require 64 MB and 1 GB, respectively, under the condition of $K = 16$ and 32 bits for each feature weight.

Given an N-tuple network and corresponding set of feature weights, we calculate the value of an evaluation function of a state as follows. Since the board of
the game 2048 is symmetric in terms of rotation and reflection, we can consider
8 sampling for each N-tuple. We take the feature weight for each sampling, and
compute the sum of those values as the evaluation value of the state. Given a
state s, the evaluation value $V(s)$ of the state is the sum of the feature weights
for all N-tuple and all symmetric boards.

Let us see an example in Fig. 4 where we use an N-tuple network with two
3-tuples. We have eight symmetric boards for a state s, and each board has two
feature weights for each tuple. Therefore, in this example, the evaluation value of
a state is the sum of 16 feature weights. If we have a network with m N-tuples,
then the evaluation value of a state is the sum of $8m$ feature weights.

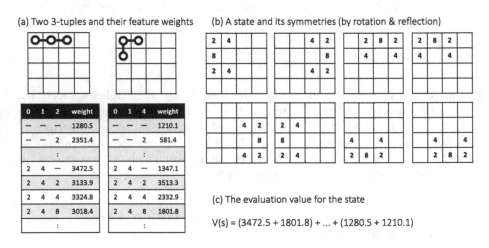

Fig. 4. An example for calculating an evaluation value of a state

The 2048 player in this paper greedily selects a move such that the sum
of score and evaluation value is the maximum. For a state s, let the set of
possible moves, the score given by move a, and the next state by move a be
$A(s) \subseteq \{\mathsf{N}, \mathsf{E}, \mathsf{S}, \mathsf{W}\}$, $R(s, a)$ and $N(s, a)$, respectively, the player selects

$$\arg\max_{a \in A(s)} \left(R(S, a) + V(N(S, a)) \right).$$

2.2 Temporal Difference Learning

Temporal difference learning (TD learning) is one of the reinforcement learning
algorithms. Though the idea of TD learning was introduced by Sutton [13], its
origins reach back to the 1950's referring to the famous program for checkers [11].
TD learning has been adapted to several games such as backgammon [15],
Othello [9], and Go [12].

In our algorithm, the evaluation values are adjusted by TD learning as follows. Let s_t be a state at time t. The player selects a move a such that the sum of score and evaluation value of the state after the move is the maximum. Let $r = R(s_t, a)$ and s'_t be the score and the state after the move, respectively (note that $s'_t \neq s_{t+1}$ because s_{t+1} is given by putting a tile on s'_t). Then, the TD error Δ for the evaluation value is defined as follows.

$$\Delta = r + V(s'_t) - V(s'_{t-1})$$

To reduce the TD error, we update the evaluation values $V_j(s_{t-1})$ for all the N-tuples by a certain portion of Δ:

$$V'_j(S_{t-1}) = V_j(S_{t-1}) + \alpha\Delta$$

where the rate α is called *learning rate* and it was set to $\alpha = 2^{-10}$ throughout the experiments.

3   Exhaustive Analysis of Usefulness of N-Tuples

Though the game 2048 is a small game, there are still a large number of N-tuples. Table 1 shows the number of all the N-tuples and connected ones. (We count N-tuples that are the same after rotation or reflection once.) In the following, we only consider connected 6- and 7-tuples to keep the number of tuples manageable.

Table 1. Number of N-tuples

N	3	4	5	6	7	8	9	10	11	12	13
All	77	252	567	1051	1465	1674	1465	1051	567	252	77
Connected C_N	8	17	33	68	119	195	261	300	257	169	66

As a first task, we would like to order the N-tuples in terms of their usefulness.

When we form N-tuple networks by randomly selecting tuples and conduct TD learning, the (average) scores differ to a degree. Therefore, we have made the following two assumptions on the usefulness of N-tuples: (1) N-tuples contribute independently from each other; (2) N-tuples contribute linearly. With these assumptions, we consider scores come simply from the sums of partial scores of N-tuples selected in the networks.

Let 6-tuples be indexed from 1 to $C_6 = 68$ and 7-tuples be from 1 to $C_7 = 119$. Let p_i be the partial score of the i-th tuple, and s_{ji} be the 0–1 variable showing that the i-th tuple is selected in the j-th experiment. We assume that the score P_j of the j-th experiment is the sum of partial scores of selected tuples, $P_j = \sum_{i=1}^{C} s_{ji} p_i$. Then, given a set of experimental results with the selected tuples and scores, we can estimate the partial scores by the least squares method: we reduce the squared error $E = \sum_j (P_j - \sum_{i=1}^{C} s_{ji} p_i)^2$.

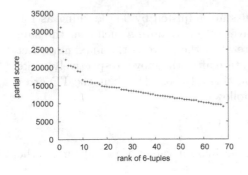

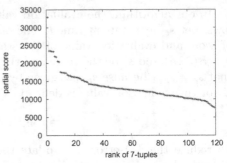

Fig. 5. Partial scores of 6-tuples   **Fig. 6.** Partial scores of 7-tuples

Here are the details of the experiments. For each experiment, we randomly selected 10 tuples and executed TD learning with 1,000,000 self-play games. We used the average of the scores of the last 10,000 games as the score of the experiment. We conducted 680 experiments for 6-tuples and 1190 experiments for 7-tuples so that each tuple was selected 100 times on average.

Figures 5 and 6 plot the partial scores in descending order. The medians of partial scores are $M_6 = 13,066$ for 6-tuples and $M_7 = 12,566$ for 7-tuples: those of the best tuples are $31,161 = 2.38M_6$ and $32,900 = 2.61M_7$, respectively; those of the worst tuples are $9,052 = 0.69M_6$ and $7,683 = 0.61M_7$, respectively. (The absolute values of partial scores may not be comparable, since we stop the experiments at 1,000,000 games before the scores saturate.)

Table 2 shows the four best and the four worst tuples for $N = 6$ and $N = 7$. In both cases, the best tuples ⟨6-01⟩ and ⟨7-001⟩ include an edge connecting two adjacent corners and are closely connected. This is reasonable for the slide-and-merge property and keep-large-tile-on-corner heuristics of the game. Seven out of the 8 worst tuples do not include corner cells and it is according to our expectation. The worst 7-tuple ⟨7-119⟩, however, includes two corner cells. We consider the following reason for this: since either of the two diagonal corners is often empty, the tuples with two diagonal corner cells have less information. We will see this again later.

Table 3 shows the results of other interesting tuples. Wu et al. [16] used the four 6-tuples ⟨6-01⟩ and ⟨6-04⟩ in Table 2 and ⟨6-40⟩ and ⟨6-48⟩ in Group 1 of Table 3. Although it is a common technique to make N-tuples by sliding existing (better) N-tuples, those N-tuples are not necessary good ones.

Group 2 of Table 3 shows N-tuples that apparently look good but are not so good. From the keep-large-tile-on-corner heuristics, one may design the 6-tuples ⟨6-24⟩ that covers the cells near a corner, but it is ranked 24th out of 68 and not so good. The case of 7-tuples is very surprising. One may design the 7-tuple ⟨7-096⟩ that has two edges among three corners, but it seems useless. This is more evidence of the reason of the worst 7-tuple. In fact, all tuples that include two diagonal corners (⟨7-119⟩ in Table 2 and ⟨7-096⟩, ⟨7-087⟩, ⟨7-079⟩ in Group 2 of Table 3) seem useless.

Table 2. Four best and four worst 6-tuples and 7-tuples

N	4 best tuples				4 worst tuples			
	⟨6-01⟩	⟨6-02⟩	⟨6-03⟩	⟨6-04⟩	⟨6-65⟩	⟨6-66⟩	⟨6-67⟩	⟨6-68⟩
6								
	31,161	24,530	22,207	20,576	9,644	9,642	9,563	9,052
	⟨7-001⟩	⟨7-002⟩	⟨7-003⟩	⟨7-004⟩	⟨7-116⟩	⟨7-117⟩	⟨7-118⟩	⟨7-119⟩
7								
	32,900	23,504	23,483	23,338	8,543	8,204	7,918	7,683

Table 3. Other interesting tuples

group 1		group 2			
⟨6-40⟩	⟨6-48⟩	⟨6-24⟩	⟨7-096⟩	⟨7-087⟩	⟨7-079⟩
12,190	11,330	14,320	10,573	10,988	11,521

group 3					
⟨6-08⟩	⟨7-007⟩	⟨7-012⟩	⟨7-034⟩	⟨7-086⟩	⟨7-096⟩
18,990	21,766	17,394	14,018	10,995	10,573

Group 3 of Table 3 tells an interesting fact. Adding a cell to an existing (good) *N*-tuple is a possible way of generating an $N + 1$-tuple. It usually works well but not in some cases. By adding to a cell to the useful 6-tuple ⟨6-08⟩ we can generate five 7-tuples, among which two are useful but other two are useless. The converse does not hold in some cases either. The 6-tuple ⟨6-08⟩ is the best among those given by removing a cell from ⟨7-007⟩, ⟨6-16⟩ from ⟨7-016⟩, and ⟨6-17⟩ from ⟨7-017⟩. Note that the numbers of 6-tuples and 7-tuples are 68 and 119, respectively.

4   Performance with Respect to Number of *N*-Tuples

In the previous section, we ordered the *N*-tuples by their usefulness. Now we select the first *m* tuples to conduct TD learning with them.

In the second set of experiments, we selected at most 45 6-tuples or at most 10 7-tuples. Since a 6-tuple requires 64 MB and a 7-tuple does 1 GB to store

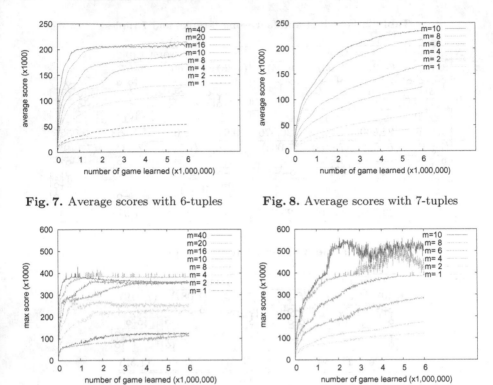

Fig. 7. Average scores with 6-tuples

Fig. 8. Average scores with 7-tuples

Fig. 9. Maximum scores with 6-tuples

Fig. 10. Maximum scores with 7-tuples

feature weights, the program with $N = 6$ and $m = 45$ consumes about 3 GB of memory and that with $N = 7$ and $m = 10$ does about 10 GB of memory. The experiments were conducted on a PC with two Intel Xeon E5645 CPU (6 cores, 2.4 GHz), 12 GB of memory, with the CentOS 5.5 (kernel 2.6.18–194.e15) and g++ 4.6.3.

For each set of N-tuples, we executed TD learning with 6,000,000 self-play games, and then had additional 10,000 games with the obtained feature weights. During the self-play and learning, we output the summary of the average score and the maximum score once every 10,000 games. For the additional games, in addition to the average and maximum scores, we measured the execution time to calculate the time for selecting a move, and the ratio of reaching 2048, 4096, 8192, 16384 and 32768 tiles. We conducted the experiments five times for each set of N-tuples and all the results (including the maximum score) were averaged among the five experiments.

Figures 7, 8, and 11 plot the average scores with respect to the number of games learned. Figures 9, 10, and 12 plot the maximum scores with respect to the number of games learned.

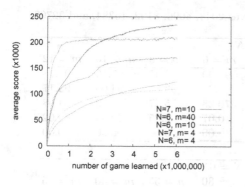 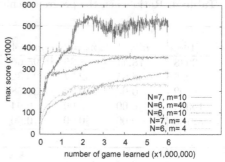

Fig. 11. Comparing average scores with 6- and 7-tuples

Fig. 12. Comparing maximum scores with 6- and 7-tuples

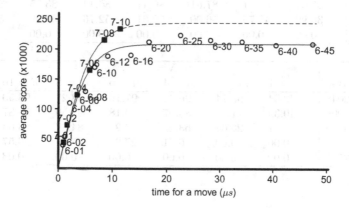

Fig. 13. Score w.r.t. computing time

In general, we confirmed the fact that the more N-tuples we use the higher score we obtain up to a certain number of N-tuples. For the case of $N = 6$, the more N-tuples we use the higher average score we obtain up to around $m = 20$, and the higher maximum score up to around $m = 10$. In terms of the learning speed, the more tuples we use the faster the learning proceeds. In the case of $N = 6$ and $m = 40$, after 1,000,000 games the learning seems to converge. For the case of $N = 7$, the more N-tuples we use the higher score we obtain (for $m \leq 10$).

Comparing $N = 6$ and $N = 7$, we can see that the learning proceeds faster for $N = 6$. This is due to the difference of numbers of features that an N-tuple contributes. For the $N = 7$ cases, 6,000,0000 games seem to be not sufficient to converge. Nonetheless, the results with $N = 7$ and $m = 10$ finally outperform all the results with $N = 6$.

Figure 13 plots the average scores to the time for selecting a move. The time for selecting a move is almost linear in the number m of used N-tuples. For the same number m, the program with 7-tuples took about 1.5 times as much time

Table 4. Ratio when the program achieves 2048, 4096, 8192, 16384, and 32768

tile	$m=1$	$m=2$	$m=4$	$N=6$ $m=6$	$m=8$	$m=10$	$m=12$
2048	78.41	88.36	95.66	96.00	97.45	97.16	97.78
4096	36.05	62.77	90.32	91.36	93.87	94.05	95.17
8192	0.07	0.33	56.38	70.28	75.67	79.29	84.08
16384	0.00	0.00	0.04	0.07	0.05	29.64	39.02
32768	0.00	0.00	0.00	0.00	0.00	0.00	0.00

tile	$m=16$	$m=20$	$m=25$	$N=6$ $m=30$	$m=35$	$m=40$	$m=45$
2048	97.87	98.38	98.45	98.42	98.46	98.41	98.30
4096	95.42	96.11	96.25	95.97	95.91	95.89	95.64
8192	85.01	86.51	87.61	86.41	86.14	85.75	86.45
16384	38.96	49.75	56.00	52.61	52.76	50.09	51.42
32768	0.00	0.00	0.00	0.00	0.00	0.00	0.00

tile	$m=1$	$m=2$	$m=4$	$N=7$ $m=6$	$m=8$	$m=10$
2048	82.54	90.74	96.43	97.16	98.27	98.50
4096	40.39	71.75	86.97	89.18	93.59	96.87
8192	0.31	26.08	63.22	73.28	84.87	83.63
16384	0.00	0.00	6.71	27.91	47.17	56.57
32768	0.00	0.00	0.00	0.00	0.00	0.03

as that with 6-tuples did. The program with $N=7$ and $m=10$ obtained better results in less time than that with $N=6$ and $m=40$ (Weak points are the memory size and the cost of learning process).

In Fig. 13, the curves are the Logistic curves through the origin at the mid-point $f(x) = L\frac{(1-e^{-kx})}{(1+e^{-kx})}$, fitted to the points (the average scores with respect to the computing times). We can see the fact that the average score peaks for the case of $N=6$. Since the average score does not peak for $N=7$ up to $m=10$, we fitted the curve with an additional result for $m=30$ (the average score 249,625 and the computation time $40\,\mu s$)[1]. These facts suggest that we should combine N-tuples with another game-tree-search technique.

Table 4 shows the ratio when the program successfully achieves tiles 2048, 4096, 8192, 16384 and 32768. Since the program did not use any game-tree-search technique, it failed suddenly with a little probability (missing 1.5 % for 2048) even with 40 6-tuples or 10 7-tuples. In contrast, with 40 6-tuples or 10 7-tuples, the program succeeded to make 16,384 once for two tries. Furthermore, the program with $N=7$ and $m=10$ happened to reach 32,768.

---

[1] Since it requires 30 GB of memory to conduct the experiment, we used a PC with 32 GB memory for this additional experiment.

5   Related Work

Several game-playing algorithms have been adapted to the game 2048 [3,7,10, 14,16,17,20]. Among them, the state-of-the-art algorithm combines expectimax with TD learning or some other heuristics.

The first application of TD learning to the 2048 player was done by Szubert and Jaśkowski [14]. They utilized hand-selected two 4-tuples and two 6-tuples and the player learned with 1,000,000 self-play games achieved the average score 100,178. The two 4-tuples were extended to two 6-tuples by Wu et al. [16] and the extension increased the average score to 142,727. The hand-selected four 6-tuples achieved better score than our systematically selected four 6-tuples (the average score was 109,983). Wu et al. also proposed the multi-staged extension of the learning algorithm, and by the combination with expectimax search the player achieved the average score 328,946 (multi-staged TD, expectimax depth = 5). They recently achieved a 65536-tile [19].

The expectimax algorithm takes much more time when the depth is large. In the competition of computer players for the game 2048, it is often required to play a move in 1–10 ms [5,18]. Our player with $N = 7$ and $m = 10$ requires a large memory (about 10 GB) but runs much faster (about 12 µs for a move).

6   Conclusion

In this paper we designed experiments, with which we can systematically evaluate the usefulness of N-tuples. In addition to confirming the usefulness of previous hand-selected N-tuples, we found several interesting properties of N-tuples for the game 2048. By selecting the N-tuples from the head of the lists, we can easily obtain N-tuple networks. From the second set of experiments, we confirmed the fact that the more N-tuples we use the higher scores we obtain up to a certain number of tuples where the score peaks. With 10 7-tuples, the program achieved the average score 234,136 and the maximum score 504,660. As far as the authors know, these scores are the highest among the TD learning players (without game-tree-search techniques).

Our future work includes the following two tasks. First, we would like to confirm the performance of our 7-tuples with expectimax search. Second, we would like to propose a better way of selecting N-tuples from the ordered list.

Acknowledgment. Most of the experiments in this paper were conducted on the IACP cluster of the Kochi University of Technology.

References

1. GPCC (games and puzzles competitions on computers) problems for 2015 (2015, in Japanese). http://hp.vector.co.jp/authors/VA003988/gpcc/gpcc15.htm
2. Abdelkader, A., Acharya, A., Dasler, P.: On the complexity of slide-and-merge games, [cs.CC] (2015). arXiv:1501.03837

3. Chabin, T., Elouafi, M., Carvalho, P., Tonda, A.: Using linear genetic programming to evolve a controller for the game 2048 (2015). http://www.cs.put.poznan.pl/wjaskowski/pub/2015-GECCO-2048-Competition/Treecko.pdf
4. Cirulli, G.: 2048 (2014). http://gabrielecirulli.github.io/2048/
5. Jaśkowski, W., Szubert, M.: Game 2048 AI controller competition @ GECCO 2015 (2015). http://www.cs.put.poznan.pl/wjaskowski/pub/2015-GECCO-2048-Competition/GECCO-2015-2048-Competition-Results.pdf
6. Langerman, S., Uno, Y.: Threes!, fives, 1024!, and 2048 are hard. CoRR abs/1505.04274 (2015)
7. Oka, K., Matsuzaki, K., Haraguchi, K.: Exhaustive analysis and Monte-Carlo tree search player for two-player 2048. Kochi Univ. Technol. Res. Bull. **12**(1), 123–130 (2015, in Japanese)
8. Oka, K., Matsuzaki, K.: An evaluation function for 2048 players: evaluation for the original game and for the two-player variant. In: Proceedings of the 57th Programming Symposium, pp. 9–18 (2016, in Japanese)
9. van der Ree, M., Wiering, M.: Reinforcement learning in the game of Othello: learning against a fixed opponent and learning from self-play. In: IEEE Symposium on Adaptive Dynamic Programming and Reinforcement Learning (ADPRL), pp. 108–115 (2013)
10. Rodgers, P., Levine, J.: An investigation into 2048 AI strategies. In: 2014 IEEE Conference on Computational Intelligence and Games, pp. 1–2 (2014)
11. Samuel, A.L.: Some studies in machine learning using the game of checkers. IBM J. Res. Dev. **44**(1), 206–227 (1959)
12. Schraudolph, N.N., Dayan, P., Sejnowski, T.J.: Learning to evaluate go positions via temporal difference methods. In: Computational Intelligence in Games, pp. 77–98 (2001)
13. Sutton, R.S.: Learning to predict by the methods of temporal differences. Mach. Learn. **3**(1), 9–44 (1988)
14. Szubert, M., Jaśkowski, W.: Temporal difference learning of N-tuple networks for the game 2048. In: 2014 IEEE Conference on Computational Intelligence and Games, pp. 1–8 (2014)
15. Tesauro, G.: TD-Gammon, a self-teaching backgammon program, achieves master-level play. Neural Comput. **6**(2), 215–219 (1994)
16. Wu, I.C., Yeh, K.H., Liang, C.C., Chang, C.C., Chiang, H.: Multi-stage temporal difference learning for 2048. In: Cheng, S.-M., Day, M.-Y. (eds.) Technologies and Applications of Artificial Intelligence. LNCS, vol. 8916, pp. 366–378. Springer, Cham (2014). doi:10.1007/978-3-319-13987-6_34
17. Xiao, R.: nneonneo/2048-ai (2015). https://github.com/nneonneo/2048-ai
18. Yeh, K.H., Liang, C.C., Wu, K.C., Wu, I.C.: 2048-bot tournament in Taiwan (2014). https://icga.leidenuniv.nl/wp-content/uploads/2015/04/2048-bot-tournament-report-1104.pdf
19. Yeh, K.H., Wu, I.C., Hsueh, C.H., Chang, C.C., Liang, C.C., Chiang, H.: Multi-stage temporal difference learning for 2048-like games, [cs.LG] (2016). arXiv:1606.07374
20. Zaky, A.: Minimax and expectimax algorithm to solve 2048 (2014). http://informatika.stei.itb.ac.id/~rinaldi.munir/Stmik/2013-2014-genap/Makalah2014/MakalahIF2211-2014-037.pdf

Human-Side Strategies in the Werewolf Game Against the Stealth Werewolf Strategy

Xiaoheng Bi$^{(\boxtimes)}$ and Tetsuro Tanaka

The University of Tokyo, Tokyo, Japan
{bi,ktanaka}@tanaka.ecc.u-tokyo.ac.jp

Abstract. The werewolf game contains unique features, such as persuasion and deception, which are not included in games that have been previously studied in AI research. Studying the werewolf game could be one of the next challenging targets for AI research. In this paper, we concentrate on a werewolf-side strategy called the "stealth werewolf" strategy. With this strategy, each of the werewolf-side players behaves like a villager, and the player does not pretend to have a special role. Even though the strategy is thought to be suboptimal, so far this has not been proved. In this paper, we limit the human-side strategies such that the seer reveals his/her role on the first day and the bodyguard never reveals his/her role. So, the advantage of the werewolves in determining the player to be eliminated by vote is nullified. We calculated the ε-Nash equilibrium of strategies for both sides under this limitation. The solution shows that the winning rates of the human-side are more than half when the number of werewolves is assigned as in common play. Since it is thought to be fair and interesting for the winning rate to stay near 50%, the result suggests that the "stealth werewolf" strategy is not a good strategy for werewolf-side players. Furthermore, the result also suggests that there exist unusual actions in the strategies that result in an ε-Nash equilibrium.

1 Introduction

The werewolf game is a popular party game played in many countries. Studying the werewolf game could make contributions to multiple fields because it includes many aspects such as gathering information, judging information, and natural language processing. Studying this game could be one of the next challenging targets for AI research.

Each player in the werewolf game belongs to either the human-side or the werewolf-side[1]. The goal of human-side players is to eliminate all werewolf-side players, and the goal of werewolf-side players is to attack and kill human-side players and gain a majority.

---

[1] Some variants of the werewolf game have third-side players. This paper does not treat these variants.

© Springer International Publishing AG 2016
A. Plaat et al. (Eds.): CG 2016, LNCS 10068, pp. 93–102, 2016.
DOI: 10.1007/978-3-319-50935-8_9

Each player has one of the following roles:

Villager (human-side) has no special abilities.

Seer (human-side) targets a player during night turns and identifies whether the player is a human.

Bodyguard (human-side) selects a player to protect during night turns. If the target coincides with the werewolf-side target, the attack fails.

Medium (human-side) recognizes whether the player eliminated by voting on the last day was a human.

Freemasons (human-side) a pair of human-side players who can recognize each other.

Werewolf (werewolf-side) communicate by gestures during night turns and decide whom to target for an attack. The attack fails if the target player is protected by the bodyguard, otherwise it succeeds and the target dies.

Possessed (werewolf-side) has no special abilities. The player belongs to the werewolf-side but will be identified by the seer or recognized by the medium as human.

By default, one werewolf player is assigned in games with less than eight players, two werewolves are assigned in games with eight to fifteen players, and three werewolves are assigned in games with sixteen to nineteen players.

The games progress as follows.

Daytime turns. Players talk freely, which includes revealing their roles and any other information that is relevant to their roles. At the end of a daytime turn, the players eliminate one player by voting. If the eliminated player is the last werewolf, the human-side wins.

Night turns. All the players close their eyes. Players who have special roles perform actions according to their roles. If the number of werewolves exceeds or equals the number of humans, the werewolf-side wins.

Several simplified variants of the werewolf game have been studied. Braverman et al. [1] studied the optimal strategies in the mafia game which is a variant of the werewolf game, and tried to calculate the winning rates. They analyzed situations with and without a seer. In the situation where no seer exists, the number of werewolves needs to be $O(\sqrt{R})$ to ensure that the winning rate is fair where R is the number of players. Conversely, the number of werewolves needs to be $O(R)$ if a seer exists.

There are also studies of the werewolf game that concentrate on aspects other than strategies. Katagami et al. [2] studied the nonverbal information in the werewolf game. They investigated how nonverbal information, such as gestures and facial expressions, contribute to the winning rate. After the investigation, they found that nonverbal information plays an important role in winning or losing the game. Furthermore, a match system for humans with life-like agents was developed by Katagami et al. [3]. With that system, Katagami et al. [4] tried to analyze nonverbal information from movies of games played by humans to verify whether a life-like agent can give impressions like a human if they mount the analyzed movements on a life-like agent.

In this paper, we concentrate on a werewolf-side strategy called the "stealth werewolf" strategy. With this strategy, all werewolf-side players act as villagers, and they do not pretend to have special roles. Even though this strategy is thought to be suboptimal, so far this has not been proved. We impose a simple limitation of the human-side strategies such that the seer reveals his/her role on the first day and the bodyguard never reveals his/her role, and the advantage of the werewolves on vote turns is nullified. We calculated the ε-Nash equilibrium of both strategies using this limitation.

In this paper, we first introduce the limitations of the strategies. Next, we calculate the ε-Nash equilibrium of both strategies in small games using the CFR+ algorithm. Then, we show the results of our experiment and discuss their implications. Finally, we formulate our conclusion.

2 Human-Side Strategies Against the Stealth Werewolf Strategy

In this paper, we only treat four roles: villager, seer, bodyguard, and werewolf. We can ignore the "possessed" because his/her actions are the same as those of a villager in the used strategy. Even though ignoring the two human-side roles, "medium" and "freemasons" is disadvantageous to the human-side, we permit this handicap.

With the stealth werewolf strategy, each of the werewolf-side players acts as a villager from the human-side players' point of view. Therefore, if a villager does nothing during daytime turns with the human-side strategy, a werewolf-side player must also do nothing during daytime turns.

Because it is difficult to calculate the optimal strategy against the stealth werewolf strategy, we limit the actions of human-side players as described below.

2.1 Deciding to Eliminate a Player

As the players eliminate a player by a majority vote, the werewolves can raise the probability of the target of the vote to be a human player. To remove this advantage to the werewolf-side, human-side players can randomly select a player from the candidate list using the following method.

All players share the candidate list, which includes all suspicious players. Although the dices are not used in a werewolf game, we may assume that players can send messages simultaneously; thus, the players can mimicking to roll a dice. Considering there are m players in the candidate list, each player can thus roll a virtual dice from 0 to $m-1$ and send out their results as messages. By taking the modulo of the sum of the players' messages including the number they rolled, we can earn a result (the modulo itself) which is random and uncontrollable. Note that it is a strategy for human-side and there is no guarantee that all the werewolves will follow human-side's strategy. However, as long as the number of human-side players excceeds the one of werewolves[2] and each human-side player follows the strategy, werewolves can do nothing to prevent the strategy from being applied. As a result, every candidate has the same probability of being eliminated.

Even though players can only talk one by one in real situations, virtually simultaneous messages can be achieved using the following protocol.

– The player i ($1 \leq i \leq n$) composes a message m_i and generates a string r_i with randomized numbers.
– From player 1 to player n, each player i reveals a value $H(m_i r_i)$ which is calculated by sufficiently strong one-way hash function H.
– From player 1 to the player n, each player i reveals $m_i r_i$.

To make the above protocol meaningful, a premise stating that it is difficult to find a pair of values where $H(mr) = H(m'r')$ is necessary. With this premise, the protocol is easier to implement than the one proposed in [1].

Because the candidate list is uniquely determined by the history of the game, the deciding process can be treated as a chance node of a game tree in the model of extensive games.

2.2   Actions of the Seer

In the strategy proposed in this paper, the seer reveals his/her role on the first day. Because all the players know that the werewolf-side has selected the stealth werewolf strategy, the seer is trusted completely. Therefore, the seer is removed from the candidate list.

During night turns, the seer randomly identifies a player from the candidate list. The seer opens the result the next morning. If the identified player is a werewolf, he/she is eliminated during the daytime. Otherwise the identified player is removed from the candidate list. The action of the seer can also be treated as a chance node of a game tree in the model of extensive games.

2.3   Actions of the Bodyguard

Even though revealing the role of the bodyguard with proper timing is effective, we do not add these actions to the human-side strategies in this paper.

We limit the bodyguard's action to only choosing a target to protect. The bodyguard protects a target each night. The bodyguard selects one of the following groups to protect.

– The seer
– White villagers—who have been identified to be villager
– Villagers who have been attacked but not killed because the bodyguard protected the player

---

[2] As mentioned above, if the number of human-side players fail to excceed the one of werewolves, the game has already ended with werewolves' victory.

- Gray players—who are still unidentified, each of them is either a villager or a werewolf

The bodyguard protects one player from the selected group randomly. Selecting which group to protect is important for human-side strategies. The human-side strategy is determined by the probabilities of this choice for each human-side information set.

2.4 Actions of Werewolves

Because each of the werewolf-side players is assumed to act as a villager, the only available action is to select the target to attack during night turns. Werewolves select their target from the following groups:

- The seer
- White villagers—the bodyguard may be included
- Attack failed villagers—a werewolf recognizes the targets of failed attacks from previous nights
- Others—the bodyguard may be included

The werewolves attack one player from the selected group randomly. Selecting which group to attack is important in the werewolf-side strategies. The werewolf-side strategy is determined by the probabilities of this choice for each werewolf-side information set.

3 Calculating ε-Nash Equilibrium

Even though the werewolf game may appear to have many players, it is theoretically a two-player zero-sum game with the limitations described. This means that the Nash equilibrium will exist for the strategies and that the utilities for every strategy are certain. The strategies of both sides proposed in the previous section have ambiguity in selecting the group to protect or attack.

To calculate the ε-Nash equilibrium, we use the CFR+ algorithm studied by Bowling et al. [5]. This algorithm is a variant of the counterfactual regret minimization algorithm, which was developed by Zinkevich et al. [6]. CFR calculates the ε-Nash equilibrium in large extensive games. Before CFR was invented, various methods based on linear programming were used to calculate the ε-Nash equilibrium in extensive games. However, these methods cannot treat large games that have millions of information sets. CFR and its variants enable the treatment of large games, such as Heads-up Limit Hold'em Poker [5].

Even though the CFR+ program used in [5] is available as open source, it is specialized for poker games. Therefore, it is not suitable to be directly applied to the werewolf game. Consequently, we designed a general-purpose Python program and ran it with pypy, which is a high-speed Python code interpreter and a just-in-time compiler[3].

---

[3] The programs and outputs are available at https://github.com/u-tokyo-gps-tanaka-lab/gpw2015.

In our Python program, we used a standardized string, as described below, to represent the information sets of the bodyguard and the werewolves. Because revealing the role of the seer in the first day is a fixed action, this action was not included in the representation of the information sets.

- There is a set number of villagers, seer, bodyguard, and werewolves as the assignment of the number of different roles. Note that the number of seer and bodyguard can only be zero or one.
- G is a villager who is suspicious (gray in other words).
- S is the seer.
- B is the bodyguard.
- W is a werewolf.
- V is a villager who is inpected to be human (white in other words).
- C is a villager who is white from the bodyguard's and werewolves' perspective because of a failed attack. The player is still gray to the other villagers because this player has still to be identified.
- I is the identified bodyguard who is identified to be white.
- v is the voting step, and the next character presents the result of the elimination.
- g is the step for the bodyguard and the werewolves to choose a target.
  - The character after 'g' is the target of the bodyguard. This will be '−' if the bodyguard has died.
  - The character after the bodyguard's target is the target of the werewolves.
  - The last character in this string shows whether the attack succeeded or failed, '+' and '−' denote success and failure, respectively.
- d is the step where the seer identifies a player.
  - The character after 'd' represents the player identified by the seer. This character may be '−' in two cases. The first case is when the seer has died. The second case is when the player identified by the seer is attacked by the werewolves on the same turn.

For example, the following string represents the information set of the bodyguard and means that four villagers, one seer, one bodyguard, and four werewolves were present at the start of the game, a gray villager was eliminated after the first vote, the attack failed because the targets of both the bodyguard and the werewolves were the seer, the seer identified the bodyguard, and a gray villager was eliminated after the next vote.

- B, 4 1 1 4, vG, gSS-, dB, vG

The following string represents one of possible situations that are the same situation as above for the werewolves' information set.

- W, 4 1 1 4, vW, gSS-, dG, vG

The differences between these two strings are that the bodyguard is not aware of the role of the eliminated player and the werewolves are not able to identify the bodyguard from the other villagers.

A strategy is the combination of possibilities for a player to choose from available actions in each information set. By calculating the pair of strategies which gives ε-Nash equilibriums, we can limit the expected utility ranges at most ε from optimal utility.

4   The Solutions

We set up four different configurations according to the existence of seer and bodyguard as below, and calculated the winning rates in the various setups of a number of roles for the experiments.

1. No seer, no bodyguard
2. With seer, no bodyguard
3. No seer, with bodyguard
4. With seer, with bodyguard

Tables 1, 2, 3 and 4 shows the human-side winning rates of each group after 500 updating iterations of CFR+[4]. It would take too long to run the program if the total number of players exceeds ten, therefore, the number of players was limited to ten.

Table 1. Human-side winning rate: no seer, no bodyguard

Werewolves\Players	3	4	5	6	7	8	9	10
1	33%	25%	47%	38%	54%	45%	59%	51%
2	-	-	13%	8%	23%	16%	30%	22%
3	-	-	-	-	6%	3%	11%	7%
4	-	-	-	-	-	-	3%	1%

Generally, one werewolf player is assigned in games with less than eight players, and two werewolves are assigned in games with eight to ten players. Table 4 shows that winning rates of the human-side are more than 50% with these werewolves/human conditions, except in the case where the number of players is four. This result suggests that the stealth werewolf strategy is not a good strategy.

Furthermore, we analyzed the strategies that give ε-Nash equilibriums and obtained some properties of the strategies. As mentioned in [5], giving a strategy combination which contains a strategy for each player, then the following holds: if for each player using his or her strategy the player can at most gain more

---

[4] The exploitabilities of the strategies are computed, and the values are less than 3×10^{-3}.

Table 2. Human-side winning rate: with seer, no bodyguard

Werewolves\Players	3	4	5	6	7	8	9	10
1	50%	33%	50%	40%	56%	46%	60%	51%
2	-	-	17%	10%	24%	17%	31%	22%
3	-	-	-	-	7%	4%	12%	7%
4	-	-	-	-	-	-	3%	1%

Table 3. Human-side winning rate: no seer, with bodyguard

Werewolves\Players	3	4	5	6	7	8	9	10
1	33%	29%	46%	42%	53%	49%	58%	54%
2	-	-	13%	11%	22%	19%	29%	25%
3	-	-	-	-	5%	5%	11%	9%
4	-	-	-	-	-	-	2%	2%

Table 4. Human-side winning rate: with seer, with bodyguard

Werewolves\Players	3	4	5	6	7	8	9	10
1	50%	33%	67%	68%	80%	81%	84%	83%
2	-	-	33%	27%	53%	52%	66%	64%
3	-	-	-	-	25%	20%	42%	40%
4	-	-	-	-	-	-	17%	15%

utility, but not over ε, by changing to other strategies; it means that the strategy combination gives ε-Nash equilibriums. As a result of calculation, the ε is at most twice the strategy's exploitability.

4.1   The Effect of the Existence of a Seer and a Bodyguard on the Winning Rates of Human-Side

Figure 1 shows the human-side winning rates of various assignments that all contain two werewolves but a different number of players. For the game where there is a seer but not a bodyguard, the seer, after revealing his/her role to the villagers during the first turn of the game, will definitely be attacked by werewolves. However, since the role of the seer has been revealed, villagers will not vote for the elimination of the seer. As a result, the possibility of a werewolf being voted for elimination is slightly increased. Therefore, the human-side winning rate will also slightly be increased. When a bodyguard is assigned but without seer, the human-side winning rates will also be influenced slightly. However, if both the seer and the bodyguard exist, the human-side winning rates will be increased drastically, sometimes even by 48%.

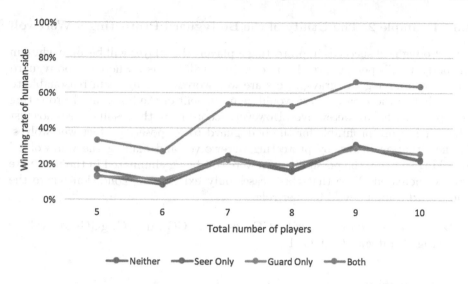

Fig. 1. Werewolves 2: comparison of winning rates

Note that there are two steps where someone will be killed, which are vote and werewolves' attack. In the cases that the human-side failed to eliminate a werewolf in a vote, which certainly happens much more than the ones in which they succeeded, there will be two villagers get killed in that turn if there is no bodyguard. Assuming there are five villagers and one werewolf assigned into the game, the maximum number of chances for them to vote is two. That number will increase by one, if we add one villager into the game. However, the number will stay the same if we add another one. However, as the number of players increases, the possibility for human-side to eliminate a werewolf will become lower. That is why the winning rate does not increase monotonically. Adding a bodyguard into the game scarcely eases that effect since the possibility of the bodyguard protecting a villager successfully is also not high.

4.2 Example 1: The Utility of the Bodyguard Protecting a Villager but Not the Seer

From the results of CFR+, we found that in the majority of situations, the bodyguard will have more utility by always protecting the seer. However, there exists cases where the bodyguard gains more benefits by protecting a gray player instead of the seer. In the following example, because there might be two were-wolves left, it is better for the bodyguard to protect one of gray players to cause the werewolves' attack to fail.

- B, 4 1 1 4, vG, gGG-, dW, vW, gSG+, d-, vG, gSS-, dB, vC
- Average Strategies[5] G: 1, S: 0

---

[5] As mentioned in [5], the average of strategies calculated in every loop gives ε-Nash equilibrium.

4.3   Example 2: The Utility of the Bodyguard Protecting a Werewolf

If the bodyguard succeeds in protecting a player, this player will become white in the bodyguard's perspective. Therefore, there will be cases where the bodyguard knows who among the gray players are werewolves. It may seem reasonable to think that in those cases there would be no benefit of the bodyguard protecting gray players who are werewolves. However, according to the results, cases do exist where it is more profitable for the bodyguard to purposely protect werewolves. In the situation below, by protecting werewolves and making the werewolves' attacking succeed, the possibility of a werewolf being eliminated in the next vote will be increased. Note that these cases only exist in the condition where the bodyguard cannot reveal his/her role.

- B, 4 1 1 4, vG, gGS+, d-, vG, gGG-, d-, vC, gGG-, d-, vG, gGG-, d-, vG
- Average Strategies C: 0, G: 1

5   Conclusion

In this paper, we proposed a limitation on the human-side strategies against the stealth werewolf strategy and calculated the strategies of both sides that result in the ε-Nash equilibrium. The solutions show that the winning rates of the human-side are more than 50% with the usual werewolves/human conditions. This suggests that the stealth werewolf strategy is not very good. Furthermore, the results also suggest that unusual actions exist in the optimal strategy.

References

1. Braverman, M., Etesami, O., Mossel, E.: Mafia: a theoretical study of players and coalitions in a partial information environment. Ann. Appl. Probab. **18**, 825–846 (2008)
2. Katagami, D., Takaku, S., Inaba, M., Osawa, H., Shinoda, K., Nishino, J., Toriumi, F.: Investigation of the effects of nonverbal information on werewolf. In: 2014 IEEE International Conference on Fuzzy Systems (FUZZ-IEEE). IEEE (2014)
3. Katagami, D., Kobayashi, Y., Osawa, H., Inaba, M., Shinoda, K., Toriumi, F.: Development of werewolf match system for human players mediated with lifelike agents. In: Proceedings of the Second International Conference on Human-Agent Interaction. ACM (2014)
4. Katagami, D., Kanazawa, M., Toriumi, F., Osawa, H., Inaba, M., Shinoda, K.: Movement design of a life-like agent for the werewolf game. In: 2015 IEEE International Conference on Fuzzy Systems (FUZZ-IEEE). IEEE (2015)
5. Bowling, M., Burch, N., Johanson, M., Tammelin, O.: Heads-up limit hold'em poker is solved. Science **347**, 145–149 (2015)
6. Zinkevich, M., Johanson, M., Bowling, M., Piccione, C.: Regret minimization in games with incomplete information. In: NIPS-20, pp. 905–912 (2008)

Werewolf Game Modeling Using Action Probabilities Based on Play Log Analysis

Yuya Hirata[1], Michimasa Inaba[1(✉)], Kenichi Takahashi[1], Fujio Toriumi[2],
Hirotaka Osawa[3], Daisuke Katagami[4], and Kousuke Shinoda[5]

[1] Hiroshima City University, 3-4-1 Ozukahigashi, Asaminami-ku, Hiroshima, Japan
hirata.y@cm.info.hiroshima-cu.ac.jp, {inaba,takahashi}@hiroshima-cu.ac.jp
[2] The University of Tokyo, 7-3-1 Hongo, Bunkyo-ku, Tokyo, Japan
[3] The University of Tsukuba, 1-1-1 Tenno-dai, Tsukubashi, Ibaraki, Japan
[4] Tokyo Polytechnic University, 1583 Iiyama, Atsugi-shi, Kanagawa, Japan
[5] The University of Electro-Communications, 1-5-1 Chifugaoka,
Chofu, Tokyo 158-8585, Japan

Abstract. In this study, we construct a non-human agent that can play
the werewolf game (i.e., AI wolf) with aims of creating more advanced
intelligence and acquire more advanced communication skills for AI-
based systems. We therefore constructed a behavioral model using information regarding human players and the decisions made by such players;
all such information was obtained from play logs of the werewolf game.
To confirm our model, we conducted simulation experiments of the werewolf game using an agent based on our proposed behavioral model, as
well as a random agent for comparison. Consequently, we obtained an
81.55% coincidence ratio of agent behavior versus human behavior.

Keywords: Werewolf game · Communication game · Player modeling ·
Multi-player

1 Introduction

In the Werewolf Game (also called Mafia), werewolves appear in a village in
the form of humans during the day, attacking villagers one-by-one every night.
The villagers decide that they must execute those who are suspected of being
werewolves, but first must determine via discussions which villagers are actually
werewolves. Since villagers are not given any information about others, information gleaned via discussion provides the only clue. Underlying the game is
how human players see through the identities of the werewolf players and how
werewolf players deceive the villagers, thus hiding their identities by providing
limited information.

Studies in game informatics that began with chess have expanded in recent
years, including games such as Go, Curling [1], and real-time simulation
(RTS) [2]. Unlike in the case of them, the werewolf game differs in a way such
that communication skills determine victory or defeat. The game requires the

© Springer International Publishing AG 2016
A. Plaat et al. (Eds.): CG 2016, LNCS 10068, pp. 103–114, 2016.
DOI: 10.1007/978-3-319-50935-8_10

use of our advanced intellectual ability, including the ability to understand the intention of others only from conversation, to therefore deduce the background of an individual and determine his or her willingness to cooperate or be persuaded. Thus, the werewolf game includes numerous communication-related problems that are significant barriers that prohibit artificial intelligence from penetrating the future society.

We, therefore, study agents that can play the werewolf game (i.e., AI wolf) with aims of creating more advanced intelligence and acquiring more advanced communication skills for AI-based systems. Construction of an AI wolf has identified numerous problems including persuading others to obtain trust, deducing an opponent model from information gleaned only from conversations, understanding and expressing non-verbal information, co-operating with other players, and applying natural language processing. We designed a protocol to discuss by AI wolves [3], released a construction kit of an AI wolf using the given protocol [4], and constructed the system that can compete with each other by anthropomorphic agent on the werewolf game. These initial studies aimed at solving the AI-specific problem of acquiring advanced communication skills by creating an environment where AI wolves can play the werewolf game and gathering collective intelligence via competitions.

To this end, in August 2015, we held the first AI wolf competition in The Computer Entertainment Developers Conference (CEDEC2015), which is the largest Japanese technical conference for game developers and engineers in Yokohama. More than 50 teams participated in the competition. We also analyzed human gameplay to obtain knowledge for realizing the AI wolf. For example, we investigated the effects of non-verbal information in the werewolf game [5], revealing gestures that impact victory or defeat by analyzing videos wherein human gestures were annotated in conjunction with the werewolf game. All these studies focused on constructing a strong agent for an AI wolf; such an agent requires not only strength but also the ability to behave much like humans.

Herein, we endeavor to realize an agent that can behave like humans by obtaining behavioral information from play logs of games played between humans, thus constructing a sound behavioral model. We used game situations obtained from play logs and action information of players in game situations to construct our behavioral model. Specific game situations and attributes, for example, the number of living villagers, number of players which have special ability, etc., can easily be obtained using the play logs; however, we could not obtain some information without analyzing utterance logs via natural language processing. We, therefore, obtained two types of information: (1) coming-out (CO) information: describing who, when, and what role is expressed, e.g., "Player A, on the first day, expressed him/herself as a seer"; and (2) decision information: describing who, when, and who was identified as either a villager or a werewolf, e.g., "Player B, on the third day, detected player C as a werewolf."

2   What is the Werewolf Game?

2.1   Gameplay

In the game, all players are randomly allocated to roles, as summarized in Table 1. Players are divided into two teams: humans and werewolves. To win as a human, the goal is to kill all werewolves, whereas to win as a werewolf, the goal is to kill humans to the number of werewolves or fewer. Players do not know what the other players' roles are, as the assigned roles are hidden. A basic course of action of a human player is to find werewolves via conversation. Conversely, werewolf players know who all of the werewolves are. A basic course of action for a werewolf player is to engage in a variety of cooperative maneuvering without other humans learning of their role.

In the werewolf game, there are two phases: day and night. In the day phase, all players discuss who the werewolves are. Players who have special abilities, as described below, lead discussions to gain an advantage for their team by using the information gained via their abilities. After a certain period of time, players identify and execute one player suspected as a werewolf; this player is selected via a collective vote. The executed player cannot play the game from then on. In the night phase, werewolf players attack human players. Attacked players are also eliminated from the game. Moreover, players with special abilities can use their abilities in the night phase. The day and night phases repeat until one group meets the conditions for winning. A crucial aspect of the werewolf game is for human players to detect the lies put forth by werewolf players. Persuading other players by using information given by their special abilities is also important. For werewolf players, the crucial aspect is to manipulate discussions to their advantage. Occasionally, werewolf players must impersonate a role.

2.2   Roles

There are many variations in the werewolf game, often including roles with special abilities. Herein, we have adopted the orthodox roles especially in Japan. Table 1 shows these roles and the ability of each role. Seers have the ability to identify werewolves in the night phase, thus comprising the most important role in the werewolf game. Counter to this, werewolf players often impersonate the role of seers to disrupt and confuse the discussion; it is not uncommon for there to be three players impersonating the role of seers in a given game. Herein, we therefore obtained CO information and decision information from utterance logs.

3   Werewolf BBS

We used data obtained from the Werewolf BBS[1], wherein users can play the game online. This site also provides discussion forums; overall, we could obtain utterance logs for all players, use history of special abilities, the role of each

---
[1] http://ninjinix.x0.com/wolf0/.

Table 1. Roles in the Werewolf Game.

Roles	Special abilities
Villager	Nothing
Werewolf	In the night phase, werewolf players attack one human player; werewolf players can attack one player in the whole of werewolf side in every night phase; werewolf players can secretly talk among themselves
Seer	In the night phase, a seer can select one player and know whether the selected player is a werewolf or not
Bodyguard	In the night phase, a bodyguard can select one player and protect the selected player from attack by a werewolf
Medium	A medium can know whether a player who is executed via a vote is a werewolf or not
Possessed	A possessed is a human, but his or her objective is the same as that of the werewolf players; a possessed is judged as human by both a seer and a medium (and is counted as a human player when victory or defeat judgments are made)

player, information of who is dead or alive at each date, and information as to the cause of death (i.e., by execution or attack); however, expressing one's own role (i.e., CO) and speaking about other players is not included. Obtaining information as to whether a player is a werewolf is a special ability, but the timing in telling other players depends on the player. Moreover, there are players who impersonate other roles. Accordingly, we analyzed utterance logs using natural language processing to obtain such information. Note that it is difficult to obtain this information because utterance logs are written in various colloquial styles. Therefore, we created numerous regular expressions to obtain CO and decision information from utterance logs to cover many such variations.

4   Acquisition of CO and Decision Information

4.1   Using Regular Expressions

We obtained CO and decision information by using regular expressions. To construct regular expressions, considering the style and expressions used (on the utterance is included CO and decision information) are efficient; however, such an approach required tremendous time and cost to obtain utterances concerning CO and decision information by hand from all utterances in the Werewolf BBS.

Therefore, we obtained information regarding "when did seer (or medium) use special ability", "which side did seer (or medium) decide", and "who did seer (or medium) decide" by checking the use history of special abilities employed by players in Werewolf BBS. Next, we obtained the utterance that includes the target player's name and result from utterances spoken by the seer and medium players on the day the special ability was used. These utterances included CO

Table 2. Example utterances.

Utterance	Type	Regular expression
I am seer	CO	⟨⟨USER⟩⟩ is ⟨⟨ROLE⟩⟩
I confirm CO of seer of Albin	CO	I confirm CO of ⟨⟨ROLE⟩⟩ of ⟨⟨USER⟩⟩
Peter is werewolf	decision	⟨⟨USER⟩⟩ is ⟨⟨DECISION⟩⟩

and decision information; we could obtain CO information because a decision was often reported at the same time as that of the CO. We, therefore, constructed regular expressions to obtain CO and decision information by using these utterances for reference.

As we analyzed the play log, for example, when player A is identified as a seer, other players sometimes also stated that "Player A is a seer." Using such utterances, we could also obtain CO information from players without special abilities. Therefore, we used other players' utterances on the same day to construct regular expressions. As such, we constructed 477 regular expressions and obtained CO and decision information via those regular expressions.

An example of utterances and regular expressions is shown in Table 2. In the table, ⟨⟨USER⟩⟩ accepts first-person pronouns and a player's name, ⟨⟨ROLE⟩⟩ accepts names of roles, and ⟨⟨DECISION⟩⟩ accepts words that represent one side or the other, i.e., "werewolf" or "human" or the like.

4.2   Performance Evaluation of Regular Expressions

We conducted an experiment to evaluate the performance of our CO and decision information acquisition method via regular expressions. In this experiment, we randomly selected 50 games for CO information and 10 for decision information. We also evaluated our method using CO and decision information acquired by hand.

We evaluated the performance by measuring precision, recall, and the f-measure. If CO information obtained via the regular expressions completely matched what we acquired by hand, we noted the obtained CO information as correct. Similarly, if decision information obtained via the regular expressions completely matched what we acquired by hand, we noted the obtained decision information as correct.

Consequently, there were 193 utterances containing CO information in 50 games. From our regular expressions, 193 were matched and 190 were correct. Furthermore, there were 156 utterances containing decision information in 10 games. By our regular expression, 137 were matched and 114 were correct. Results are shown in Table 3, from which we observe that CO information yielded a very high precision and recall. Results regarding decision information were worse than those of CO information. In the case of decision information, depending on whether the speaker had a special ability, the meaning of utterances (e.g., "Player A is a werewolf") was changed to a decision based on either

Table 3. Precision and recall rates.

	Precision	Recall	F-measure
CO	98.4(190/193)	98.4(190/193)	0.98
Decision	83.2(114/137)	73.1(114/156)	0.78

their ability or just speculation. Thus, obtaining decision information was more difficult than obtaining CO information, as is evident in our experimental results.

5   Behavioral Model Based on Action Selection Probabilities

Here, we describe a method used to construct our behavioral model using data obtained from the Werewolf BBS. Our proposed model is targeted only at the behaviors and utterances shown in Table 4.

We define the probability that a player performs action $a(a \in A)$ in situation $s(s \in S)$ by the following equation:

$$p(a|s) = \frac{n_{s,a}}{\sum_{a \in A} n_{s,a}} \tag{1}$$

Here, $p(a|s)$ represents the action selection probability and $n_{s,a}$ is the number of times a player has performed action a in situation s in the given play logs. Situation s is defined based on the basis of a decision result reported by a player who is identified as a seer or medium and number of player which expressed him/herself as a seer or medium. For cases 1 and 2 of Table 4, $A = \{CO, not\ CO\}$. For cases 3, 4, 6, 7, and 8 from Table 4, $A = \{p_1, p_2, ..., p_k\}$, assuming p_i is a player and k is the number of players. Here, p_i is defined by the number of CO players, the CO type (i.e., seer or medium), and the reported results of their decision. For case 5 from Table 4, $A = \{$human side player, werewolf side player$\}$.

To clarify our model, we describe a specific example wherein we focus on the selection of an attack target of a werewolf. Given that there are 10 players and a situation s, as described in Table 5, the game situation consists of two seers, a werewolf or a possessed expressing him/herself as a seer; furthermore, there are two players inspected as humans by those players who expressed themselves as seers. Other players did not express themselves and were not inspected by any special abilities. Here, executable action a (i.e., the player that can be an attack target) is shown in Table 6, but the werewolf is not included in action a because a werewolf cannot attack another werewolf. We assume that the numbers of occurrences of each action that the player took in the same situation in the play log were $n_{s,p_1} = 854$, $n_{s,p_2} = 3077$, and $n_{s,p_3} = 1320$. We then obtained $p(p_1|s) = 854/(854 + 3077 + 1320) = 854/5251 = 0.163$, $p(p_2|s) = 3077/5251 = 0.586$, $p(p_3|s) = 1320/5251 = 0.251$ by Eq. (1). Accordingly, given the situation of Table 5, the probability that a werewolf attacks a player who expressed him/herself as a seer is 16.3%; as for the player who was

Table 4. Modeled actions.

Num	Action
1	Whether a seer (or medium) expresses his/her role
2	Whether a werewolf (or possessed) expresses his/her fake role
3	Selection of divination target by a seer
4	Selection of a target possessing a special ability by a werewolf (or a possessed) impersonating a seer
5	Selection of a decision result of a special ability by a werewolf (or a possessed) impersonating a role
6	Selection of a vote target
7	Selection of an attack target by a werewolf
8	Selection of a protected target by a bodyguard

Table 5. Examples of situation s.

Factor	number of players
The number of players identified as a seer	2
The number of players inspected twice as human players by a seer	2
The number of players who have not been identified as any specific type and have not been inspected by a seer	6

inspected two times as a human player by a seer, this probability is 58.6%; and for the player who did not express him/herself and was not inspected by a seer, the probability is 25.1%.

As to why such probabilities occurred, the player who was inspected two times as a human player by a seer is trusted by human players because the player is very likely to be a human player. If there is a player who can be trusted, human players can advantageously discuss because by leading discussion by the player, werewolf players face increased difficulty in disrupting such discussions. Thus, the werewolf players prefer to attack players inspected two times as human players by a seer.

Table 6. Examples of action A.

A	Target player
p_1	The player who has been identified as a seer
p_2	The player who was inspected twice as human by a seer
p_3	The player who was not identified as any specific type and was not inspected by a seer

6 Degree of Coincidence Between Agents and the Play Logs

6.1 Outline

In this section, we investigate the degree of coincidence between agents using action selection probabilities and human behaviors from play logs. For comparison, we also created a random agent that randomly selects its action. Herein, we created our agents using the AI wolf server [4] released on the Artificial Intelligence Werewolf site[2]. We used data from 467 instances of the werewolf game with 223 villager wins and 224 werewolf wins as the action selection probability of the agent. We used K-fold cross-validation with K = 10 to calculate the coincidence ratio; here, the coincidence ratio is the ratio that the agent's highest-probability action in the situations defined in Sect. 5 above coincides with all human behaviors in the play logs in the same situation. Actions used to calculate the coincidence ratio include those of our proposed behavioral model, as shown in Table 4. For example, "I am a villager" is not used to calculate the coincidence ratio because it is not available in our proposed behavioral model. Furthermore, when the situation is as summarized in Table 5, the selectable actions regarding the attack target of a werewolf are shown in Table 6. The agent's highest-probability action from among selectable actions is p_2 of Table 6. We could thus investigate whether the agent's action coincides with human behavior by comparing p_2 with human behaviors obtained from play logs from the Werewolf BBS.

6.2 Results

Figure 1 shows the degree of coincidence between the actions determined by our behavioral model and human behavior. In this figure, green bars indicate the number of games. As the game can be finished in five days at the earliest, the number of games gradually decreases from the sixth day onward. The average degree of coincidence of our proposed model was 81.55%, whereas that of the random model was 33.73%. From Fig. 1, the agent based on our behavioral model of action selection probability behaved like a human substantially more so than the random agent. The number of executable actions of the agent, e.g., execute, attack, and guard, increased in the middle days of the game given the increase in the number of CO actions and players inspected by a seer. Therefore, as the game reaches its middle, the degree of coincidence of the random agent further decreases. Furthermore, the degree of coincidence of the agent based on our behavioral model of action selection probability decreased, too, but obtained higher values than that of the random agent.

In the final phase of the werewolf game, the coincidence ratio of the agent based on our behavioral model of action selection probability increased; however, the tendency that this degree of coincidence decreases was seen in days 8 and 9. This tendency is not seen in the random agent because the action selection

---

[2] http://www.aiwolf.org/en/.

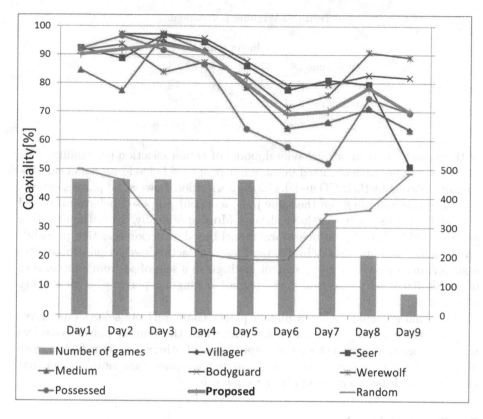

Fig. 1. Degree of coincidence (Color figure online)

probability cannot be obtained for day 9 given that the situation information is insufficient. There are only 74 games remaining on day 9.

6.3 Consideration

We conducted our simulation experiments 10,000 times on agents based on our behavioral model of action selection probability to investigate its influence on victory or defeat. In our simulation experiment, we prepared 15 agents based on our behavioral model of action selection probability; these agents played the werewolf game between the same agents. As noted above, we also conducted the same simulation experiments using the random agent to compare our results.

The winning percentage of our simulation experiments is shown in Table 7. We calculated the winning rate of actual games by using the data of the afore-mentioned 467 instances (with 223 villager wins and 224 werewolf wins). As summarized in the table, the obtained winning rate of agents based on our behavioral model of action selection probability was closer to the winning rate of the actual games when compared to that of the random agent; however, there is still a substantial difference between the winning percentage of actual games and that

Table 7. Winning percentage.

	Villager win	Werewolf win
Actual game	47.8%	52.2%
Proposed method	32.6%	67.4%
Random method	22.0%	78.0%

of the agents based on our behavioral model of action selection probability. This discrepancy may have occurred because our proposed behavioral model can distinguish players by their CO and decision information; however, if players express the same role and are given the same judgment, our proposed behavioral model cannot distinguish between those players. More specifically, given the situation summarized in Table 5, our behavioral model based on action selection probability identifies actions from Table 6 as well as each action's selection probability; however, our behavioral model cannot distinguish a seer of p_1 from another seer of p_1. Similarly, our behavioral model cannot distinguish player p_2 from another player of p_2.

In actual gameplay, when a human player comparatively selects one player as a target of an action in the above situation, the human player considers discrepancies from past utterances, impressions of others, etc. Our future work aims to incorporate these aspects to construct a refined behavioral model that can distinguish between players in the same role.

7 Related Work

Related studies include Monopoly [6] and The Settlers of Catan [7,8]. Both these games attempt to include communication in the gameplay via the computer; however, utterances of these games target negotiation, e.g., in the trading and exchange of properties, utilities, and the like. This only requires the ability to estimate the intentions of others. These studies are related to automated negotiation, which is widely studied in the field of multi-agent systems (e.g. [9,10]). Conversely, in the werewolf game, the ability to persuade and earn credibility is as important as estimating the intentions of other parties through logical thinking.

Taylor investigated "The Resistance Game" wherein trust affects the game result in common with the werewolf game [11]. However, this study focuses on the game without communication among players.

There are a few existing studies on the werewolf game. Braveman [12] and Yao [13] both showed that the probability of a werewolf-side win, $w(n, m)$, is proportional to $m/\sqrt{n}$, where n is the number of players at the start of the game and m is the number of werewolves. Furthermore, Migdal showed the exact formula of probability $w(n, m)$ [14].

In these studies, players with special abilities (e.g., seers) are not included, thus simplifying the mathematical modeling. The game is performed using only villagers and werewolves; however, actual games include many more roles, as seen on the Werewolf BBS. We also note that there are substantial differences regarding the process and nature of the game when roles other than just villager and werewolf are included. For example, if the aforementioned Werewolf BBS data were applied to the expression provided by Migdal (assuming the roles with special abilities are lumped into the villager role, i.e., $n = 15$ and $m = 3$), we obtain a werewolf winning rate of 97.1%; however, according to our research, the actual werewolf winning percentage on the Werewolf BBS was 52.2%.

There are studies that have focused on human behavior and the psychological aspects of playing a werewolf that used various features for determining whether a player is a werewolf. For example, there was a study that used each player's utterances, utterance lengths, and the number of interruptions [15]; a study that used hand and head movements [16]; and a study that used the number of words in each utterance [17] to determine whether a player was a werewolf. Furthermore, several audio–visual corpus containing dialogue data in the werewolf game were constructed to analyze group communication [18,19]. However, these studies do not focus on playing the werewolf game with a computer.

8   Conclusion

In this study, we constructed a behavioral model by obtaining behavioral information from play logs describing play between humans; our model identifies an action selection probability to realize an agent that can behave like humans. We first obtained two types of information, i.e., CO and decision information via regular expressions to obtain behavioral information, and then acquired information regarding the dead or alive state at each date, the role of each player, etc. Consequently, we obtained a precision of 98.4%, a recall of 98.4%, and an f-measure of 0.98 for CO information acquisition; for decision information, we obtained a precision of 83.2%, a recall of 73.1%, and an f-measure of 0.78. We constructed a behavioral model based on action selection probability using information acquired from play logs and conducted simulation experiments. Consequently, agents based on our behavioral model of action selection probability behaved like humans much more so than a random agent; however, action selection probabilities could not be obtained in some instances due to insufficient situation information. In future work, we aim to include more game data and work to distinguish between players that express themselves as the same role and are inspected by the same side.

Acknowledgements. We heartily thank Mr. Ninjin for allowing us to use the data of the Werewolf BBS. This study received a grant of JSPS Grants-in-aid for Scientific Research 15K12180.

References

1. Ito, T., Kitasei, Y.: Proposal and implementation of "digital curling". In: 2015 IEEE Conference on Computational Intelligence and Games (CIG), pp. 469–473 (2015)

2. Garcia-Sanchez, P., Tonda, A., Mora, A.M., Squillero, G., Merelo, J.J.: Towards automatic StarCraft strategy generation using genetic programming. In: 2015 IEEE Conference on Computational Intelligence and Games (CIG), pp. 284–291 (2015)
3. Osawa, H., Toriumi, F., Katagami, D., Shinoda, K., Inaba, M.: Designing protocol of werewolf game: protocol for inference and persuasion. In: The 24th Fuzzy, Artificial Intelligence, Neural Networks and Computational Intelligence (FAN 2014) (2014)
4. Toriumi, F., Kajiwara, K., Osawa, H., Inaba, M., Katagami, D., Shinoda, K.: Development of AI wolf platform: development of game ai by using collective intelligence. In: Digital Games Research Association JAPAN 2014 (DiGRA JAPAN 2014) (2015)
5. Katagami, D., Takaku, S., Inaba, M., Osawa, H., Shinoda, K., Nishino, J., Toriumi, F.: Investigation of the effects of nonverbal information on werewolf. In: 2014 IEEE International Conference on Fuzzy Systems (FUZZ-IEEE), pp. 982–987 (2014)
6. Yasumura, Y., Oguchi, K., Nitta, K.: Negotiation strategy of agents in the Monopoly game. In: Proceedings 2001 IEEE International Symposium on Computational Intelligence in Robotics and Automation, pp. 277–281 (2001)
7. Guhe, M., Lascarides, A., O'Connor, K., Rieser, V.: Effects of belief and memory on strategic negotiation. In: Proceedings of the SEMDIAL, vol. 2013, pp. 82–91 (2013)
8. Guhe, M., Lascarides, A.: The effectiveness of persuasion in the settlers of catan. In: IEEE Conference on Computational Intelligence and Games (CIG), pp. 1–8. IEEE (2014)
9. Okumura, M., Fujita, K., Ito, T.: An implementation of collective collaboration support system based on automated multi-agent negotiation. In: Ito, T., Zhang, M., Robu, V., Matsuo, T. (eds.) Complex Automated Negotiations. SCI, vol. 435, pp. 125–141. Springer, Heidelberg (2013)
10. Lang, F., Fink, A., Brandt, T.: Design of automated negotiation mechanisms for decentralized heterogeneous machine scheduling. Eur. J. Oper. Res. **248**(1), 192–203 (2016)
11. Taylor, D.P.: Investigating approaches to ai for trust-based, multi-agent board games with imperfect information; with don eskridge's "the resistance", Discovery, Invention & Application, no. 1 (2014)
12. Braverman, M., Etesami, O., Mossel, E.: Mafia: a theoretical study of players and coalitions in a partial information environment. Ann. Appl. Probab. **18**(3), 825–846 (2008)
13. Yao, E.: A theoretical study of mafia games, arXiv preprint arXiv:0804.0071 (2008)
14. Migdał, P.: A mathematical model of the Mafia game, arXiv preprint arXiv:1009.1031 (2010)
15. Chittaranjan, G., Hung, H.: Are you awerewolf? detecting deceptive roles and outcomes in a conversational role-playing game. In: 2010 IEEE International Conference on Acoustics Speech and Signal Processing (ICASSP), pp. 5334–5337 (2010)
16. Xia, F., Wang, H., Huang, J.: Deception detection via blob motion pattern analysis. In: Affective Computing and Intelligent Interaction, pp. 727–728 (2007)
17. Zhou, L., Sung, Y.W.: Cues to deception in online Chinese groups. In: Hawaii international conference on system sciences. In: Proceedings of the 41st Annual, pp. 146–146 (2008)
18. Hung, H., Chittaranjan, G.: The idiap wolf corpus: exploring group behaviour in a competitive role-playing game. In: Proceedings of the International Conference on Multimedia, pp. 879–882. ACM (2010)
19. Prévot, L., Yao, Y., Gingold, A., Bel, B., Chan, K.Y.J.: Toward a scary comparative corpus: the werewolf spoken corpus. In: SEMDIAL 2015, pp. 204–205 (2015)

Nash Equilibrium in Mastermind

François Bonnet[(✉)] and Simon Viennot[(✉)]

Graduate School of Advanced Science and Technology, JAIST, Nomi, Japan
{f-bonnet,sviennot}@jaist.ac.jp

Abstract. Mastermind is a famous two-player deduction game. A Code-maker chooses a secret code and a Codebreaker tries to guess this secret code in as few guesses as possible, with feedback information after each guess. Many existing works have computed optimal worst-case and average-case strategies of the Codebreaker, assuming that the Codemaker chooses the secret code uniformly at random. However, the Codemaker can freely choose any distribution probability on the secret codes. An optimal strategy in this more general setting is known as a Nash Equilibrium. In this research, we compute such a Nash Equilibrium for all instances of Mastermind up to the most classical instance of 4 pegs and 6 colors, showing that the uniform distribution is not always the best choice for the Code-maker. We also show the direct relation between Nash Equilibrium computations and computations of worst-case and average-case strategies.

1 Introduction

1.1 A Simple Deduction Game

Before studying the famous game of Mastermind, let us start by describing a much simpler deduction game to illustrate some notions. We consider the two-player game *Guess-A-Number*, played by Alice and Bob. Initially, Alice chooses a *secret number* between 1 and N, where N is a parameter of the game (known by both players). Bob has to discover Alice's secret number. To find this number, Bob makes successive *guesses*; each guess being a number. The game ends when Bob correctly guesses her number. After each guess, Alice gives a *feedback* informing Bob whether (a) his guess is the secret number, or (b) his guess is lower than the secret number, or (c) his guess is higher. Based on that feedback, Bob eventually finds Alice's secret number. In this game, Bob's goal is to win using as few guesses as possible. Note that Alice does not have any choice except at the beginning, when she chooses her number.

Example. Let consider the smallest non-trivial instance of this game, with $N = 3$, and let us analyze what are the possible strategies of the players:

- Alice chooses a number from the set $\{1, 2, 3\}$.
- Bob is clever; he knows that his first guess should be the number 2. It is the only first guess that guarantees him to discover Alice's number in at most two steps *in the worst case*. Indeed, (a) if Alice chose the number 2, Bob wins

© Springer International Publishing AG 2016
A. Plaat et al. (Eds.): CG 2016, LNCS 10068, pp. 115–128, 2016.
DOI: 10.1007/978-3-319-50935-8_11

in a single guess; while (b) if Alice chose 1 or 3, he wins using two guesses. Assuming that Alice chooses her number *uniformly* at random, Bob's strategy requires $\frac{2+1+2}{3} \simeq 1.67$ steps in *average*.

- Alice is also clever; she is expecting Bob to first guess the number 2. To counter him, she decides to avoid choosing number 2 as her secret number; she selects now her secret number only between 1 and 3 with equal probability. This change in her strategy increases the average number of guesses of Bob; it becomes $\frac{2+0+2}{2} = 2$.
- Bob is even more clever. He knows that Alice never chooses the number 2 as her secret number. Then he updates his strategy too. Instead of guessing first the number 2, he only needs to guess 1 and 3 successively. His average number of guesses reduces to $\frac{1+0+2}{2} = 1.5$.
- Alice is ...

Such reasoning could continue forever and Alice's and Bob's strategies will never converge. Fortunately, many years ago, Nash introduced the notion of Nash Equilibrium (NE) [11]. There exist some pairs of players' strategies for which none of the players benefit in changing their strategy. In the previously-described game, when both players are playing optimal strategies (in the NE sense), Bob discovers the number in an average of $\frac{9}{5} = 1.8$ guesses. Alice has to choose number 1 with probability $\frac{2}{5}$, number 2 with probability $\frac{1}{5}$, and number 3 with probability $\frac{2}{5}$.[1]

Mastermind is a more complex game, but a similar analysis can be done, as we will see in this paper.

1.2 The Game of Mastermind

Mastermind is a two-player game in which Alice (*aka.* the Codemaker) chooses a *secret code* and Bob (*aka.* the Codebreaker) has to discover this secret code. The code is a sequence of n pegs, each of them taken from a set of k colors. The original game, invented and sold in the 1970s, proposed a code of length $n = 4$ and $k = 6$ colors, leading to $6^4 = 1\,296$ possible secret codes. Later, to increase the level of difficulty, a *Super Mastermind* version was commercialized with $n = 5$ pegs and $k = 8$ colors.

After Alice has chosen her secret code, Bob makes successive *guesses*; each guess being a sequence of n pegs chosen among k colors (*i.e.* a guess corresponds to one of the possible codes). After each guess, Alice gives a feedback (*aka. grade*) informing Bob about the quality of his guess. The grade is a pair of two integers[2] (b, w), where b indicates the number of correct pegs in the guess with respect to the secret code, and w indicates the number of pegs with correct colors but incorrect positions (see Sect. 2 for a more formal definition).

---

[1] The straightforward proof is left to the reader.
[2] We use (b, w) since the original game use *b*lack and *w*hite pins to display the grade.

Example. Consider the game instance with $n = 5$ and $k = 8$, where colors are represented by numbers 1 to 8. Alice chooses the secret code 72321 and Bob proposes the guess 23523. In Bob's guess, only one single peg is correct (good position, good color); the one at position 4 with color 2. There are also two pegs with a correct color but an incorrect position: the peg with color 2 at position 1 and the peg with color 3 at position 2. Consequently, the grade is $(b, w) = (1, 2)$. Note that since the secret code contains a single peg with color 3; only one peg with color 3 from Bob's guess is counted in the number w.

1.3 Related Work

Due to its mathematical nature, the game has been widely studied. In 1976, Knuth analyzed the original game $(n, k) = (4, 6)$ and proved that any code can be found using at most 5 guesses [9], and one cannot do better; there is no strategy solving all codes in 4 guesses. After this optimal *worst case* result, researchers started naturally to look for an optimal *average case* result. In 1993, Koyama and Lai finally proved that the best strategy finds the code in $\frac{5625}{1296} \simeq 4.34$ guesses in average (assuming that the secret code is chosen *uniformly at random* among the 1296 possible codes) [10]. Similar worst and average cases have later been computed for larger instances; latest results up to $(4, 7)$ are given by Ville [13].

A general average case solution for two pegs and arbitrary number of colors is given by Goddard [5] and Chen and Lin [1]. General worst case solutions for three pegs (and arbitrary number of colors) or two colors (and arbitrary number of pegs) have been proposed by Jager [7]. Asymptotic bounds for large number of pegs were first proposed in 1983 by Chvátal [2] and recently improved by Doerr *et al.* [3]. Related works also include variants of the game with only black pegs [6,8] or in a static version [2,4] where the goal is to determine the code by asking simultaneously many guesses (without waiting for the feedback).

1.4 Motivation and Contributions

All related work mentioned in the previous paragraph deals with Codebreaker strategies. This is quite natural, since this is what makes the game interesting for human players. However Mastermind, similarly to the Guess-A-Number game, is in fact a two-player game. One should also investigate the strategies of the Codemaker. She plays only a single move in the game (choosing the secret code) but this choice may have an impact on the strategies of the Codebreaker.

To the best of our knowledge, only one paper has been published on this specific problem. In 1982, Pearson proposed an analysis of *two person, zero sum games* and illustrated his theory using a small instance of Mastermind [12]. When playing with $n = 2$ pegs and $k = 3$ colors, the codebreaker should choose any *unicolor*[3] code with probability $\frac{1}{6}$ and any *bicolor* code with probability $\frac{1}{12}$. This distribution of secret codes guarantees the highest possible average case for

---

[3] A unicolor (resp. bicolor) code is a code with both pegs with same (resp. different) color. There are 3 unicolor codes and 6 bicolor codes. Note that $3 \times \frac{1}{6} + 6 \times \frac{1}{12} = 1$.

the Codebreaker, namely $\frac{29}{12} \simeq 2.42$ guesses (compared to $\frac{21}{9} \simeq 2.33$ guesses if the Codemaker plays uniformly at random).

In 1995, Wiener posted a message on `sci.math` newsgroup [14] stating that he has "done a full game-theoretic analysis of the 4-peg, 6-colour version of mastermind [...]". He concluded that an optimal Codemaker must not play any unicolor code, but should play any other code uniformly at random, *i.e.* with probability $\frac{1}{1290}$. Such distribution of code leads to an average case of $\frac{5600}{1290} \simeq 4.34$ guesses for an optimal Codebreaker.

However, as far as we know, Wiener did not release any publication of this result, except this short newsgroup message. The result has never been computed independently and there is also no existing description of the computation algorithms. In this research, our goal is then to compute such optimal Codemaker strategy (more precisely, to compute the Nash Equilibrium) for different instances of Mastermind. We confirm the announced result of Wiener and we also show that smaller instances of Mastermind exhibit interesting Nash Equilibria.

1.5 Outline

The remaining of the paper is organized as follows. Section 2 formalizes the game and summarizes some of the known results. Section 3 explains how we computed Nash Equilibria. Section 4 presents our results emphasizing some unexpected cases. Section 5 finally concludes the paper.

2 Definitions and Notations

2.1 Rules of the Game

As described in the Introduction, Mastermind is a two-player game where Alice (the Codemaker) chooses a secret code that Bob (the Codebreaker) has to discover. The game is parametrized by a pair of integers (n, k) where n denotes the number of pegs (*i.e.* the length of a code) and k denotes the number of colors (*i.e.* the cardinality of the alphabet). In this paper, we use integers to represent colors; an alphabet of k colors is represented by the set $\{0, 1, 2, \ldots, k-1\}$. A code C is therefore a sequence of n integers; $C = (C_1, C_2, C_3, \ldots, C_n)$. Since all proposed examples contain at most ten colors, we simplify notations as follows: code $(1, 0, 3, 2, 0)$ becomes 10320.

To discover the secret code, the Codebreaker makes successive guesses, each guess being a code. The game ends when he successfully guesses the correct code. The Codemaker grades each submitted guess with respect to her secret code. The grading function $g_{n,k}$ is a symmetric function taking two codes as inputs and returning a pair of integers (b, w) as output. For an instance (n, k) of the game of Mastermind, a secret code S and a guess G, $g_{n,k}(S, G) = (b, w)$ with:

$$b = \sum_{i=1}^{n} \delta(S_i, G_i) \qquad \text{and} \qquad w = \max_{\tilde{G} \in Perm(G)} \left(\sum_{i=1}^{n} \delta(S_i, \tilde{G}_i) \right) - b,$$

where δ denotes the Kronecker symbol and $Perm(G)$ denotes the set of all permutations of G (formalization inspired from [2]).

Combinatorial observations. Given an instance (n, k) of the game, there are k^n possible codes. Both integers b and w output by the grading function belong to the set $\{0, \ldots, n\}$ and they satisfy the inequality $b + w \leq n$. There is clearly no pair of codes with relative grade equal to $(n - 1, 1)$. Thus, for a given instance (n, k) of Mastermind with $k > 2$, there are $\frac{n(n+3)}{2}$ possible grades.[4]

2.2 Strategies in the Game

In the following, we assume a fixed instance (n, k) of the game. Formally, all functions defined below (such as wc) are parametrized with n and k (and should be denoted $wc_{n,k}$). For clarity, we do not subscript these functions.

Codemaker's Strategies. The only move of the Codemaker is to choose a secret code. A pure strategy is to choose a given code. Usually we consider only mixed strategies where the Codemaker plays according to a distribution of probability over the set of all possible codes. One particular strategy is the Uniform strategy where she chooses a secret code uniformly at random among the k^n codes.

Codebreaker's Strategies. The Codebreaker has to find the secret code. In the game of Mastermind, pure strategies of the Codebreaker can easily be represented by trees where nodes are guesses and edges are grades. To play a given strategy/tree, the Codebreaker starts with the root node as initial guess, and then follows the edge corresponding to the grade received from the Codemaker, until it reaches a leaf meaning that the secret code has been found.

The Codebreaker wants to win *as quickly as possible*. Formally, this notion can be interpreted in (at least) three ways. Given a (pure or mixed) strategy S of the Codebreaker, we define the three following values:

1. **Worst case:** $wc(S)$ denotes the smallest integer such that S is guaranteed to discover any secret code in at most $wc(S)$ guesses. A strategy S is said to be wc-optimal if there is no strategy S' with $wc(S') < wc(S)$.
   For a pure strategy S, $wc(S)$ equals the height of the corresponding tree.
2. **Average case:** $avg(S)$ denotes the average number of guesses required to discover any code, assuming that the Codemaker plays her Uniform strategy. A strategy is said to be avg-optimal if there is no strategy S' with $avg(S') < avg(S)$.
   For a pure strategy S, $avg(S)$ equals the average depth of all leaves.

---

[4] This formula is incorrect when $k = 1$ since there exists a single code, hence a single possible grade $(n, 0)$. For $k = 2$ colors, there are also some unreachable grades such as $(b, w) = (0, n)$ when n is odd.

3. **Weakest case:** $weak(S)$ denotes the largest average number of guesses required when playing against all possible Codemaker strategies. Said differently, it corresponds to the average number of guesses required when the adversary is playing the strongest possible strategy that counters the Codebreaker's strategy.

For a pure strategy S, $weak(S) = wc(S)$ since the Codemaker can choose to play (one of) the pure strategy corresponding to (one of) the worst case. Thus this notion of $weak(S)$ is really interesting only for mixed strategies.

When considering an instance (n, k) of Mastermind, we define $\mathrm{WC}(n, k)$ to denote the value of some wc-optimal strategy. Similarly, we use the notation $\mathrm{AVG}(n, k)$ for avg-optimal strategy:

$$\mathrm{WC}(n, k) = \min_{S \in \mathbb{S}_B} (wc(S)) \quad \text{and} \quad \mathrm{AVG}(n, k) = \min_{S \in \mathbb{S}_B} (avg(S)),$$

where $\mathbb{S}_B$ denotes the set of all strategies of the Codebreaker, including mixed strategies.[5] As already mentioned in Sect. 1.3, existing related work deals with computing these values $\mathrm{WC}(n, k)$ and $\mathrm{AVG}(n, k)$.

Nash Equilibrium. The definitions of WC and AVG are based on the notions of wc-optimality and avg-optimality respectively. Similarly one can use the third notion of weakest case to define a last optimality criteria, corresponding to the Nash Equilibrium $\mathrm{NE}(n, k)$:

$$\mathrm{NE}(n, k) = \min_{S \in \mathbb{S}_B} (weak(S)).$$

2.3   Example with $(n, k) = (3, 2)$

To illustrate the previous definitions, let us consider a simple instance of Mastermind with 3 pegs and 2 colors. There are $2^3 = 8$ codes; 000, 001, 010, 011, 100, 101, 110, 111. Figure 1 depicts a possible strategy S for the Codebreaker. Note that there is no edge labeled $(0, 0)$, $(0, 1)$, $(0, 3)$, or $(1, 1)$ starting from the root since no secret code can lead to such grade when compared with guess 001.

Using this strategy, in the worst case, the Codebreaker wins in four guesses (to find the secret code 101), hence $wc(S) = 4$. Globally, one code is found in 1 guess, four codes in 2 guesses, two codes in 3 guesses, and one code in 4 guesses, hence $avg(S) = \frac{1 \times 1 + 4 \times 2 + 2 \times 3 + 1 \times 4}{8} = \frac{19}{8} \simeq 2.38$. This strategy S is neither wc-optimal nor avg-optimal. Indeed there exists better strategies for both metrics; $\mathrm{WC}(3, 2) = 3$ and $\mathrm{AVG}(3, 2) = \frac{18}{8} = 2.25$ (finding them is left to the reader).

---

[5] To compute WC and AVG, it is sufficient to consider only pure strategies. However for NE, it is required to consider also mixed strategies.

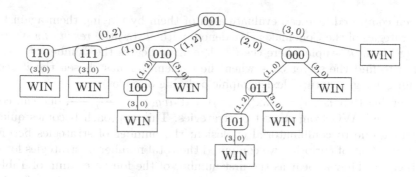

Fig. 1. A Codebreaker's strategy S for the instance $(3, 2)$ of Mastermind

Since S is a pure strategy, as already mentioned earlier, $weak(S) = wc(S) = 4$. Indeed, knowing that the Codebreaker is playing S, the Codemaker may decide to always choose the secret code 101.

2.4   Known Results

Table 1 summarizes known values of AVG for Mastermind. As far as we know, blank entries (*e.g.* AVG(5, 5)) are still unknown; indeed even relatively small instances are hard to compute due to combinatorial explosion. This table is not exhaustive; Ville lists additional values, such as AVG(4, 7) [13].

Table 1. Some known values of $AVG(n, k)$

		Number of colors k				
		2	3	4	5	6
Nb. of pegs n	2	$8/4 = 2$	$21/9 \approx 2.33$	$45/16 \approx 2.81$	$81/25 = 3.24$	$132/36 \approx 3.67$
	3	$18/8 = 2.25$	$73/27 \approx 2.70$	$206/64 \approx 3.22$	$451/125 \approx 3.61$	$854/216 \approx 3.95$
	4	$44/16 = 2.75$	$246/81 \approx 3.04$	$905/256 \approx 3.54$	$2463/625 \approx 3.94$	$5625/1296 \approx 4.34$
	5	$97/32 \approx 3.03$	$816/243 \approx 3.36$	$3954/1024 \approx 3.86$		

3   How to Compute Optimal Values

This section explains how to compute WC, AVG, and NE values.

3.1   Basic Approach

The naive approach involves generating all pure strategies for the Codebreaker[6] and analyzing them to obtain the desired values. Once the list of all strategies

---

[6] Pure strategies of the Codemaker are trivially computed. There are exactly k^n pure strategies, one for each possible code.

has been computed, one can evaluate each of them by playing them against all pure strategies of the Codemaker. We denote with $res(S)$ the *result* of a strategy S; $res(S)$ is an k^n-tuple where the ith element indicates the number of guesses required to find the secret code when the Codemaker has chosen the ith code (assuming, wlog. a natural lexicographic ordering of codes).

Observing that $wc(S) = \max(res(S))$ and $avg(S) = \frac{\sum res(S)}{k^n}$, one can compute WC and AVG from the set of strategies. This approach becomes quickly impractical due to combinatorial explosion; the number of strategies becomes intractable. Out of curiosity, we computed the total number of strategies for the Codebreaker. They appear as the first number of the fourth column of Table 2. The second number of the same fourth column indicates the number of unique strategy results. Indeed, many strategies lead to the same result. Considering only unique results already reduces greatly the order of magnitude.

Example (continued). Considering the strategy S of Fig. 1, one can check that $res(S) = (2, 1, 2, 3, 3, 4, 2, 2)$.

Table 2. Some interesting numbers about the combinatorial explosion. #strategies represents the total number of strategies and the total number of unique results. #results represents, with respect to equivalence classes, (i) the total number of unique results, (ii) the total number after eliminating results dominated by other results, (iii) an approximate number of non-dominated results (domination by linear combination).

(n, k)	#codes	#grades	#strategies		#classes	#results (wrt classes)		
$(2, 2)$	4	5	8	– 8	2	2	– 2	– 2
$(2, 3)$	9	5	26 760	– 1 278	2	33	– 3	– 3
$(2, 4)$	16	5	2.08×10^{11}	– 6 043 176	2	188	– 6	– 3
$(2, 5)$	25	5	9.91×10^{21}	–	2	557	– 8	– 5
$(2, 6)$	36	5	9.29×10^{36}	–	2	1 377	– 11	– 5
$(3, 2)$	8	9	1 776	– 648	2	16	– 3	– 3
$(3, 3)$	27	9	2.47×10^{23}	–	3	2 489	– 17	– ~12
$(3, 4)$	64	9	1.47×10^{79}	–	3	124 852	– 112	– ~24
$(3, 5)$	125	9	6.72×10^{190}	–	3	1 201 354	– 286	– ~69
$(3, 6)$	216	9		–	3	6 793 325	– 619	– ~123
$(4, 2)$	16	14	2.29×10^{11}	– 14 578 420	3	230	– 4	– 4
$(4, 3)$	81	14	4.13×10^{107}	–	4	2 669 925	– 509	– ~143
$(4, 4)$	256	14		–	5		– 107 274	– ~12 430
$(4, 5)$	625	14		–	5		– 4 650 433	– ~200 604
$(4, 6)$	1296	14		–	5		–	– ~899 057

Table 3. Number of codes ($= k^n$) and number of equivalence classes

		Number of colors k				
		2	3	4	5	6
Nb. of pegs n	2	$4 \Rightarrow 2$	$9 \Rightarrow 2$	$16 \Rightarrow 2$	$25 \Rightarrow 2$	$36 \Rightarrow 2$
	3	$8 \Rightarrow 2$	$27 \Rightarrow 3$	$64 \Rightarrow 3$	$125 \Rightarrow 3$	$216 \Rightarrow 3$
	4	$16 \Rightarrow 3$	$81 \Rightarrow 4$	$256 \Rightarrow 5$	$625 \Rightarrow 5$	$1\,296 \Rightarrow 5$
	5	$32 \Rightarrow 3$	$243 \Rightarrow 5$	$1\,024 \Rightarrow 6$	$3\,125 \Rightarrow 7$	$7\,776 \Rightarrow 7$

3.2 Equivalence Classes

The combinatorial explosion can be greatly limited by noting that from a theoretical point of view, playing a blue, red, or green peg does not make any difference. Hence any permutation of colors in a strategy S of the Codebreaker has no effect on the values of $wc(S)$, $avg(S)$, and $weak(S)$. Similarly any permutation of the pegs has also no effect. The same reasoning applies to the strategies of the Codemaker. Instead of evaluating Codebreaker's strategies against all possible codes (*i.e.* all pure Codemaker's strategies), one can "simply" evaluate strategies with respect to equivalence classes. Given a strategy S, instead of computing a k^n-tuple result, one can study a much smaller tuple whose cardinality equals the number of equivalence classes (see Table 3). $res_{eq}(S)$ is computed from $res(S)$ by summing elements corresponding to codes belonging to the same class.

Example (continued). Based on the example of Sect. 2.3 with $(n, k) = (3, 2)$, the 8 codes can be grouped in 2 equivalence classes: the class of unicolor codes $\{000, 111\}$ and the class of bicolor codes $\{001, 010, 011, 100, 101, 110\}$. Based on these classes, the new evaluation of the strategy S of Fig. 1 becomes $res_{eq}(S) = (2 + 2, 1 + 2 + 3 + 3 + 4 + 2) = (4, 15)$.

3.3 Recursive Computation with Pruning

There is in fact no need to list all possible strategies of the Codebreaker for computing the values that we are interested in. The strategies can be explored recursively by exploring alternately all possible guesses of the Codebreaker after some grade answer of the Codemaker (a grade node), and then exploring all possible grades after some guess (a guess node). Figure 2 gives an example of exploration tree for the instance $(3, 3)$.[7]

The main point of this recursive exploration is that instead of listing the strategies, we only compute the cost of grade nodes and guess nodes, which is equivalent to prune the under-optimal strategies progressively. This recursive exploration is classical for computations of worst-case and average-case, and

---

[7] Figures 2, 3, 4 and 5 appear only in Appendix A.

it can also be used for Nash Equilibrium. The only difference is the kind of information (cost) that will be propagated upward.

3.4 Computing WC and AVG Values

In the case of the worst-case computation, the cost of a strategy corresponds to the maximal number of guesses needed by the strategy. The cost of a grade node is the cost of the best guess choice for the Codebreaker, hence the minimal cost over the guesses. The cost of a guess node is the cost of the worst possible grade, hence the maximal cost over the grades. WC computations are similar to a mini-max algorithm.

In the case of the average-case computation, the cost of a strategy is the total number of guesses. The cost of a grade node is still the minimal cost over the guesses, but the cost of a guess node is now the sum of cost over the grades. AVG computations are similar to a mini-max algorithm but with a sum operation instead of a max operation.

3.5 Computing NE Values

The algorithm that we used to compute the Nash-Equilibrium is quite similar. The first difference is that the cost of a strategy is now represented not by a single number but by a list of numbers, *i.e.* the number of guesses needed for each equivalence class. In the case of Sect. 2.3 example, it is a couple of numbers. In the case of the usual $(4,6)$ game, it is a 5-tuple. Also, for each grade and guess node, we cannot retain the cost of a unique optimal strategy. We need to retain the cost of all strategies that are not dominated by others.

At a grade node, the CodeBreaker can choose its next guess, so that a strategy at a grade node is any strategy for any of the guesses. The complete list of costs at a grade node is obtained by a union of the list of costs for each guess. At a guess node, a strategy of the CodeBreaker is the choice of a strategy for each of the grades. The complete list of costs is obtained by an operation that is called a Minkowski sum over the list of costs of the possible grades.[8]

The final complete list of costs that is obtained can be turned into a system of inequalities that represent the constraints on the Nash-Equilibrium. This system can be solved with classical Linear Programming methods (we used Mathematica in this research).

4 Our Results

NE Values. Table 4 summarizes the Nash Equilibrium values that we have computed. We highlighted in red the differences with AVG values of Table 1.

Strategies Achieving NE Values. Table 5 gives Alice's strategies at the equilibrium. Strategies are given with respect to classes of equivalence ordered lexicographically. For example, considering the instance $(4, 4)$, Alice should never

---

[8] A full description will be given in a longer version of this article.

Table 4. Computed values of NE(n, k)

| | | \multicolumn{5}{c}{Number of colors k} | | | | |
		2	3	4	5	6
Nb. of pegs n	2	2	$29/12 \approx 2.42$	$45/16 \approx 2.81$	$49/15 \approx 3.27$	$11/3 \approx 3.67$
	3	$23/10 = 2.3$	$73/27 \approx 2.70$	$219/68 \approx 3.22$	$1591/440 \approx 3.62$	$619/156 \approx 3.97$
	4	$39/14 \approx 2.79$	$67/22 \approx 3.05$	$1629/460 \approx 3.54$	$2463/625 \approx 3.94$	$5600/1290 \approx 4.34$
	5	$46/15 \approx 3.07$	$118/35 \approx 3.37$			

Table 5. Computed Codemaker's strategy achieving NE(n, k)

| | | \multicolumn{5}{c}{Number of colors k} | | | | |
		2	3	4	5	6
Nb. of pegs n	2	$\frac{1}{4}, \frac{1}{4}$	$\frac{1}{6}, \frac{1}{12}$	$\frac{1}{16}, \frac{1}{16}$	$\frac{1}{15}, \frac{1}{30}$	$\forall \alpha \in \left[\frac{1}{36}, \frac{1}{21}\right], \alpha, \frac{1-6\alpha}{30}$
	3	$\frac{1}{5}, \frac{1}{10}$	$\frac{1}{27}, \frac{1}{27}, \frac{1}{27}$	$\frac{1}{34}, \frac{1}{68}, \frac{1}{68}$	$\frac{1}{110}, \frac{1}{110}, \frac{3}{440}$	$\frac{1}{156}, \frac{1}{156}, \frac{1}{312}$
	4	$0, \frac{1}{14}, \frac{1}{14}$	$0, \frac{1}{66}, \frac{1}{66}, \frac{1}{99}$	$0, \frac{2}{345}, \frac{1}{276}, \frac{1}{276}, \frac{1}{345}$	$\frac{1}{625}, \frac{1}{625}, \frac{1}{625}, \frac{1}{625}, \frac{1}{625}$	$0, \frac{1}{1290}, \frac{1}{1290}, \frac{1}{1290}, \frac{1}{1290}$
	5	$0, \frac{1}{30}, \frac{1}{30}$	$0, \frac{3}{770}, \frac{3}{770}, \frac{1}{330}, \frac{2}{385}$			

play any of the 4 codes of the first class (class of 0000), should play each of the 48 codes of the second class (class of 0001) with probability $\frac{2}{345}$, each of the 36 codes of the third class (class of 0011) with probability $\frac{1}{276}$, each of the 144 codes of the fourth class (class of 0012) with probability $\frac{1}{276}$, each of the 24 codes of the fifth class (class of 0123) with probability $\frac{1}{345}$.[9]

Observations. These results lead to many interesting comments.

- NE values are often different from AVG value. In most cases, Alice can increase the number of guesses required by Bob. Surprisingly, for some non-trivial instances of the game, such as $(4, 5)$, she cannot improve her play; playing uniformly at random is her best option in such case.
- NE values are generally very close to AVG values. While from a theoretical point of view, both values are different, in practice it is not so bad for Alice to play uniformly at random.
- Results on optimal strategies are not trivial. No generic pattern can be deduced from the current known optimal strategies.
- Intuitively, unicolor codes are easier to solve for Bob so they should be played less frequently by Alice. This intuition is generally verified for "large" instances $(n \geq 4)$, but this is not always verified, especially for small instances

---

[9] Fortunately, $4 \times 0 + 48 \times \frac{2}{345} + 36 \times \frac{1}{276} + 144 \times \frac{1}{276} + 24 \times \frac{1}{345} = 1$.

of the game. Sometimes, Alice has to play these unicolor codes even more frequently (*e.g.* for the game instance $(3, 4)$).
- For most of solved instances, the given optimal solution is unique.[10] Only for
the game instance $(2, 6)$, Alice has an infinite number of optimal strategies.

5 Conclusion

In this research, we have computed the Nash Equilibrium of all small instances of
Mastermind. We could confirm an announced but never published result about
the most classical size of 4 pegs and 6 colors, which states that a uniform distribution of secret codes is not the best one for the Codemaker. She should not play
unicolor secret codes. However, we found that for different numbers of pegs and
colors, there is no simple rule. In the future, we plan to extend our computations
to bigger sizes, and we are also working on a general result for the case of 2 pegs
and an arbitrary number of colors.

Acknowledgments. This research was supported in part by JSPS KAKENHI Grant
Number 26870228.

A Example for Game Instance $(n, k) = (3, 3)$

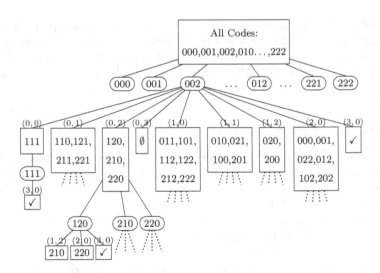

Fig. 2. Exploration tree. Squared nodes correspond to grade nodes and rounded nodes
to guess nodes. Grade nodes include the list of codes still possible as the secret code.
Edges from a guess node to a grade node are labeled with the corresponding grade.

---

[10] We could not prove yet the uniqueness for instances $(5, 3)$, $(4, 5)$, and $(4, 6)$, but it
should be obtained very soon.

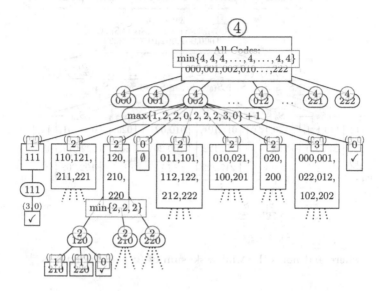

Fig. 3. Computing WC value using Min and Max operations

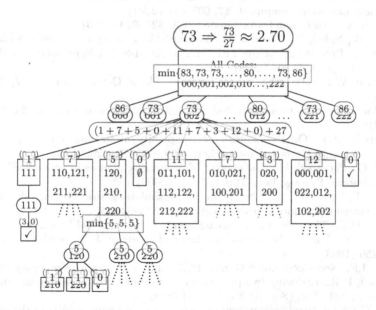

Fig. 4. Computing AVG value using Min and Sum operations

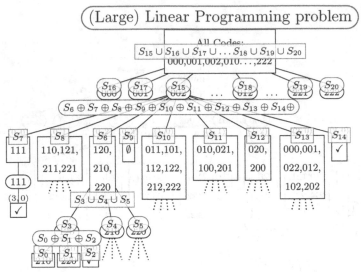

where $\oplus$ denotes the Minkowski sum of (convex) polytopes.

Fig. 5. Computing NE value using Union and MinkowskiSum operations

References

1. Chen, S.T., Lin, S.S.: Optimal algorithms for $2 \times n$ mastermind games-a graph-partition approach. Comput. J. **47**, 602–611 (2004)
2. Chvátal, V.: Mastermind. Combinatorica **3**, 325–329 (1983)
3. Doerr, B., Sphel, R., Thomas, H., Winzen, C.: Playing mastermind with many colors. In: Proceedings of the 24th Annual ACM-SIAM Symposium on Discrete Algorithms, pp. 695–704 (2013)
4. Goddard, W.: Static mastermind. J. Comb. Math. Comb. Comput. **47**, 225–236 (2003)
5. Goddard, W.: Mastermind revisited. J. Comb. Math. Comb. Comput. **51**, 215–220 (2004)
6. Goodrich, M.T.: On the algorithmic complexity of the mastermind game with black-peg results. Inform. Process. Lett. **109**, 675–678 (2009)
7. Jäger, G., Peczarski, M.: The number of pessimistic guesses in generalized mastermind. Inform. Process. Lett. **109**, 635–641 (2009)
8. Jäger, G., Peczarski, M.: The number of pessimistic guesses in generalized black-peg mastermind. Inform. Process. Lett. **111**, 933–940 (2011)
9. Knuth, D.E.: The computer as master mind. J. Recreational Math. **9**, 1–6 (1976)
10. Koyama, K., Lai, T.: An optimal mastermind strategy. J. Recreational Math. **25**, 251–256 (1993)
11. Nash, J.F.: Non-Cooperative Games. Ph.D. thesis, Princeton University (1950)
12. Pearson, K.R.: Reducing two person, zero sum games with underlying symmetry. J. Aust. Math. Soc. (Ser. A) **33**, 152–161 (1982)
13. Ville, G.: An optimal mastermind $(4, 7)$ strategy and more results in the expected case, May 2013, eprint arXiv:1305.1010
14. Wiener, M.: Re: sci.math faq: Master mind, post in sci.math newsgroups on 29 Nov 1995 at 20: 44: 49

11 × 11 Domineering Is Solved:
The First Player Wins

Jos W.H.M. Uiterwijk[✉]

Department of Data Science and Knowledge Engineering (DKE),
Maastricht University, Maastricht, The Netherlands
uiterwijk@maastrichtuniversity.nl

Abstract. We have developed a program called MUDoS (Maastricht University Domineering Solver) that solves Domineering positions in a very efficient way. It enables the solution of known positions (up to the 10 × 10 board) to be much quicker.

More importantly, it enables the solution of 11 × 11 Domineering, a board size that up till now was far out of the reach of previous Domineering solvers. The solution needed the investigation of 259,689,994,008 nodes, using almost half a year of computation time on a single simple desktop computer. The results show that under optimal play the first player wins 11 × 11 Domineering, irrespective whether Vertical or Horizontal starts.

In addition, several other new boards were solved. Using the convention that Vertical starts, the 8 × 15, 11 × 9, 12 × 8, 12 × 15, 14 × 8, and 17 × 6 boards are all won by Vertical, whereas the 6 × 17, 8 × 12, 9 × 11, and 11 × 10 boards are all won by Horizontal.

1 Introduction

Domineering is a two-player perfect-information game invented by Göran Andersson around 1973. It was popularized to the general public in an article by Martin Gardner [12]. It can be played on any subset of a square lattice, though mostly it is restricted to rectangular $m \times n$ boards, where m denotes the number of rows and n the number of columns. The version introduced by Andersson and Gardner was the 8 × 8 board.

Play consists of the two players alternately placing a 1×2 tile (domino) on the board, where the first player may place the tile only in a vertical alignment, the second player only horizontally. The first player being unable to move loses the game, his opponent (who made the last move) being declared the winner. Since the board is gradually filled, i.e., Domineering is a converging game, the game always ends, and ties are impossible. With these rules the game belongs to the category of *combinatorial games*, for which a whole theory (the Combinatorial Game Theory, or CGT in short) has been developed.

Among combinatorial game theorists Domineering received quite some attention, but this was limited to rather small or irregular boards [1,3,4,10,14,23]. Larger (rectangular) boards were solved using α-β search [15], leading to solving

A. Plaat et al. (Eds.): CG 2016, LNCS 10068, pp. 129–136, 2016.
DOI: 10.1007/978-3-319-50935-8_12

all boards up to the standard 8×8 board [7], later extended to the 9×9 board [13,17], and finally extended to larger boards up to 10×10 [8,9].

2   Three Approaches

The following subsections give a rough characterization of the two main programs used to systematically solve Domineering positions so far, and of the program used to obtain the new results, as described in this paper.

2.1   A Brute-Force Appoach: DOMI

The first systematic analysis of rectangular Domineering boards was performed by Breuker et al. [7,13,17]. They developed the program DOMI, using a straight-forward variant of the α-β technique [15], enhanced with a transposition table. The algorithm did not use perfect domain knowledge for classifying positions as wins or losses and hence can be characterized as a pure brute-force approach. Transposition tables with 2M (2^{21}) entries were used with a two-level replacement scheme called *TwoBig* [6], in which each entry can store two table positions. Mirror symmetries are taken into account. The newest position is always stored, overwriting the less important position in terms of nodes investigated.

2.2   A Knowledge-Based Approach: OBSEQUI

A few years later Nathan Bullock published results on solving Domineering boards up to the 10×10 board [9]. His program OBSEQUI used a sophisticated evaluation function which can determine statically the winner at a shallower point in the search tree than DOMI did. This allowed the elimination of large portions of the search space, resulting in much more efficient solving of Domineering boards. OBSEQUI used a transposition table (taking mirror symmetries into account) with 2^{23} entries with either a two-level *TwoBig* replacement scheme or a one-level replacement scheme called *FindFirst* [8]. Also, a much better move-ordering heuristic was used, plus the use of a dominance relation to prune prov-ably irrelevant moves. Since the main advantage of Bullock's program is based on game-specific knowledge, we can characterize his approach as a knowledge-based approach.

2.3   A Knowledge-Intensive Approach: MUDOS

Uiterwijk continued using game-specific knowledge to an even more detailed extent. His program MUDOS incorporated deep knowledge of Domineering posi-tions with known result. These knowledge rules are so intense, that it even enables solving many game boards without any search at all (i.e., investigating a single node, the empty board under consideration). This was called *perfectly solving* [18]. The most important feature of these knowledge rules is the number of safe moves that a player provably can reach in a position [19–21]. The transposition table used (again taking mirror symmetries into account) contained 2^{26} entries, with a simple one-level *Deep* replacement scheme. Due to the heavy use of very knowledge-intense rules based on game-specific properties we can characterize his approach as a knowledge-intensive approach.

3   New Results

After almost half a year of computation time, 11×11 Domineering was solved. We give some data in Sect. 3.1. As a sidetrack, we solved several other new boards. Data are given in Sect. 3.2. An overview of updated combinatorial-game-theoretic values of Domineering boards is given in Sect. 3.3.

3.1   The Solution of 11 × 11 Domineering

The solution of 11 × 11 Domineering took 174 days and 15 h on a standard desktop computer (a HP with duo core Intel E8400 3.00 GHz CPU with a 64-bit Windows 7 operating system and 4 GB internal memory). The MUDoS program is written in C#.

The result is that the first player under optimal play wins the game. Since the board is square, this is irrespective of Vertical or Horizontal moving first.

To put the solution of the 11 × 11 board into perspective, we show in Table 1 the results and number of nodes investigated to solve square boards up to 11 × 11 by the three programs mentioned in the previous section.

Table 1. Results and number of nodes investigated to solve square Domineering boards. Vertical always starts. A "1" and "2" in the results column indicate a first-player (Vertical) and second-player (Horizontal) win, respectively. A "–" in a column indicates that the program was unable to solve the position.

Board	Result	DOMI [7]	OBSEQUI [9]	MUDoS
2 × 2	1	1	1	1
3 × 3	1	1	1	1
4 × 4	1	40	23	1
5 × 5	2	604	259	17
6 × 6	1	17,232	908	1
7 × 7	1	408,260	31,440	1
8 × 8	1	441,990,070	2,023,301	24,147
9 × 9	1	~25,000,000,000[a]	1,657,032,906	4,917,736
10 × 10	1	–	3,541,685,253,370	13,506,805
11 × 11	1	–	–	259,689,994,008

[a]This result was obtained with an improved version of DOMI, around 2000 [5]. The exact number of nodes investigated was lost.

For the result the investigation of 259,689,994,008 nodes was needed, with an average speed of 17,211 nodes/sec. While this is some ten times slower than OBSEQUI's speed, this decrease in speed is by far compensated by the much higher pruning efficiency, as evidenced by the ratio's of the number of nodes investigated by MUDoS and OBSEQUI. For the 8×8, 9×9 and 10×10 boards these are 1.19%, 0.30%, and 0.00038%, respectively. Of course the latest number is so low, since OBSEQUI solved the 10×10 board on a distributed network of several computers (no further details given), without memory sharing, by which transposition tables will be far less effective. But as a striking fact, whereas OBSEQUI needed several months of computation time on this network, MUDoS needs only 21 min on a single computer to solve the 10×10 board.

3.2   The Solution of New Other Domineering Boards

Besides 11×11 Domineering we were able to solve several other new Domineering boards. The results are given in Table 2.

Table 2. Results and number of nodes investigated to solve other new Domineering boards. Vertical always starts. A "1" and "2" in the results column indicate a first-player (Vertical) and second-player (Horizontal) win, respectively. The 10×11 board was solved before (see below). A "–" in a column indicates that the program was unable to solve the position and hence the game-theoretic value is still unknown.

Board	Result	# nodes	Board	Result	# nodes
10×11	1	1	11×10	2	1
9×11	2	84,145,153	11×9	1	23,183,077
6×17	2	25,670,138,842	17×6	1	810,774,495
8×12	2	273,559,795	12×8	1	11,960,354
8×14	–	–	14×8	1	490,146,677
8×15	1	1	15×8	–	–
12×15	1	1	15×12	–	–

The most notable results and their consequences are given below. We there use the notion of outcome class $[1, 4, 10]$ of an $m \times n$ board, denoted by $[m \times n]$, where an outcome class is N, P, V, or H, where N stands for a Next player win (i.e., a win for the player to move), P for a Previous player win (i.e., a loss for the player to move), V for a Vertical win (irrespective of who starts), and H for a Horizontal win (irrespective of who starts).

Other Boards with Width or Height 11. Although the 10×11 board was already solved (Vertical wins), using the translational symmetry rules of Lachmann c.s. [16], and even perfectly solved [18], the 11×10 board was not. However, MUDoS solves it investigating just 1 node, showing that Horizontal wins.[1] As a result $[10 \times 11] = V$ (and $[11 \times 10] = H$). Further, with some more work, we were able to solve the 9×11 board (Horizontal wins) and the 11×9 board (Vertical wins). Consequently, $[9 \times 11] = H$ (and $[11 \times 9] = V$).

Boards with Width or Height 6. The 6×17 and 17×6 boards were also solved (wins for Horizontal and Vertical, respectively). Consequently, $[6 \times 17] = H$. Moreover, using the translational symmetry rules of Lachmann c.s. [16] and the facts that $[6 \times 4] = N$ and $[6 \times n]$ with $n = 8$, 12, and 14 are H, it follows that $[6 \times 21]$ $(17 + 4) = N$ or H, and $[6 \times 25]$ $(17 + 8) = H$, $[6 \times 29]$ $(17 + 12) = H$, and $[6 \times 31]$ $(17 + 14) = H$. Moreover, in [11] it was shown that $[6 \times n]$ for $n > 31 = N$ or H for widths 33, 35, 37, 39, 43, 45, 47, 51, and 59. Using the result for $[6 \times 17]$ all these values analogously are determined to be H, the only exception being width 35 (still N or H). This shows that the holes in the results for boards of height 6 have considerably been filled. The outcome classes for all $6 \times n$ boards are known now, the only exceptions being the 6×18, 6×21, 6×23, 6×27, and 6×35 boards, all five having outcome classes N or H, which means that Horizontal at least wins as first player. Of course the results for $[m \times 6]$ can similarly be updated, replacing H by V.

Boards with Width or Height 8. The 8×12 and 12×8 boards were also solved (wins for Horizontal and Vertical, respectively). Consequently, $[8 \times 12] = H$, but also, using the translational symmetry rules and the facts that $[8 \times 10]$ and $[8 \times 16]$ are H, it follows that $[8 \times 22]$ $(12 + 10) = H$, $[8 \times 24]$ $(12 + 12) = H$, and $[8 \times 28]$ $(12 + 16) = H$. Moreover, since $[8 \times 10] = H$ and all $[8 \times n]$ for even n from 20–28 are H, it follows that all $[8 \times n]$ with even $n \geq 20$ are H. This makes the entries in the $8 \times n$ row completely regular for even n from $n = 20$ onwards, in contrast to [11], were (in an irregular way) some of those were determined to be H, the others as N or H. We also were able to solve the 14×8 board (Vertical wins), but not the 8×14 board yet. It means that $[8 \times 14] = N$ or H. This leaves the 8×14 and 8×18 boards as the only holes in this row for even width. Finally, the 8×15 (and 12×15) board is trivially solved to be a Vertical win (so outcome class N or V), but the rotated 15×8 (and 15×12) board could not yet be determined. Again, of course the results for $[m \times 8]$ can similarly be updated, replacing H by V, including that all $[m \times 8]$ with even $m \geq 20$ are V.

3.3   Updated Table of CGT Values of Domineering

In Table 3 we give a complete updated overview of all results for solved Domineering boards, as outcome classes. The results are taken from [11] and includes

---

[1] We note that solving a board investigating a single node is not exactly the same as perfectly solving a board, since in the latter the board is solved using characteristics of the board solely, without generating the possible moves, whereas in the former the possible moves are generated, but immediately proven to contain at least one winning move or only losing moves.

Table 3. Updated results for outcome classes of Domineering boards. An entry like NH means that the value is either N or H. -V (or -H) means that all we know is that the outcome class is not V (or H). The notes are explained in the text. New results obtained are shaded.

m\n	1	2	3	4	5	6	7	8	9	10	11	12	13	14	15	16	17	18	19	20	21	22	23	24	25	26	27	28	29	30	31	>31
1	P	H	H	H	H	H	H	H	H	H	H	H	H	H	H	H	H	H	H	H	H	H	H	H	H	H	H	H	H	H	H	H
2	V	H	H	N	V	N	N	N	H	N	N	H	H	N	N	H	N	N	N	H	H	H	N	H	H	H	1	H	H	H	H	H
3	V	N	N	N	V	N	N	V	H	V	N	P	P	N	N	H	H	H	H	H	H	H	H	H	H	H	H	H	H	H	H	H
4	V	N	N	N	V	N	H	H	H	H	H	H	H	H	H	H	H	H	H	H	H	H	H	H	H	H	H	H	H	H	H	H
5	V	H	V	H	P	H	H	H	V	H	V	H	P	H	H	H	H	H	H	H	H	H	H	H	H	H	H	H	H	H	H	H
6	V	N	N	N	V	N	H	N	V	N	N	H	V	H	N	H	H	NH	N	H	NH	H	NH	H	H	H	NH	H	H	H	H	1)
7	V	V	N	H	V	N	N	N	H	N	N	H	V	H	N	H	H	H	N	H	H	H	N	H	H	H	H	H	H	H	H	H
8	V	H	V	H	V	H	V	N	H	H	H	H	V	NH	NV	H	H	NH	H	H	H	H	H	H	H	H	H	H	H	H	H	2)
9	V	H	V	H	V	H	V	H	V	H	V	H	V	H	NV	H	H	H	H	H	H	H	H	H	H	H	H	H	H	H	H	H
10	V	N	V	H	V	N	V	V	H	H	V	H	H	H	NV	H	H	H	H	H	H	NH	H	H	H	NH	H	H	NH	H	H	H
11	V	N	N	H	V	N	V	H	V	V	H	V	-H	-V	NV	H	NH	-V	NH	NH	NH	H	NH	H	NH	NH	NH	NH	NH	H	H	H
12	V	P	V	P	V	V	V	H	H	V	N	H	NP	H	-V	H	H	H	H	H	H	H	H	H	H	H	H	H	H	H	H	H
13	V	N	V	V	V	H	H	H	V	H	-H	NP	NP	NP	NV	NP	NH	H	NH	H	NH	H	NH	H	NH	H	NH	H	NH	H	NH	3)
14	V	N	V	V	V	H	V	V	V	H	V	H	H	NP	NV	NP			NH					H						NH	H	
15	V	N	V	V	V	N	V	NH	V	NH	NV	NH	V	NH	NP	NP		NH														
16	V	V	V	V	V	V	V	V	V			H	V	H	NP	NP																
17	V	N	V	V	V	V	V	V	V			V	-H	NV	NV		NP		NP													
18	V	N	V	V	V	NV	V	NV	V			NH		NH				NP		NP												
19	V	N	V	V	V	N	V		V			V	NV	NP					NP		NP											
20	V	V	V	V	V	V	V		V		V		V	NV	NV					NP			NP									
21	V	N	V	V	V	NV	V	V	V	NV	V		V	NP	NP						NP				NP							
22	V	N	V	V	V	V	V		V			V	NV	V								NP				NP						
23	V	N	V	V	V	NV	V		V	NV		V	NV	NV									NP				NP					
24	V	V	V	V	V	V	V		V			V	NV											NP				NP				
25	V	V	V	V	V	V	V		V			V	NV		V										NP				NP			
26	V	V	V	V	V	NV	V		V	NV		V	NV													NP				NP		
27	V	N	V	V	V	NV	V		V			V	NV														NP					
28	V	V	V	V	V	V	V	V	V			V	NV	V														NP			
29	V	V	V	V	V	V	V		V			V	NV	NV															NP		
30	V	V	V	V	V	V	V		V		NV	V	NV	V																NP	
31	V	V	V	V	V	V	V	V	V			V	NV																	NP	
>31	V	V	V	V	V	4)	V	5)	V			V	6)																		

results from $[3,4,7,9–11,13,16,17]$.[2] In addition, our new results have been added. This table is also available at [22], where any future updates will be made public.

In this table the following notes apply: (1) the outcome classes for all $n > 31$ are H, except that the outcome class for $n = 35$ is N or H; (2) the outcome classes for all even $n \geq 20$ are H; (3) the outcome classes are alternating H (even n) and N or H (odd n); (4)–(6): equivalent to notes (1)–(3) by replacing n with m and H with V.

For boards with one or both dimensions larger than 31, besides the results in the notes above, nothing is known about their outcome classes, except of course that $m \times m$ boards have outcome classes N or P, that $m \times 2km$ boards have outcome classes H, and that $2kn \times n$ boards have outcome classes V.

4   Conclusions and Future Work

As can be seen from the results it is clear that MUDoS is a very efficient Domineering solver. All boards solved before are solved in an equal amount (for the trivial boards) or far smaller (for the more complex boards) number of investigated nodes than by previous solvers.

The efficiency of our solver enabled the solution of the 11×11 Domineering board. The result indicates that the first player wins. Moreover, several new rather complex boards have been solved. Applying these together with the use of the translational symmetry rules updated the Domineering outcome class landscape considerably.

Regarding future work, foremost this condensed overview will be extended to a full publication. This will include a detailed description of MUDoS' knowledge rules and heuristics employed. Moreover, the impact of the rules and heuristics on solving performance, separately and in combination, will be illlustrated with experiments.

As a follow-up we moreover intend as a last step to enhance the solving power of our Domineering program by incorporating knowledge from Combinatorial Game Theory into our solver. A preliminary experiment using endgame databases up to 16 squares filled with CGT values, combined with a very simplistic α-β solver showed reductions up to 99% for boards up to 7×7 [2].

References

1. Albert, M.H., Nowakowski, R.J., Wolfe, D.: Lessons in Play: An Introduction to Combinatorial Game Theory. A K Peters, Wellesley (2007)
2. Barton, M., Uiterwijk, J.W.H.M.: Combining combinatorial game theory with an α-β solver for Domineering. In: Grootjen, F., Otworowska, M., Kwisthout, J. (eds.) BNAIC 2014 - Proceedings of the 26th Benelux Conference on Artificial Intelligence, pp. 9–16. Radboud University, Nijmegen (2014)

---

[2] Although Drummond-Cole determined the outcome classes for 8×26 and 26×8 (H and V), these results were not included in his table of known outcome classes for Domineering [11].

3. Berlekamp, E.R.: Blockbusting and Domineering. J. Comb. Theor. (Ser. A) **49**, 67–116 (1988)
4. Berlekamp, E.R., Conway, J.H., Guy, R.K.: Winning Ways for Your Mathematical Plays. Academic Press, London (1982). 2nd edn. A K Peters, Wellesley, MA, in four volumes: vol. 1 (2001), vols. 2, 3 (2003), vol. 4 (2004)
5. Breuker, D.M.: Personal communication (2014)
6. Breuker, D.M., Uiterwijk, J.W.H.M., van den Herik, H.J.: Replacement schemes and two-level tables. ICCA J. **19**, 175–180 (1996)
7. Breuker, D.M., Uiterwijk, J.W.H.M., van den Herik, H.J.: Solving 8 × 8 Domineering. Theor. Comput. Sci. (Math Games) **230**, 195–206 (2000)
8. Bullock, N.: Domineering: solving large combinatorial search spaces. M.Sc. thesis, University of Alberta (2002)
9. Bullock, N.: Domineering: solving large combinatorial search spaces. ICGA J. **25**, 67–84 (2002)
10. Conway, J.H.: On Numbers and Games. Academic Press, London (1976)
11. Drummond-Cole, G.C.: An update on Domineering on rectangular boards. Integers **14**, 1–13 (2014)
12. Gardner, M.: Mathematical games. Sci. Am. **230**, 106–108 (1974)
13. van den Herik, H.J., Uiterwijk, J.W.H.M., van Rijswijck, J.: Games solved: now and in the future. Artif. Intell. **134**, 277–311 (2002)
14. Kim, Y.: New values in Domineering. Theor. Comput. Sci. (Math Games) **156**, 263–280 (1996)
15. Knuth, D.E., Moore, R.W.: An analysis of alpha-beta pruning. Artif. Intell. **6**, 293–326 (1975)
16. Lachmann, M., Moore, C., Rapaport, I.: Who wins Domineering on rectangular boards? In: Nowakowski, R.J. (ed.) More Games of No Chance, vol. 42, pp. 307–315. Cambridge University Press, MSRI Publications, Cambridge (2002)
17. Uiterwijk, J.W.H.M., van den Herik, H.J.: The advantage of the initiative. Inf. Sci. **122**, 43–58 (2000)
18. Uiterwijk, J.W.H.M.: Perfectly solving Domineering games. In: Cazenave, T., Winands, M.H.M., Iida, H. (eds.) Computer Games, Workshop on Computer Games, CGW at IJCAI 2013, Beijing, China, Revised Selected Papers, vol. 408, pp. 97–121. Communications in Computer and Information Science (2014)
19. Uiterwijk, J.W.H.M.: The impact of safe moves on perfectly solving Domineering boards. Part 1: analysis and experiments with 1-step safe moves. ICGA J. **37**(2), 97–105 (2014)
20. Uiterwijk, J.W.H.M.: The impact of safe moves on perfectly solving Domineering boards. Part 2: analysis and experiments with multi-step safe moves. ICGA J. **37**(3), 144–160 (2014)
21. Uiterwijk, J.W.H.M.: The impact of safe moves on perfectly solving Domineering boards. Part 3: theorems and conjectures. ICGA J. **37**(4), 207–213 (2014)
22. Uiterwijk, J.W.H.M.: Updated game theoretic values for Domineering boards. https://dke.maastrichtuniversity.nl/jos.uiterwijk/?page_id=39
23. Wolfe, D.: Snakes in Domineering games. Theor. Comput. Sci. (Math Games) **119**, 323–329 (1993)

A Reverse Hex Solver

Kenny Young and Ryan B. Hayward$^{(\boxtimes)}$

Department of Computing Science, UAlberta, Edmonton, Canada
hayward@ualberta.ca
http://webdocs.cs.ualberta.ca/~hayward/

Abstract. We present SOLREX, an automated solver for the game of
Reverse Hex. Reverse Hex, also known as Rex, or Misère Hex, is the
variant of the game of Hex in which the player who joins her two sides
loses the game. SOLREX performs a mini-max search of the state space
using Scalable Parallel Depth First Proof Number Search, enhanced by
the pruning of inferior moves and the early detection of certain winning
strategies.

SOLREX is implemented on the same code base as the Hex program
SOLVER, and can solve arbitrary positions on board sizes up to 6×6,
with the hardest position taking less than four hours on four threads.

1 Introduction

In 1942 Piet Hein invented the two-player board game now called Hex [10].
The board is covered with a four-sided array of hexagonal cells. Each player is
assigned two opposite sides of the board. Players move in alternating turns. For
each turn, a player places one of their stones on an empty cell. Whoever connects
their two sides with a path of their stones is the winner.

In his 1957 *Scientific American* Mathematical Games column, *Concerning
the game of Hex, which may be played on the tiles of the bathroom floor*, Martin
Gardner mentions the misère version of Hex known as Reverse Hex, or Rex, or
Misére Hex: whoever joins their two sides *loses* [5]. See Fig. 1.

So, for positive integers n, who wins Rex on $n \times n$ boards? Using a strategy-
stealing argument, Robert O. Winder showed that the first (resp. second) wins
when n is even (odd) [5]. Lagarias and Sleator further showed that, for all n,
each player has a strategy that can avoid defeat until the board is completely
covered [13].

Which opening (i.e. first) moves wins? Ronald J. Evans showed that for n
even, opening in an acute corner wins [4]. Hayward et al. further showed that,
for n even and at least 4, opening in a cell that touches an acute corner cell and
one's own side also wins [9].

The results mentioned so far prove the existence of winning strategies. But
how hard is it to *find* such strategies? In his 1988 book Gardner commented that
"*4 × 4 [Rex] is so complex that a winning line of play for the first player remains*

The authors gratefully acknowledge the support of NSERC.

A. Plaat et al. (Eds.): CG 2016, LNCS 10068, pp. 137–148, 2016.
DOI: 10.1007/978-3-319-50935-8_13

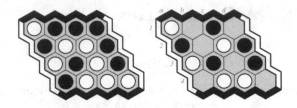

Fig. 1. Left: the end of a Rex game. White has joined both White sides, so loses. Right: a Rex puzzle by Ronald J. Evans. White to play and win. [7]

unknown" [7,8]. In 2012, based on easily detected pairing strategies, Hayward et al. explained how to find winning strategies for all but one (up to symmetry) opening move on the 4 × 4 board [9].

In this paper, we present SOLREX, an automated Rex solver that solves arbitrary Rex positions on boards up to 6 × 6. With four threads, solving the hardest 6 × 6 opening takes under 4 h; solving all 18 (up to symmetry) 6 × 6 openings takes about 7 h.

The design of SOLREX is similar to the design of the Hex program SOLVER. So, SOLREX searches the minimax space of gamestates using Scalable Parallel Depth-First Proof Number Search, the enhanced parallel version by Pawlewicz and Hayward [14] of Focussed Depth-First Proof Number Search of Arneson, Hayward, and Henderson [2]. Like SOLVER, SOLREX enhances the search by inferior move pruning and early win detection. The inferior move pruning is based on Rex-specific theorems. The win detection is based on Rex-specific virtual connections based on pairing strategies.

In the next sections we explain pairing strategies (Sect. 2), inferior cell analysis (Sect. 3), win detection (Sect. 4), the details of SOLREX (Sect. 5), and then present experimental results (Sect. 6).

2   Death, Pairing, Capture, Joining

Roughly, a dead cell is a cell that is useless to both players, as it cannot contribute to joining either player's two sides. Dead cells can be pruned from the Rex search tree. Related to dead cells are captured cells, roughly cells that are useless to just one player and so can be colored for the other player. In Hex, each player wants to capture cells; in Rex, each player wants to force the opponent to capture cells. In Rex, such opponent-forced capture can be brought about by pairing strategies. As we will see in a later section, pairing strategies can also be used to force the opponent to join their two sides.

Before elaborating on these ideas, we give some basic terminology. Let $\overline{X}$ denote the opponent of player X.

For a given position, *player X colors cell c* means that player X moves to cell c, i.e., places a stone of her color on cell c. A cell is *uncolored* if it is unoccupied. To *X-fill* a set of cells is to X-color each cell in the set; to *fill* a set is either to X-fill or $\overline{X}$-fill the set.

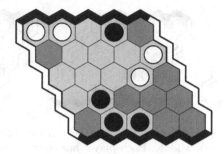

Fig. 2. Shaded cells are dead. All other uncolored cells are live.

A *state* $S = P^X$ is a position P together with the specified player X to move next. The *winner* of S is whoever has a winning strategy from S.

For a position P and a player X, a *X-joinset* is a minimal set of uncolored cells which when X-colored joins X's two sides; a *joinset* is an X-joinset or an $\overline{X}$-joinset; an uncolored cell is *live* if it is in a joinset, otherwise it is *dead*; a colored cell is *dead* if uncoloring it would make it dead (Fig. 2).

For an even size subset C of uncolored cells of a position or associated state, a *pairing* Π is a partition of C into *pairs*, i.e., subsets of size two. For a cell c in a pair $\{c, d\}$, cell d is c's *mate*. For a state S, a player Y, and a pairing Π, a *pairing strategy* is a strategy for Y that guarantees that, in each terminal position reachable from S, at most one cell of each pair of Π will be Y-colored.

For a state $S = P^X$, *Last* is that player who plays last if the game ends with all cells colored, and *Notlast* is the other player, i.e., she who plays second-last if the game ends with all cells uncolored. So, Last (Notlast) is whoever plays next if and only if the number of uncolored cells is odd (even). For example, for $S = P^X$ with P the empty 6×6 board, Last is $\overline{X}$ and Notlast is X, since X plays next and P has 36 uncolored cells.

Theorem 1. *For state S and pairing Π, each player has a pairing strategy for S.*

Proof. It suffices to follow these rules. Proving that this is always possible is left to the reader.

First assume Y is Last. In response to $\overline{Y}$ coloring a cell in Π, Y colors the mate. Otherwise, Y colors some uncolored cell not in Π. Next assume Y is Notlast. In response to $\overline{Y}$ coloring a cell in Π with uncolored mate, Y colors the mate; otherwise, Y colors a cell not in Π; otherwise (all uncolored cells are in Π, and each pair of Π has both or neither cell colored), Y colors any uncolored cell of Π.   □

For a player X and a pairing Π with cell set C of a position P or associated state $S = P^Y$, we say Π *X-captures* C if X-coloring at least one cell of each pair of Π leaves the remaining uncolored cells of C dead; and we say Π *X-joins* P if X-coloring at least one cell of each pair of Π joins X's two sides (Fig. 3).

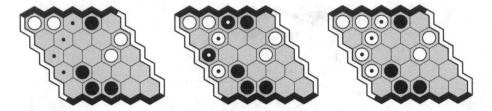

Fig. 3. Left: dots show a White-captured set (the top two cells form one pair, the bottom two form the other). Middle: Each player has colored one cell from each pair, and the two Black cells are dead. Right: original position after filling White-captured cells.

Notice that every captured set (as defined here, i.e., for Rex) comes from a pairing and so has an even number of cells, as does every X-join set.

3   Inferior Cell Pruning and Early Win Detection

We now present the Rex theorems that allow our solver to prune inferior moves and detect wins early.

For a position P, a player X, and a set of cells C, $P + C_X$ is the position obtained from P by X-coloring all cells of C, and $P - C$ is the position obtained from P by uncoloring all colored cells of C. For clarity, we may also write $P - C_X$ in this case where X is the player who originally controlled all the cells of C. Similarly, for a state $S = P^Y$, where $Y = X$ or $\overline{X}$, $S + C_X$ is the state $(P + C_X)^Y$. Also, in this context, when C has only one cell c, we will sometimes write c_X instead of $\{c\}_X$.

For states S and T and player X, we write $S \geq_X T$ if X wins T whenever X wins S, and we write $S \equiv T$ if the winner of S is the winner of T, i.e., if $S \geq_X T$ and $T \geq_X S$ for either player X.

An X-strategy is a strategy for player X.

Theorem 2. *For an even size set C of uncolored cells of a state S, $S \geq_X S + C_X$.*

Proof. Assume π^+ is a winning X-strategy for $S^+ = S + C_X$. Let π be the X-strategy for S obtained from π^+ by moving anywhere in C whenever $\overline{X}$ moves in C. For any terminal position reachable from S, the set of cells occupied by $\overline{X}$ will be a superset of the cells occupied by $\overline{X}$ in the corresponding position reachable from S^+, so X wins S.   □

Theorem 3. *For a position P with uncolored cell c, $(P + c_{\overline{X}})^Y \geq_X P^Y$.*

Proof. First assume $Y = \overline{X}$. Assume X wins $S = P^{\overline{X}}$. Then, for every possible move from S by $\overline{X}$, X can win. In particular, X can win after $\overline{X}$ colors c. So X wins $(P + c_{\overline{X}})^X$.

Next assume $Y = X$. Assume X wins $S = P^X$. We want to show X wins $S' = (P + c_{\overline{X}})^X$. Let c' a cell to which $\overline{X}$ moves from S', let $C = \{c, c'\}$, and let S'' be the resulting state $(P + C_{\overline{X}})^X$. X wins S so, by Theorem 2, X wins S''. So, for every possible move from S', X wins. So X wins S'. □

Theorem 4. *For an X-captured set C of a state S, $S + C_X \geq_X S$.*

Proof. Assume $\overline{X}$ wins $S^+ = S + C_X$ with strategy π^+. We want to show that $\overline{X}$ wins S. Let Π be an X-capture pairing for C, and modify π^+ by adding to it the Π pairing strategy for $\overline{X}$.

Let Z be a terminal state reachable from S by following π. Assume by way of contradiction that Z has an $\overline{X}$-colored set of cells joining $\overline{X}$'s two sides. If such a set Q^* exists, then such a set Q exists in which no cell is in C. (On C $\overline{X}$ follows a Π pairing, so in Z at most one cell of each pair of Π is $\overline{X}$-colored. Now X-color any uncolored cells of C. Now at least one cell of each pair is X-colored, and C is X-captured, so each $\overline{X}$-colored cell of C is dead, and these cells can be removed one at a time from Q^* while still leaving a set of cells that joins $\overline{X}$'s two sides. Thus we have our set Q.) But then the corresponding state Z^+ reachable from S^+ by following π^+ has the same set Q, contradicting the fact that $\overline{X}$ wins S^+. □

Corollary 1. *For an X-captured set C of a state S, $S \equiv S + C_X$.*

Proof. By Theorems 2 and 4. □

Theorem 5. *For a player X and a position P with uncolored dead cell d, $(P + d_X)^{\overline{X}} \geq_X P^X$. A move to a dead cell is at least as good as any other move.*

Proof. Coloring a dead cell is equivalent to opponent-coloring the cell. So this theorem follows by Theorem 3. □

Theorem 6. *For a position P with uncolored cells c, k with c dead in $P + k_X$, $(P + c_X)^{\overline{X}} \geq_X (P + k_X)^{\overline{X}}$. Prefer victim to killer.*

Proof. $(P + k_X)^{\overline{X}} \equiv (P + k_X + c_X)^X \geq_X (P + c_X)^X$. □

Theorem 7. *For a position P with uncolored cells c, k with c dead in $P + k_{\overline{X}}$, $(P + c_X)^{\overline{X}} \geq_X (P + k_X)^{\overline{X}}$. Prefer vulnerable to opponent killer.*

Proof. Assume k is a winning move for X from P^X, i.e., assume X wins $S = (P + k_X)^{\overline{X}}$. Consider any such winning strategy π. We want to show c is also a winning move for X from P^X, i.e., that X wins $S' = (P + c_X)^{\overline{X}}$.

To obtain a winning X-strategy π' for S', modify π by replacing c with k: whenever X (resp. $\overline{X}$) colors c in π, X ($\overline{X}$) colors k in π'. In P, $\overline{X}$-coloring k kills c: so in P, if some X-joinset J contains c, then J must also contain k. But a continuation of π' has both k and c X-colored if and only if the corresponding continuation of π has them both X-colored. So, since X wins S following π, X wins S' following π'. □

Theorem 8. *For a position P with uncolored cell d and set C that is X-captured in $(P+d_x)^{\overline{X}}$, for all $c \in C$, $(P+c_x)^{\overline{X}} \geq_X (P+d_x)^{\overline{X}}$. Prefer capturee to capturer.*

Proof. $(P + c_X)^{\overline{X}} \geq_X (P + C_X + d_X)^{\overline{X}} \equiv (P + d_X)^{\overline{X}}$. □

Our next results concern *mutual fillin* (Figs. 4 and 5), namely when there are two cells a, b such that X-coloring a $\overline{X}$-captures b and $\overline{X}$-coloring b X-captures a.

Theorem 9. *Let P be a position with sets A, B containing cells a, b respectively, such that A is X-captured in $(P + b_{\overline{X}})$, and B is $\overline{X}$-captured in $(P + a_X)$. Then $P \equiv P + a_X + b_{\overline{X}}$.*

Proof. By if necessary relabelling $\{X, a, A\}$ and $\{\overline{X}, b, B\}$, we can assume X plays next. We claim that a X-dominates each cell in $A + B$. Before proving the claim, observe that it implies the theorem, since after X colors a, all of B is Y-captured, so Y can then color any cell of B, in particular, b.

To prove the claim, consider a strategy that X-captures A in $P + b_{\overline{X}}$. Now, for all α in $A + B$,

$$(P + \alpha_X)^{\overline{X}} \leq_X \qquad (P + b_{\overline{X}})^{\overline{X}} \qquad \text{(Theorem 3 twice: remove } \alpha_X, \text{ add } b_{\overline{X}})$$

$$\equiv \quad (P + A_X + b_{\overline{X}})^{\overline{X}} \qquad \text{(capture)}$$

$$\leq_X \quad (P + a_X + B_{\overline{X}})^{\overline{X}} \qquad \text{(Theorem 3, repeatedly for } X \text{ and then } \overline{X})$$

$$\leq_X \qquad (P + a_X)^{\overline{X}} \qquad \text{(capture)}$$

So the claim holds, and so the theorem. □

Theorem 10. *Let c be any X-colored cell in a position P as described in Theorem 9. Then $(P - c + a_X)^{\tilde{X}} \geq_X P^{\tilde{X}}$. Prefer filled to mutual fillin creator.*

Proof. Define b' to be the mate of b in the $\overline{X}$-capture strategy for B in $(P+a_X)$.

$$P^{\tilde{X}} \equiv \qquad (P + a_X + b_{\tilde{X}})^{\tilde{X}} \qquad \text{(Theorem 9)}$$

$$\equiv \quad (P + a_X + B_X - b'_{\tilde{X}})^{\tilde{X}} \qquad \text{(filling captured cells, now } b' \text{ dead)}$$

$$\equiv \qquad (P + a_X + B_X)^X \qquad \text{(coloring } b')$$

$$\equiv \qquad (P + a_X)^X \qquad \text{(capture)}$$

$$\leq_X \qquad (P - c + a_X)^{\tilde{X}} \qquad \text{(Theorem 3)}$$

□

Finally, we mention join pairing strategies.

Theorem 11. *For a state $S = P^X$ with an $\overline{X}$-join pairing Π, X wins P^X.*

Proof. It suffices for X to follow the Π strategy. In each terminal state Z player X will have colored at most one cell of Π. From Z obtain Z' by $\overline{X}$-coloring any uncolored cells: this will not change the winner. But in Z' at least one cell of each pair of Π is $\overline{X}$-colored, and Π is an $\overline{X}$-join pairing. So in Z' $\overline{X}$'s two sides are joined, so in Z $\overline{X}$'s two sides are joined. So X wins. □

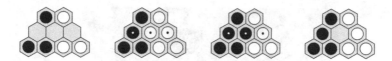

Fig. 4. Mutual fillin. If B colors left cell, the other two cells are W-captured. If W colors right cell, the other two cells are B-captured. So we can replace first position with this.

Fig. 5. Mutual fillin domination. Off-board stone shows B to play. Black move would create mutual fillin pattern. So, for these three states, Black prefers large dot to small.

4   Early Win Detection

For a position P, a *X-join-pairing strategy* is a pairing strategy that joins X's two sides, and an *X-pre-join-pairing strategy* is an uncolored cell k together with an X-join-pairing strategy of $P + k_X$; here k is the *key* of this strategy. The key to our algorithm is to find opponent (pre-)join-pairing strategies. When it is clear from context that the strategies join a player's sides, we call these simply *(pre)-pairing strategies.*

Theorem 12. *Let P be a position with an X-join-pairing strategy. Then $\overline{X}$ wins P^X and also $P^{\overline{X}}$.*

Proof. This follows from Theorem 7 in [9]: $\overline{X}$ can force X to follow the X-join-pairing strategy.

Theorem 13. *Let P be a position with an X-pre-join-pairing strategy and with $X = Last$. Then $\overline{X}$ wins P^X and also $P^{\overline{X}}$.*

Proof. This follows from Theorem 6 in [9]. $\overline{X}$ can avoid playing the key of the pre-pairing strategy, forcing X to eventually play it.

5   Solrex

SOLREX is based on SOLHEX, the Hex solver of the Benzene code repository [3]. The challenge in developing SOLREX was to identify and remove any Hex-specific, or Rex-unnecessary, aspects of SOLHEX — e.g., permanently inferior cells apply to Hex but not Rex — and then add any Rex-necessary pieces. For instance, it was necessary to replace the methods for finding Hex virtual connections with methods that find Rex (pre-) pairing strategies.

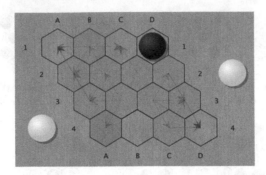

Fig. 6. Inferior cells of a Rex position. Each arrow end is inferior to its arrow head.

Search follows the Scalable Parallel Depth First variant of Proof Number Search, with the search focusing only on a limited number of children (as ranked by the usual electric resistance model) at one time [14].

When reaching a leaf node, using a database of fillin and inferior cell patterns, we apply the theorems of Sect. 3. We find dead cells by applying local patterns and by searching for any empty cells of which the neighbourhood of empty cells, after stone groups have been removed and neighbouring empty cells contracted, is a clique. We iteratively fillin captured cells and even numbers of dead cells until no more fillin patterns are found. We also apply any inferior cell domination that comes from virtual connection decompositions [2,11].

We then look into the transposition table to see if the resulting state win/loss value is known, either because we previously solved, or because of color symmetry (a state which looks the same for each player is a win for Notlast). Then inferior cells are pruned. Then, using H-search [1] in which the or-rule is limited to combining only 2 semi-connections, we find (pre)-join-pairing strategies. Then, for X the player to move, we prune each key of every X-pre-join-strategy.

H-search is augmented by observing that semi-connections that overlap on a captured set of endpoints do not conflict and so can be combined into a full connection [2,11]. Notice that augmented H-search is not complete: some pairing strategies (e.g. the mirror pairing strategy for the $n \times (n-1)$ board [6]) cannot be found in this way.

Figure 7 shows the start of SOLREX's solution of 1.Bd1, the only unsolved 4×4 opening from [9]. First, inferior cells are found: White b1 captures a1,a2; a2 kills a1; b2 captures a2,a3; c2 leaves c1 dominated by b2; d2 captures d3,d4; etc. See Fig. 6. Only 5 White moves remain: a1,c1,a4,b4,d4. After trying 2.Wa4, a White pre-join-pairing strategy is found, so this loses. Similarly, 2.Wb4 and 2.Wd4 also lose. Now 2 White moves remain: a1,a3. From 2.Wa1, search eventually reveals that 3.Bc1 wins (a2 also wins). From 2.Wc1, search reveals that 3.Ba1 wins (b2 and d4 also win). The deepest line in solving this position is 1.Bd1 2.Wc1 3.Bd4 4.Wc4 5.Bb2 6.Wa3 7.Ba4 8.Wb4.

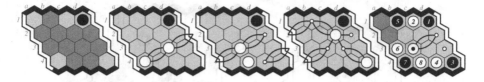

Fig. 7. Solving 1.Bd1. Left: White inferior cells after 1.Bd1. Then White pre-join-pair strategies after 2.Wa4, 2.Wb4, 2.Wd4. Search reveals that 2.Wa1 loses. Search reveals that 2.Wc1 loses. So 1.Bd1 wins. The last diagram shows the deepest line of search and the final pre-join-pair strategy: the shaded cells are Black-captured.

5×5 knockout tests	
version	time ratio
all features on	1.0 (13.9s)
no dead clique cutset	.97
unaugmented H-search	.99
no mutual fillin	1.00
no color symmetry pruning	1.01
no VC decomp	1.06
no dead fillin	1.07
no resistance move ordering	1.62
no capture fillin	2.02
no inferior pruning	2.30
no H-search	89.83

6×6 knockout test	
version	time ratio
all features on	1.0 (13646 s)
unaugmented H-search	1.10
no color symmetry pruning	1.13
no dead clique cutset	1.37
no mutual fillin	1.44
no VC decomp	1.95

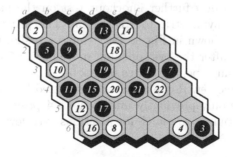

Fig. 8. Principal variation of 1.Black[e3], hardest 6 × 6 opening. From here Black forces White to connect with pairs {C4,C5} {D6,E5}{F4,F5} and last cell D5.

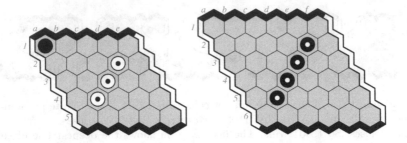

Fig. 9. Left: all losing replies. Right: all losing openings.

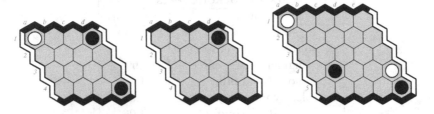

Fig. 10. Three new Rex puzzles. Left: White to play: find the only winning move. Middle: White to play: find White's best move, and Black's best reply. Right: White to play: find the only winning move.

6   Experiments

We ran our experiments on Torrington, a quad-core i7-860 2.8GHz CPU with hyper-threading, so 8 pseudo-cores. For 5×5 Rex, our test suite is all 24 replies to opening in the acute corner:[1] this takes SOLREX 13.2 s. For 6×6 Rex, our test suite is all 18 (up to symmetry) 1-move opening states: this takes SOLREX 25900 s. To measure speedup, we also ran the 18 1-move 6×6 openings on a single thread, taking 134635 s.

To show the impact of Solrex's various features, we ran a features knockout test on the 5×5 test suite. For features which showed negligible or negative contribution, we ran a further knockout test on the hardest 6×6 position, 1.White[d2], color-symmetric to 1.Black[e3]. The principal variation for this hardest opening is shown in Fig. 8. The results are shown below. Figure 9 shows all losing moves after the best opening move on 5×5 (all opening 5×5 moves lose), and all losing opening moves on 6×6.

Figure 10 shows three new Rex puzzles we discovered by using SOLREX. The middle puzzle was the only previously unsolved 4×4 position. The other two were found by using SOLREX to search for positions with few winning moves.

---

[1] All opening 5×5 Rex moves lose, so we picked all possible replies to the presumably strongest opening move.

7   Conclusions

All features listed in the knockout tests contributed significantly to shortening search time: the four features that contributed no improvement on 5×5 boards all contributed significantly on 6×6 boards. The effectiveness of these pruning methods – which exploit pruning via local patterns in a search space that grows exponentially with board size — explained by Henderson for Hex, is clearly also valid for Rex [11]:

> "In almost all cases, we see that feature contributions improved with board size. We believe this is partly because the computational complexity of most of our algorithmic improvements is polynomial in the board size, while the corresponding increase in search space pruning grows exponentially. Furthermore, as the average game length increases, more weak moves are no longer immediately losing nor easily detectable via previous methods, and so these features become more likely to save significant search time."

Of these features, by far the most critical was H-search, which yielded a time ratio of about 90 on 5×5 Rex when omitted. The enormous time savings resulting from H-search is presumably because our general search method does not learn to recognize the redundant transpositions that correspond to the discovery of a (pre-) pairing strategy. So H-search avoids some combinatorial explosion.

SOLREX takes about 7 h to solve all 18 (up to symmetry) 6×6 boardstates; by contrast, SOLHEX takes only 301 h to solve all 32 (up to symmetry) 8×8 boardstates [12]. So why is SOLHEX faster than SOLREX?

One reason is because Hex games tend to be shorter than Rex games: in a balanced Rex game, the loser can often force the winner to play until the board is nearly full. A second reason is there are Hex-specific pruning features that do not apply to Rex: for example, the only easily-found virtual connections for Rex that we know of are pairing strategies, and there seem to be far fewer of these than there are easily-found virtual connections in Hex. A third reason is, in Hex, if the opponent can on the next move create more than one winning virtual connection, then the player must make a move which interferes with each such connection or lose the game; we know of no analogous property for Rex.

The general approach of SOLHEX worked well for SOLREX, so this approach might work for other games, for example connection games such as Havannah or Twixt.

Solutions to Puzzles. Evans' puzzle: b1 (unique). Three new puzzles: Left: a2 (unique). Middle: Black wins; best move for White is a1, which leaves Black with only 2 winning replies (a2, c1); all other White moves leave Black with at least 3 winning replies (e.g., c1 leaves a1, b2, d4). Right: e3 (unique).

Acknowledgments. We thank Jakub Pawlewicz for helpful comments.

References

1. Anshelevich, V.V.: The game of Hex: an automatic theorem proving approach to game programming. In: AAAI/IAAI, pp. 189–194. AAAI Press/The MIT Press, Menlo Park (2000)
2. Arneson, B., Hayward, R.B., Henderson, P.: Solving Hex: beyond humans. In: Herik, H.J., Iida, H., Plaat, A. (eds.) CG 2010. LNCS, vol. 6515, pp. 1–10. Springer, Heidelberg (2011). doi:10.1007/978-3-642-17928-0_1
3. Arneson, B., Henderson, P., Hayward, R.B.: Benzene (2009). http://benzene. sourceforge.net/
4. Evans, R.J.: A winning opening in reverse Hex. J. Recreational Math. **7**(3), 189–192 (1974)
5. Gardner, M.: Mathematical games: concerning the game of hex, which may be played on the tiles of the bathroom floor. Sci. Am. **197**(1), 145–150 (1957)
6. Gardner, M.: Mathematical games: four mathematical diversions involving concepts of topology. Sci. Am. **199**(4), 124–129 (1958)
7. Gardner, M.: Mathematical games: games of strategy for two players: star nim, meander, dodgem, and rex. Sci. Am. **232**(6), 106–111 (1975)
8. Gardner, M.: Hexaflexagons and other mathematical diversions: the first scientific American book of puzzles and games, Chap. 8, pp. 73–83. University of Chicago Press, Chicago, USA (1988)
9. Hayward, R.B., Toft, B., Henderson, P.: How to play reverse hex. Discrete Math. **312**, 148–156 (2012)
10. Hein, P.: Vil de laere Polygon? Politiken, December 1942
11. Henderson, P.: Playing and solving Hex. Ph.D. thesis, UAlberta (2010). http:// webdocs.cs.ualberta.ca/hayward/theses/ph.pdf
12. Henderson, P., Arneson, B., Hayward, R.B.: Solving 8 × 8 Hex. In: Boutilier, C. (ed.) IJCAI, pp. 505–510 (2009)
13. Lagarias, J., Sleator, D.: The mathemagician and pied puzzler: a collection in tribute to martin gardner. In: Berlekamp, E., Rodgers, T. (eds.) Chap. 3, pp. 237–240. A.K. Peters (1999)
14. Pawlewicz, J., Hayward, R.B.: Scalable parallel DFPN search. In: Herik, H.J., Iida, H., Plaat, A. (eds.) CG 2013. LNCS, vol. 8427, pp. 138–150. Springer, Heidelberg (2014). doi:10.1007/978-3-319-09165-5_12

Computer-Aided Go: Chess as a Role Model

Ingo Althöfer[✉]

Fakultät für Mathematik und Informatik, Friedrich-Schiller-Universität,
07743 Jena, Germany
ingo.althoefer@uni-jena.de

Abstract. Recently computers have gained strength in the Asian board game Go. The Chess community experienced some 15 to 30 years ago that teams with humans and computers may be much stronger than each of their components. This paper claims that time is ripe for computer-aided Go on a large scale, although neither most users nor the Go programmers have realized it. A central part of the paper describes successful pioneers in Go play with computer help. Progress in computer-aided Go may also lead to progress in human Go and in computer Go itself.

1 Introduction

As learned in Chess some decades ago (mainly between the years 1985 and 2000), humans and computers have teamed up to achieve levels of play that are much better than the single strengths of the agents involved [1]. A similar development is possible in Go. Progress in computer-aided Go may also lead to progress in computer Go as well as in the theoretical understanding of the game Go itself.

We present and discuss recent developments in computer-aided Go in different fields: we look both at over-the-board play and at (long-time) analysis. It is our expectation that computer-aided Go with commercial bots will surpass top human levels soon, in particular years before commercial bots alone will achieve this.

The paper is organised as follows. The first half deals with the histories of computer-aided Chess and Go: in Sect. 2 the Chess scene is discussed as a role model; Sect. 3 tells the stories of four pioneers in computer-assisted Go play. The second half is a sort of an opinion paper: Sect. 4 contains a wish list of six points for features in commercial Go bots; and the paper concludes with miscellaneous thoughts in Sect. 5.

2 Chess as a Role Model

In Chess, commercial bots became interesting as opponents and for analysis purposes around 1985. The approach of computer-assisted analysis made a great step forward, when PC-based Chess programs became popular in the late 1980's. In particular, the leading company ChessBase engaged world champion Garry Kasparov from 1987 on for several PR events where the champion demonstrated how Chess databases and analysis tools might be used to prepare for an opponent.

A. Plaat et al. (Eds.): CG 2016, LNCS 10068, pp. 149–155, 2016.
DOI: 10.1007/978-3-319-50935-8_14

The World Championship match from 1990 was the first where one of the teams (challenger Karpov) used a commercial Chess computer ("Fidelity Elite") for analysing adjourned games.

Already in 1988, one of the top Eastern German correspondence Chess players (Heinrich Burger) used several small commercial Chess bots around the clock to analyse positions from his games in the Correspondence Chess Olympiad. This helped East Germany to get a Bronze medal in that tournament. In the meantime, every serious correspondence Chess player is using intensive computer help.

In 1994, Chess programs for the PC with k-best analysis modes came up and made the machines interesting tools for testing new lines, refutations, and ideas [5,6] in openings. A recent interview with Matthias Wüllenweber (chief of the ChessBase company for 30 years already) [8] shows that even today more new analysis features and tools for Chess programs are just around the corner, both welcomed and are to be expected soon by strong Chess players. Currently, every Chess professional depends on computer analysis in his or her preparation for tournament games.

This author was successfully involved in early developments of interactive analysis tools. He used them in settings like 3-Hirn [1,4], where in realtime a human has the final choice amongst candidate moves provided by two different Chess bots. It turned out that 3-Hirn plays about 200 rating points stronger than the Chess bots involved, independently of the absolute Chess strength of the human controller [3,5].

3   Successful Pioneers in Computer-Assisted Go

So far, commercial Go bots are not really user-friendly for interactive analysis mode. Nevertheless, a handful of creative Go players found successful ways of interactive analysis. Here we portrait some of them.

3.1   Thomas Redecker and His Use of Komi Fans

MCTS bots do not give expected scores, but instead winning probabilities. In the analysis of positions (in particular endgame positions) a technique called "komi fan" helps to find the likely score for (score-)perfect play on both sides: the position under investigation is analysed for different values of (artificial) komi. Figure 1 shows a sample position.

Analysing this position with the bot CRAZYSTONE2013 gives the winning probabilities of Table 1 for Black, depending on the komi value.

According to these data, the likely perfect score (without komi) seems to be about +5 for Black. We analysed the same position with another bot, MANY FACES OF GO, version 12.022. The outcomes are shown in Table 2. Again, the likely perfect score seems to be +5 for Black. Funnily, both bots have a slight anomaly at komi 3.5/4.5: Black achieved slightly better scores at komi 4.5. Each

Fig. 1. Position on 9 × 9 board for a komi-fan test; White to move

Table 1. Winning percents computed by CRAZYSTONE

komi	1.5	2.5	3.5	4.5	5.5	7.5	9.5
percent	72.7	68.1	61.6	62.3	46.4	34.5	22.6

Table 2. Winning percents computed by MANY FACES OF GO

komi	1.5	2.5	3.5	4.5	5.5	7.5	9.5
percent	69.9	69.2	54.4	57.1	44.2	30.4	22.4

of the searches in this example was performed with two minutes of computing time on a quad core notebook.

Thomas Redecker wrote a whole book on the analysis of one specific and very difficult Go position [9]. In several positions he used this komi fan technique with MANY FACES OF GO to find the "correct" value of the position.

3.2 Strong Correspondence Go with Computer Help on 9 × 9: Darren Cook

The internet game server www.LittleGolem.net is one of the few places where Go with very long thinking times (i.e., in correspondence mode) can be played with a western interface. In a typical tournament on LittleGolem the player has in average 36 h for each of his moves.

Between 2002 and 2011, Darren Cook was the operator/player behind the account "sm9" on LittleGolem. sm9 played only games on 9 × 9-board. In the paper [7] Cook revealed that he had used the help of strong Go bots to find moves for sm9. For several championship cycles on 9×9, sm9 was the dominating player, ahead of VALKYRIA9 and Gerhard Knop (see in the next subsection for more infos on them).

3.3   Strong Correspondence Go with Computer Help on 19 × 19: Gerhard Knop

Currently (on April 15, 2016), the highest-ranked Go account (9.7 dan) on LittleGolem is the VALKYRIA9_bot, the bot programmed by Magnus Persson which only plays games on 9 × 9-board. The second-highest rating has Gerhard Knop (9.4 dan), the player on rank 3 is 6.3 dan. Knop plays with intensive computer help (using ZEN, CRAZYSTONE and other bots).

In normal "over-the-board" Go, Knop was slightly active in tournaments some years ago (2008–2013) with a highest EGF rating around 1,700 (meaning 4 kyu). His 9.4 dan on LittleGolem is the more impressive when one takes into account that Knop mainly plays games on 19 × 19 whereas VALKYRIA9 with its 9.7 dan "works" only on 9 × 9-board. (Explanation: www.LittleGolem.net gives only one overall Go rating for each account. In this single number the performances for 9 × 9, 13 × 13, and 19 × 19-board are combined.)

3.4   Team "Crazy Manja" in "Over the Board"-Play

In Winter 2014/15, a team "Crazy Manja" played three games against 5-dan amateur Stefan Kaitschick (EGF rating 2,380). Crazy Manja consisted of top German female player Manja Marz (EGF rating 2,280) and bot CRAZYS-TONE_2013 in analysis mode (running on a standard quad core notebook; estimated strength around 2,300 on that hardware). Marz was free in her choice for a move but got all the information from CRAZYSTONE's analysis screen.

After a loss in round 1, Crazy Manja won two games convincingly [2]. This author was involved in the experiment, operating CRAZYSTONE without any influence on the move decisions. Two more games did not end so pleasantly: in late May 2015, Crazy Manja lost a single no-handicap game narrowly against FJ Dickhut (6-dan, EGF rating 2,537) and another exhibition match during the European Go Congress 2015 clearly against 5-dan pro player Guo Yuan (who gave 3 handicap stones).

It seems that it takes a lot of experience for the human in the team to read and interpret the analysis screen of CRAZYSTONE properly. A similar statement will likely be true for future human players using DCNN-based Go bots in analysis mode.

4   A Wish List for Go Bot Features

The comparative look on Chess software makes clear that there is large space for improvement of interfaces in commercial Go bots. Here is a list of sic points we have in mind.

– Analysis modes have to be comfortable. The current situation where up to five mouse clicks are needed to undo and substitute a move is not satisfactorily.

– Programs need large score windows for possible komi values. Changing the komi value in a position should become a simple task, with only few mouse clicks.

– MCTS bots need something like a k-playout mode for small integers k. It is not sufficient that all candidate moves with their playout numbers and percents are shown. In particular this is not too helpful, when one candidate move gets more than 90 percent of the playouts in normal MCTS. Instead, it should be possible to force that each block of k playouts is distributed over k different moves. By such a spreading no move would get more than fraction $1/k$ of all playouts (rare exceptions may be positions with less than k feasible moves).

– Having in mind the analysis screen of CRAZYSTONE 2013, it would be nice not only to have a single histogram where the results of all playouts are collected, but one such histogram for each (prominent) candidate move.

– Due to the probabilistic nature of MCTS and its variants, independent runs for the same position may lead to different results. As an example one can look at game 1 between Lee Sedol and ALPHAGO in March 2016, at the position after move 101. In post-mortem analysis, Lee Sedol remarked that 102.R10 by ALPHAGO was the winning move. Interestingly, CRAZYSTONE 2013 proposes this move too in its analysis mode. However, a test with 30 independent runs (with about 3 min for each one) resulted in a first proposal of R10 for seven times, whereas in other twenty runs R14 became at rank 1. An analysis program should allow the "simultaneous" execution of m independent runs for a given position. The results should automatically be put together, showing frequencies for the (top) candidate moves.

– It would be nice to have simple switches between Japanese and Chinese rules during analysis mode. Sometimes play and analysis under the other rule set gives nontrivial insights into the difficulties of a position for a human controller.

Another experience from the history of computer-aided Chess is as following. As soon as Go bots become common tools in analysis, more features will surely be proposed by strong players. In particular, programs with neural nets should give insight into the proper values of certain "key neurons". It would then no longer be necessary that the programmers gave elaborate explanations what which value means. Instead, analysing players would soon learn by themselves to interpret neuron values in appropriate ways.

5 Miscellaneous Thoughts

This is no conclusion section in the traditional sense. The design of interactive systems for the game of Go (and also for other games) is a never-ending work in permanent progress. It will also remain a relevant task for the times when Go bots (without human help) will be stronger than all human players (without computer help).

In March 2016 a 5-game match was played between top human professional Lee Sedol and AlphaGo [10]. The games were transmitted to server KGS and commented live by hundreds of spectators. It turned out that for large sections of the games human estimates (those of professionals and amateurs) on the likely outcome of a game were far less accurate than the evaluations of the commercial bots CRAZYSTONE and ZEN. For many traditional Go players it will be a hard learning process to accept commercial Go bots as strong predictors and advisors.

As sequel to the above stories, we may conclude with our conviction: Advance in computer-aided Go is no one-way road! Progress in human+bot Go will also lead to progress in playing strength of autonomous bots and in the theoretical understanding of Go.

Acknowledgements. Gerhard Knop was so kind to tell the author about his playing style on LittleGolem. Thanks to Manja Marz for her participation in the "Crazy Manja" experiments. Student Toni Strobel at Jena University helped by analysing "crazy analysis" histograms with respect to representation as the sum of overlapping normal distributions. Thanks to the editorial board and anonymous referees for their constructive criticism. Raphael Thiele was a disciplined proof reader and also helped with the LaTeX formatting.

References

1. Althöfer, I., Donninger, C., Lorenz, U., Rottmann, V.: On timing, permanent brain and human intervention. In: Van den Herik, H., Herschberg, I.S., Uiterwijk, J., (ed.) Advances in Computer Chess 7, pp. 285–296. University of Limburg Press (1994)
2. Althöfer, I., Kaitschick, S., Marz, M.: Computer-aided go on high-dan level. In: IGGSC Proceedings, Charles University, Prague (2015)
3. Althöfer, I., de Koning, J., Lieberum, J., Meyer-Kahlen, S., Rolle, T., Sameith, J.: Five visualisations of the k-best mode. ICGA J. **26**, 182–189 (2003)
4. Althöfer, I.: 13 Jahre 3-Hirn: Meine Schach-Experimente mit Mensch-Maschinen-Kombinationen. 3-Hirn-Verlag (1998)
5. Althöfer, I.: Improved game play by multiple computer hints. Theor. Comput. Sci. **313**(3), 315–324 (2004)
6. Althöfer, I., Snatzke, R.G.: Playing games with multiple choice systems. In: Schaeffer, J., Müller, M., Björnsson, Y. (eds.) CG 2002. LNCS, vol. 2883, pp. 142–153. Springer, Heidelberg (2003). doi:10.1007/978-3-540-40031-8_10
7. Cook, D.: A human-computer team experiment for 9x9 go. In: Herik, H.J., Iida, H., Plaat, A. (eds.) CG 2010. LNCS, vol. 6515, pp. 145–155. Springer, Heidelberg (2011). doi:10.1007/978-3-642-17928-0_14
8. Metz, H., Wüllenweber, M.: Interview on the history and current role of the chessbase company in the chess world. Schach-Magazin 64, January 2016
9. Redecker, T.: The Most Difficult Problem Ever: Igo Hatsuyoron 120. Brett und Stein Verlag, Frankfurt am Main (2011). http://www.brett-und-stein.de/08-Impressum.php

10. Silver, D., Huang, A., Maddison, C., Guez, A., Sifre, L., van den Driessche, G., Schrittwieser, J., Antonoglou, I., Panneershelvam, V., Lanctot, M., Dieleman, S., Grewe, D., Nham, J., Kalchbrenner, N., Sutskever, I., Lillicrap, T., Leach, M., Kavukcuoglu, K., Graepel, T., Hassabis, D.: Mastering the game of Go with deep neural networks and tree search. Nature **529**(7587), 484–489 (2016)

Quantified Integer Programs with Polyhedral Uncertainty Set

Michael Hartisch[1(✉)], Thorsten Ederer[2], Ulf Lorenz[1], and Jan Wolf[1]

[1] Chair of Technology Management, University of Siegen, Siegen, Germany
{michael.hartisch,ulf.lorenz,jan.wolf}@uni-siegen.de
[2] Discrete Optimization, Technische Universität Darmstadt, Darmstadt, Germany
ederer@mathematik.tu-darmstadt.de

Abstract. Quantified Integer Programs (QIPs) are integer programs with variables being either existentially or universally quantified. They can be interpreted as a two-person zero-sum game with an existential and a universal player where the existential player tries to meet all constraints and the universal player intends to force at least one constraint to be not satisfied.

Originally, the universal player is only restricted to set the universal variables within their upper and lower bounds. We extend this idea by adding constraints for the universal variables, i.e., restricting the universal player to some polytope instead of the hypercube created by bounds. We also show how this extended structure can be polynomial-time reduced to a QIP.

1 Introduction

Integer linear programming has become a successful modeling and solution framework for a wide range of applications in the Operations Research community. Today, one can solve instances with thousands up to millions of variables and constraints. As problems get more complex, uncertainty becomes a relevant concern. Solutions to optimization problems can be sensitive to perturbations in the parameters, which can render them suboptimal or even infeasible in practice. Methods such as stochastic or robust programming are able to cope with parameter uncertainty and give average-case or worst-case optimal solutions, respectively.

A special class of optimization problems under uncertainty are quantified programs. Quantified Integer Programs (QIPs) are integer linear programs, where variables are either existentially or universally quantified. QIPs are PSPACE-complete [9, p. 92] and they can be interpreted as a two-person zero-sum game, where an existential player tries to stay feasible and a universal player tries to violate at least one constraint. In [1] it was shown that QIPs can be used to model and solve the game Gomoku.

In the original definition, a QIP is comparable to a multi-stage robust integer program with a cubic uncertainty set. This uncertainty set is rather conservative,

A. Plaat et al. (Eds.): CG 2016, LNCS 10068, pp. 156–166, 2016.
DOI: 10.1007/978-3-319-50935-8_15

since it allows for worst-case realizations of each universal variable at the same time. Therefore, we restrict the uncertainty set.

Such a restriction can also be seen from a gaming point of view: On the one hand, only a certain set of moves are legal moves for the opposing player according to the rules. On the other hand, when planning a move the aspect of opponent modeling [7] can be seen as restricting the response of the opponent by prohibiting unlikely moves during the analysis. This does not only help us to adapt more efficiently to a well known opponent but also shrinks the game tree of interest noticeably.

We will now generally and in an abstract manner define our problem. In contrast to the original QIP problem we restrict the universal player not only within some rigid bounds, but also dynamically, i.e., the permitted range of the variables depends on previous and possible future universal decisions. When setting a variable the universal player must check some conditions, depending only on own actions.

2 Previous and Related Work

Quantified Constraint Satisfaction Problems have been studied since at least 1995 [3]. In 2003, Subramani revived the idea of universal variables in Constraint Satisfaction Problems and coined the term Quantified Linear Program (QLP). His QLP did not have an objective function and the universal variables could only take values in their associated intervals. In the following year he extended this approach by integer variables and called them Quantified Integer Programs (QIPs) [6]. Later Wolf and Lorenz added a linear objective function [4] and enhanced the problem to: "Does a solution exist and if yes which one is the best." Within the scope of his dissertation [9], Wolf gave some theoretical results and adapted a solving procedure known from Stochastic Programming: With his implementation of Multistage Benders Decomposition it is possible to solve QLPs with millions of scenarios.

We will basically follow the notation used in [4]. Transposes are omitted when they are clear.

Definition 1 (Quantified Integer Program). *Let $x = (x_1, \ldots, x_n)^\top \in \mathbb{Z}^n$ be a vector of $n \in \mathbb{N}$ integer variables and $l, u \in \mathbb{Z}^n$ lower and upper bounds. Let $\mathcal{D} = \{x \in \mathbb{Z}^n \mid x \in [l, u]\}$. Let $A \in \mathbb{Q}^{m \times n}$ be the coefficient matrix with rational entries, $b \in \mathbb{Q}^m$ the right-hand side vector and $Q = (Q_1, \ldots, Q_n)^\top \in \{\exists, \forall\}^n$ a vector of quantifiers. The term $Q \circ x \in \mathcal{D}$ with the component wise binding operator $\circ$ denotes the quantification vector $(Q_1 x_1 \in [l_1, u_1] \cap \mathbb{Z}, \ldots, Q_n x_n \in [l_n, u_n] \cap \mathbb{Z})^\top$ such that every quantifier Q_i binds the variable x_i ranging in the associated interval $[l_i, u_i]$. We call a maximal consecutive subsequence of Q consisting of identical quantifiers a quantifier block and denote the i-th corresponding subsequence of x by x^i and call it a variable block B_i. Let $\beta \in \mathbb{N}$ be the number of such blocks. Let $c \in \mathbb{Q}^n$ be a vector of objective coefficients and let c^i denote the segment of c associated with B_i.*

We call

$$\min_{B_1} \left(c^1 x^1 + \max_{B_2} \left(c^2 x^2 + \min_{B_3} \left(c^3 x^3 + \max_{B_4} \left(\ldots + \min_{B_\beta} c^\beta x^\beta \right) \right) \right) \right)$$

$$s.t. \quad Q \circ x \in \mathcal{D} : Ax \leq b$$

a quantified integer program (QIP) and denote it with (c, Q, l, u, A, b).

Note that the universal variables are only restricted to be in their associated intervals. From now on the existential player will be referred to as "he" and the universal player as "she".

3   An Extension with Regard to the Uncertainty Set

We extend the idea of quantified variables by restricting the universal variables to a polytope that can be described through a second system $A^\forall x \leq b^\forall$ with $A^\forall \in \mathbb{Q}^{m^\forall \times n}$ and $b^\forall \in \mathbb{Q}^{m^\forall}$ for $m^\forall \in \mathbb{N}$. For a given QIP (c, Q, l, u, A, b) we only restrict the universal variables in such way that their range only depends on other universal variables. In other words, we assume that existential variables have no influence on universal decisions. Thus, we demand

$$A_{i,j}^\forall = 0 \quad \forall\, i \in \{1, \ldots, m^\forall\}\ \forall j \in \{k \in \{1, \ldots, n\} \mid Q_k = \exists\}, \tag{1}$$

i.e., each entry of $A^\forall$ belonging to an existential variable is zero.

Definition 2 (QIP with Polyhedral Uncertainty Set $(QIP^\circledcirc)$**).** *Let* (c, Q, l, u, A, b) *be a given QIP. Let* $b^\forall \in \mathbb{Q}^{m^\forall}$ *and* $A^\forall \in \mathbb{Q}^{m^\forall \times n}$ *with (1). Let* $\mathcal{D}^\circledcirc = \{x \in \mathcal{D} \mid A^\forall x \leq b^\forall\} \neq \emptyset$. *The quantified integer program with polyhedral uncertainty set* $(QIP^\circledcirc)$ *is given by* $(c, Q, l, u, A, b, A^\forall, b^\forall)$ *with*

$$\min_{B_1} \left(c^1 x^1 + \max_{B_2} \left(c^2 x^2 + \min_{B_3} \left(c^3 x^3 + \max_{B_4} \left(\ldots + \min_{B_\beta} c^\beta x^\beta \right) \right) \right) \right)$$

$$s.t.\ Q \circ x \in \mathcal{D}^\circledcirc : Ax \leq b.$$

Note that we forbid an empty domain $\mathcal{D}^\circledcirc$ since it would complicate the following definitions.

Definition 3 (Legal Allocation). *A legal allocation of an existential variable* x_i *demands this variable to be integer and within its bounds* $[l_i, u_i]$. *The same is true for universal variables in standard QIPs. In a* $QIP^\circledcirc$, *however, the legal allocation options also depend on the (legal) allocation of previous variables* $x_1, \ldots, x_{i-1}$. *Thus, when assigning a value to the universal variable* x_i *there must exist a series of legal moves* $x_{i+1}, \ldots, x_n$ *such that the resulting vector* x *fulfills* $A^\forall x \leq b^\forall$. *The legal range* $[l_i^\forall, u_i^\forall]$ *of* x_i *can be determined by Fourier-Motzkin elimination [8] of the domain* $\mathcal{D}^\circledcirc$ *and fixating the previous variable allocations.*

Definition 4 (Strategy). *A strategy $S = (V, E, c)$ is an edge-labeled finite arborescence[1] with a set of nodes $V = V_\exists \cup V_\forall$, a set of edges E and a vector of edge labels $c \in \mathbb{Q}^{|E|}$. Each level of the tree consists either of only nodes from $V_\exists$ or only of nodes from $V_\forall$, with the root node at level 0 being from $V_\exists$. The i-th variable is represented by the inner nodes at depth $i - 1$. Each edge connects a node at some level i to a node at level $i + 1$. Outgoing edges represent moves of the player at the current node, the corresponding edge label encodes the variable allocation of the move. Each node $v_\exists \in V_\exists$ has exactly one child, and each node $v_\forall \in V_\forall$ has as many children as legal allocation options.*

A path from the root to a leaf represents a game sequence and the edge labels along this path encode the corresponding variable allocation. Such a leaf at the end of a path corresponding to x has the value $c^\top x$.

Definition 5 (Winning Strategy). *A strategy is called a winning strategy (for the existential player) if all paths from the root to a leaf represent a vector x such that $Ax \leq b$.*

Definition 6 (Optimal Winning Strategy). *A winning strategy is optimal if the minimax value of the root is smaller than or equal to the minimax values of all other winning strategies. The vector $\tilde{x}$ representing the path which obeys the minimax rule is called the principal variation (PV), i.e., it consists of the optimal moves when both players play perfectly. The optimal objective value is $c^\top \tilde{x}$.*

4   The Polynomial-Time Reduction to a QIP

Hereafter we provide an easy method to transform any given QIP$^\oplus$ (with a polyhedral uncertainty set) into a QIP (only restricted by bounds). This enables us to use our solver Yasol, which is specialized in solving quantified programs [2]. Further, the deterministic equivalent program can be computed much more easily. It also enables us to model problems in a straightforward way (by stating both systems $A^\forall x \leq b^\forall$ and $Ax \leq b$) and transform them later into a QIP to solve them.

Our goal is to transfer the condition $A^\forall x \leq b^\forall$ out of the domain of the variables into the system of constraints. We rewrite the problem as a QIP as given in Definition 1. Note that we cannot simply add $A^\forall x \leq b^\forall$ to the constraint system. This would not restrict the universal player but tighten the conditions the existential player has to meet. Instead, the universal polyhedral constraints are not enforced a priori. We introduce helper constraints and variables that ensure that a violation of the universal constraints is detected, with the effect that the existential player's constraints are relaxed. That is, "the existential player wins by default if the universal player cheats". In addition to making all constraints feasible, the universal player is penalized via the objective function.

---

[1] An arborescence is a directed, rooted tree.

Let us consider the k-th row of the system $A^\forall x \leq b^\forall$ which is given by

$$\sum_{i=1}^{n} A_{k,i}^{\forall} \cdot x_i \leq b_k^{\forall} . \tag{2}$$

It is solely the universal player's task to meet this condition, since the existential player cannot influence the left hand side because of (1). Thus

$$\sum_{i=1}^{n} A_{k,i}^{\forall} \cdot x_i > b_k^{\forall} \tag{3}$$

$$\Longleftrightarrow \sum_{i=1}^{n} A_{k,i}^{\forall} \cdot x_i \geq b_k^{\forall} + \epsilon_k \tag{4}$$

holds for some $\epsilon_k > 0$. To determine an assignment for the parameter ϵ_k we need to find the smallest possible gap between the sum of integral multiples of the coefficients $A_{k,i}^{\forall}$ and $b_k^{\forall}$. It is sufficient to underestimate this smallest possible gap in order to ensure (3) $\Leftrightarrow$ (4). This can be achieved by using the reciprocal of the (lowest) common multiplier of the denominators (LCD) of the universal polytope's coefficients. Let R_k^{LCD} be the reciprocal of the LCD of $b_k^{\forall}$ and of the coefficients $A_{k,i}^{\forall}$ for $i \in \{1, \ldots, n\}$. Then

$$\sum_{i=1}^{n} A_{k,i}^{\forall} \cdot x_i \geq b_k^{\forall} + R_k^{LCD} \tag{5}$$

is fulfilled if and only if the original constraint (2) is not satisfied. Note, that $R_k^{LCD} = 1$ if all entries of row k are integer.

We now introduce a new binary existential variable $y_k \in \{0,1\}$ with the property

$$y_k \begin{cases} = 0, & \text{if } \sum_{i=1}^{n} A_{k,i}^{\forall} \cdot x_i \leq b_k^{\forall} \\ \in \{0,1\}, & \text{if } \sum_{i=1}^{n} A_{k,i}^{\forall} \cdot x_i > b_k^{\forall} \end{cases} . \tag{6}$$

This is achieved by using the following constraint

$$\sum_{i=1}^{n} A_{k,i}^{\forall} \cdot x_i \geq L_k + (-L_k + b_k^{\forall} + R_k^{LCD}) \cdot y_k \tag{7}$$

with

$$L_k = \sum_{\substack{1 \leq i \leq n \\ A_{k,i}^{\forall} < 0}} A_{k,i}^{\forall} \cdot u_i + \sum_{\substack{1 \leq i \leq n \\ A_{k,i}^{\forall} \geq 0}} A_{k,i}^{\forall} \cdot l_i \tag{8}$$

which is the smallest value the left hand side of the original universal constraint can take with respect to the bounds. Let us take a closer look at (7). If $y_k = 0$ the constraint is always fulfilled, since

$$\sum_{i=1}^{n} A_{k,i}^{\forall} \cdot x_i \geq L_k \tag{9}$$

is always true due to the definition of L_k. If and only if the original constraint is violated y_k also can take the value 1 since (5) is met. However, if the original constraint is satisfied y_k must be bound to zero. Thus, we embedded the variable y_k in a new constraint such that (6) is fulfilled. We now introduce the binary variable $p \in \{0, 1\}$ with

$$p \begin{cases} = 0, & \text{if } \forall\, k \in \{1, \ldots, m^\forall\} : y_k = 0 \\ \in \{0, 1\}, & \text{if } \exists\, k \in \{1, \ldots, m^\forall\} : y_k = 1 \end{cases}. \tag{10}$$

This variable can be embedded using the constraint

$$p \leq \sum_{k=1}^{m^\forall} y_k. \tag{11}$$

Thus, we introduced a variable that can indicate the violation of the system $A^\forall x \leq b^\forall$. If a universal constraint is violated we require each constraint of the systems $Ax \leq b$ to be trivially satisfied: If the universal player did not abide by her rules the existential player should not be punished for a violation of his system. Thus, the system is modified as follows

$$Ax - Mp \leq b \tag{12}$$

using the parameter vector $M \in \mathbb{Q}^m$ with

$$M_k = \max_{x \in \mathcal{D}} A_{k,*} x - b_k \tag{13}$$

$$= \sum_{\substack{1 \leq i \leq n \\ A_{k,i} < 0}} A_{k,i} \cdot l_i + \sum_{\substack{1 \leq i \leq n \\ A_{k,i} \geq 0}} A_{k,i} \cdot u_i - b_k \tag{14}$$

for each $k \in \{1, \ldots, m\}$. Hence, if $p = 1$ the inequality (12) is always satisfied.

The global indicator p is now used to punish the universal player by reducing the objective value massively. Since the universal player is trying to maximize the objective function we can penalize a violation of the universal constraints by subtracting this new variable p with a sufficiently large coefficient $\tilde{M}$ in the innermost term of the objective function. Note that this block is w.l.o.g. an existential block and thus the existential player will set this variable to 1 if possible, i.e., if the universal player did not meet her conditions. For the value of $\tilde{M}$ we choose

$$\tilde{M} = \sum_{\substack{1 \leq i \leq n \\ c_i < 0}} c_i \cdot (l_i - u_i) + \sum_{\substack{1 \leq i \leq n \\ c_i \geq 0}} c_i \cdot (u_i - l_i) + 1.$$

Note that

$$\max_{x \in \mathcal{D}} c^\top x - \tilde{M} < \min_{x \in \mathcal{D}} c^\top x \tag{15}$$

holds. Thus, when subtracting this value the objective function will definitely yield a better objective value for the existential player than he could have achieved without it. However, the universal player can counteract by meeting her system of equations and thus forcing p to be zero.

The final transformed problem looks as follows

$$\min_{B_1} \left(c^1 x^1 + \max_{B_2} \left(c^2 x^2 + \min_{B_3} \left(c^3 x^3 + \max_{B_4} \left(\ldots + \min_{B_\beta, y, p} \left(c^\beta x^\beta - \tilde{M}p \right) \right) \right) \right) \right)$$

$$\text{s.t. } Q \circ x \in \mathcal{D} \quad \exists y \in \{0,1\}^{m^\vee} \quad \exists p \in \{0,1\}:$$

$$Ax - Mp \le b \tag{16}$$

$$-A^\vee x - (L - b^\vee - R^{LCD})y \le -L \tag{17}$$

$$p - \sum_{k=1}^{m^\vee} y_k \le 0 \tag{18}$$

Note, that $L \in \mathbb{Q}^{m^\vee}$ is a vector with entries according to (8) and $R^{LCD} \in \mathbb{Q}^{m^\vee}$ is the vector of the reciprocals of the lowest common multiplier of the denominators of the rows of $A^\vee$ and $b^\vee$. Further note, that the values for $\tilde{M}$, M and L can be calculated easily by using the upper and lower bound of x appropriately, depending on the sign of the corresponding entries in c and A, respectively. Also the number of auxiliary variables and constraints is linear in the input size. This problem has the structure of a QIP since the variables are only restricted to be within their bounds ($\mathcal{D}$ is a cubical integer lattice). For further investigations the PV of a solution (a strategy) of this transformed problem will be denoted by $z = (x, y, p) \in \mathcal{D} \times \{0,1\}^{m^\vee} \times \{0,1\}$.

In the following we show how the transformed QIP and the QIP$^\oslash$ are connected.

Theorem 1. *If* QIP$^\oslash$ *has an optimal winning strategy with PV $\tilde{x}$ and objective value $v = c^\top \tilde{x}$ the transformed QIP has an optimal winning strategy with PV $\tilde{z} = (\tilde{x}, \tilde{y}, \tilde{p})$ with $\tilde{y}_i = 0$ for $i = 1, \ldots, m^\vee$ and $\tilde{p} = 0$ with objective value v.*

Proof. Since $\tilde{x}$ is the PV of an optimal winning strategy of QIP$^\oslash$ it satisfies $A\tilde{x} \le b$ and $A^\vee \tilde{x} \le b^\vee$. Thus, $\tilde{z} = (\tilde{x}, \tilde{y}, \tilde{p})$ with $\tilde{y} = 0$ and $\tilde{p} = 0$ is feasible for the transformed problem with objective value $c^\top \tilde{x} - M\tilde{p} = v$. Let $\hat{z} = (\hat{x}, \hat{y}, \hat{p})$ be the PV of the optimal winning strategy of the transformed problem and thus $c^\top \hat{x} - M\hat{p} \le c^\top \tilde{x}$. If $\hat{x} \notin \mathcal{D}^\oslash \hat{z}$ would also fulfill $\hat{p} = 1$, since at least one row of the system $A^\vee \hat{x} \le b^\vee$ is violated. However, because of (15) the resulting value of the objective function is smaller than any other solution obeying $A^\vee \hat{x} \le b^\vee$. This is a contradiction to the minimax optimality of $\hat{z}$ since the universal player can avoid this by assigning her variables such that $A^\vee \hat{x} \le b^\vee$ holds. Thus, the assignment $\hat{x} \in \mathcal{D}^\oslash$ is true and $A^\vee \hat{x} \le b^\vee$. Further, $y = 0$ and $p = 0$ and $\hat{x}$ is also feasible for QIP$^\oslash$ with $c^\top \hat{x} \ge c^\top \tilde{x}$. Therefore, $c^\top \hat{x} = c^\top \tilde{x} = v$.

Theorem 2. *If* QIP$^\oslash$ *has no winning strategy, then the transformed QIP also has no feasible solution.*

Proof. Let QIP$^{\oslash}$ have no winning strategy. Assume $S = (V, E, c)$ were a winning strategy for the transformed QIP, i.e., in each leaf the system of inequalities (16)-(18) is fulfilled. Note that this arborescence has a depth of $n + m^{\forall} + 1$. We consider the arborescence $\bar{S} = (\bar{V}, \bar{E}, \bar{c})$ with $\bar{V} \subseteq V$, $\bar{E} \subseteq E$ and $\bar{c}(e) = c(e)$ for each $e \in \bar{E}$. $\bar{V}$ contains no node of a level larger than n and $\bar{E}$ contains no edges leading to such nodes. Further, edges describing illegal allocations (see Definition 3) in terms of the QIP$^{\oslash}$ are deleted as well as their whole underlying subtrees. This designed arborescence $\bar{S}$ describes a strategy for the underlying QIP$^{\oslash}$, because

- the depth is n and thus for each variable a decision level exists,
- nodes of universal variables have only legal allocation options leading out,
- the remaining strategy properties are adopted from S.

This strategy $\bar{S}$ is also a winning strategy for QIP$^{\oslash}$, since each path from the root to a leaf represents a vector x such that $Ax \leq b$; for each such path $A^{\forall} x \leq b^{\forall}$ holds, because illegal allocations were deleted.

Let us consider such a path $x_1, \ldots, x_n$ in $\bar{S}$ and the unique[2] associated overlying path $z = (x_1, \ldots, x_n, y_1, \ldots, y_{m^{\forall}}, p)$ in S. Since $A^{\forall} x \leq b^{\forall}$ and (16)-(18) we may conclude $p = 0$ and $y_i = 0$ for all $i \in \{1, \ldots, m^{\forall}\}$. Thus, because of (16), also $Ax \leq b$ holds for the leaf. Hence, we have found a winning strategy for QIP$^{\oslash}$ which contradicts the assumption.

Note that the first-stage solution of the transformed QIP is identical[3] to the first-stage solution of the QIP$^{\oslash}$.

Corollary 1. *QIP$^{\oslash}$ is in PSPACE. Since the QIP with cubical uncertainty set is a special case of the QIP$^{\oslash}$ it is even PSPACE-complete.*

5   Example

We consider a simple graph game where one player has to traverse a given graph while the opponent is allowed to erase some edges. However, the opponent is not allowed to erase edges arbitrarily but must obey some rules. This problem is closely related to the Dynamic Graph Reliability problem [5] with the difference that edges have weights and an objective function should be minimized. Further, edges are erased depending on the point in time instead of the location of the player. The underlying graph is given in Fig. 1.

The starting node is labeled with 0 and the target node with 7. The question is:

Is there a strategy for the existential player which allows him to reach the target node no matter how the opponent acts? And if there are multiple strategies: Which one is the winning strategy with the shortest worst-case path to the target node (according to the weights of the edges).

---

[2] The path is unique, because all nodes with level $\geq n$ belong to existential variables and thus have only one successor in a strategy.
[3] except for auxiliary variable p in single-stage instances.

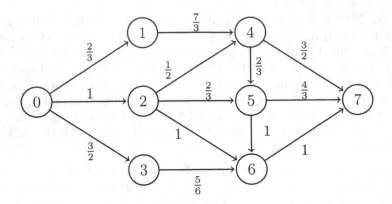

Fig. 1. Directed acyclic weighted graph with starting node 0 and target node 7

Let $G = (V, E, c)$ describe the graph given in Fig. 1 with V being the set of vertices, E the set of edges and $c : E \to \mathbb{Q}$ a function assigning weights to each edge. Let $x_{i,j} \in \{0, 1\}$ be variables indicating whether the existential player uses edge $(i, j) \in E$ or not. For each edge $(i, j) \in E$ with $i \neq 0$ let $d_{i,j} \in \{0, 1\}$ indicate whether the universal player deleted this edge or not. The turn order is given by the following quantifier string:

$$\exists x_{0,1}, x_{0,2}, x_{0,3} \ \forall d_{1,4}, d_{2,4}, d_{2,5}, d_{2,6}, d_{3,6} \ \exists x_{1,4}, x_{2,4} x_{2,5}, x_{2,6}, x_{3,6}$$
$$\forall d_{4,7}, d_{4,5}, d_{5,7}, d_{5,6}, d_{6,7} \ \exists x_{4,7}, x_{4,5}, x_{5,7}, x_{5,6}, x_{6,7}$$

Both players take turns while fixing some variables. The universal player is allowed to deactivate edges before the existential player is able to use them. In doing so the existential player wants to meet the system of equations given below.

$$\sum_{(0,j) \in E} x_{0,j} = 1 \tag{19}$$

$$\sum_{(i,7) \in E} x_{i,7} = 1 \tag{20}$$

$$\sum_{(i,k) \in E} x_{i,k} = \sum_{(k,j) \in E} x_{k,j} \qquad \forall k \in \{1, \ldots, 6\} \tag{21}$$

$$x_{i,j} \leq 1 - d_{i,j} \qquad \forall (i,j) \in E, i \neq 0 \tag{22}$$

It consists of constraints ensuring the flow from node 0 to 7 (viz. (19), (20) and (21)) and constraints forbidding to use edges that have been deleted by the universal player (22). However, the universal player is also restricted by her system $A^\forall x \leq b^\forall$ as follows:

$$\sum_{\substack{(i,j) \in E \\ i \neq 0}} d_{i,j} \leq 3, \qquad \sum_{\substack{(i,j) \in E \\ i \neq 0}} c(i,j) \cdot d_{i,j} \geq \frac{3}{2}, \qquad \sum_{\substack{(i,j) \in E \\ i \neq 0}} c(i,j) \cdot d_{i,j} \leq 2 \tag{23}$$

This system states that the universal player is allowed to delete at most 3 edges and the sum of the weights of the deleted edges must be between 1.5 and 2. Note, that we did not convert either system into a "less or equal" system in order to make their actual use more clear. Yet, this must be done to use the transformation described in Sect. 4. The final transformed QIP is displayed below. For convenience the repeating variable domains $\{0,1\}$ are omitted in the quantifier string.

$$\min_{B_1} \left(\frac{2}{3}x_{0,1} + x_{0,2} + \frac{3}{2}x_{0,3} + \max_{B_2} \left(\min_{B_3} \left(\frac{7}{3}x_{1,4} + \frac{1}{2}x_{2,4} + \frac{2}{3}x_{2,5} + x_{2,6} \right. \right. \right.$$
$$\left. \left. \left. + \frac{5}{6}x_{3,6} + \max_{B_4} \left(\min_{B_5,y,p} \left(\frac{3}{2}x_{4,7} + \frac{2}{3}x_{4,5} + \frac{4}{3}x_{5,7} + x_{5,6} + x_{6,7} - 15p \right) \right) \right) \right) \right)$$

s.t. $\exists x_{0,1}, x_{0,2}, x_{0,3} \ \forall d_{1,4}, d_{2,4}, d_{2,5}, d_{2,6}, d_{3,6} \ \exists x_{1,4}, x_{2,4}, x_{2,5}, x_{2,6}, x_{3,6}$
$\forall d_{4,7}, d_{4,5}, d_{5,7}, d_{5,6}, d_{6,7} \ \exists x_{4,7}, x_{4,5}, x_{5,7}, x_{5,6}, x_{6,7}, y_1, y_2, y_3, p :$

$$- \sum_{(0,j)\in E} x_{0,j} - p \leq -1 \ , \quad \sum_{(0,j)\in E} x_{0,j} - 2p \leq 1 \tag{24}$$

$$- \sum_{(i,7)\in E} x_{i,7} - p \leq -1 \ , \quad \sum_{(i,7)\in E} x_{i,7} - 2p \leq 1 \tag{25}$$

$$\sum_{(i,k)\in E} x_{i,k} - \sum_{(k,j)\in E} x_{k,j} - \deg^-(k) \cdot p \leq 0 \qquad \forall k \in \{1,\dots,6\} \tag{26}$$

$$\sum_{(k,j)\in E} x_{k,j} - \sum_{(i,k)\in E} x_{i,k} - \deg^+(k) \cdot p \leq 0 \qquad \forall k \in \{1,\dots,6\} \tag{27}$$

$$x_{i,j} + d_{i,j} - p \leq 1 \qquad \forall (i,j) \in E, i \neq 0 \tag{28}$$

$$4y_1 - \sum_{\substack{(i,j)\in E \\ i\neq 0}} d_{i,j} \leq 0 \tag{29}$$

$$\sum_{\substack{(i,j)\in E \\ i\neq 0}} c(i,j) \cdot d_{i,j} + 9.5y_2 \leq \frac{65}{6} \tag{30}$$

$$- \sum_{\substack{(i,j)\in E \\ i\neq 0}} c(i,j) \cdot d_{i,j} + \frac{13}{6}y_3 \leq 0 \tag{31}$$

$$p - \sum_{k=1}^{3} y_k \leq 0 \tag{32}$$

Constraints (24)-(28) describe the transformed existential system (cf. (16)), (29)-(31) are the embedded universal constraints (cf. (17)), and (32) is similar to (18). In (26) and (27) the coefficients of p are the number of incoming edges $\deg(k)^- = |\{(i,j) \in E \mid j = k\}|$ and the number of outgoing edges of node k $\deg(k)^+ = |\{(i,j) \in E \mid i - k\}|$, respectively. In (30) the coefficients result from

$L_2 = -\frac{65}{6}$, $R_2^{LCD} = \frac{1}{6}$ and $b_2^\forall = -\frac{3}{2}$. This standard QIP is easily solved by the QIP-solver Yasol. It turns out that there is a winning strategy for the existential player. The objective value of the PV is $\frac{11}{3}$ and the optimal first decision is moving from the starting node to node 2. The (perfect) universal player will then delete the edge between 2 and 4. The existential player then must move to node 5. After that the edge between node 5 and 7 is deleted and finally the target node is reached by passing node 6.

6 Conclusion

We extended the concept of quantified integer programs to a polyhedral uncertainty set. Thus, the universal variables can be restricted explicitly by using a second linear system of inequations $A^\forall x \leq b^\forall$. We also presented a general polynomial-time transformation of this new problem statement permitting us to solve a standard QIP instead of inventing new methods for solving QIP$^\varnothing$. Thus, the concept of QIPs can be put into practice in new areas of application in an easy and straightforward way. In particular, rules of games that must be obeyed by each player can be modeled easily. Therefore, the possibility of modeling and solving more complicated two-person zero-sum games with the help of quantified programming is provided.

References

1. Ederer, T., Lorenz, U., Opfer, T., Wolf, J.: Modeling games with the help of quantified integer linear programs. In: Herik, H.J., Plaat, A. (eds.) ACG 2011. LNCS, vol. 7168, pp. 270–281. Springer, Heidelberg (2012). doi:10.1007/978-3-642-31866-5_23
2. Ederer, T., Lorenz, U., Opfer, T., Wolf, J.: An Algorithmic Framework for 0/1-QIP solvers. Technical Report Number 2667, TU Darmstadt (2013)
3. Gerber, R., Pugh, W., Saksena, M.: Parametric dispatching of hard real-time tasks. IEEE Trans. Comput. **44**(3), 471–479 (1995)
4. Lorenz, U., Wolf, J.: Solving multistage quantified linear optimization problems with the alpha-beta nested Benders decomposition. EURO J. Comput. Optim. **3**(4), 349–370 (2015)
5. Papadimitriou, C.H.: Games against nature. J. Comp. Sys. Sc. **69**, 288–301 (1985)
6. Subramani, K.: Analyzing selected quantified integer programs. In: Basin, D., Rusinowitch, M. (eds.) IJCAR 2004. LNCS (LNAI), vol. 3097, pp. 342–356. Springer, Heidelberg (2004). doi:10.1007/978-3-540-25984-8_26
7. van den Herik, H.J., Donkers, H., Spronck, P.H.M.: Opponent modelling and commercial games. In: Proceedings of IEEE 2005 Symposium on Computational Intelligence and Games CIG 2005, pp. 15–25 (2005)
8. Paul, W.H.: Fourier-Motzkin elimination extension to integer programming problems. J. Comb. Theor. Ser. A **21**(1), 118–123 (1976)
9. Wolf, J.: Quantified Linear Programming (Forschungsberichte zur Fluidsystemtechnik, vol. 7), Ph.D thesis, Aachen, Shaker Verlag (2015)

A Class Grammar for General Games

Cameron Browne[✉]

Queensland University of Technology, Gardens Point, Brisbane 4000, Australia
c.browne@qut.edu.au

Abstract. While there exist a variety of *game description languages* (GDLs) for modeling various classes of games, these are aimed at game *playing* rather than the more particular needs of game *design*. This paper describes a new approach to general game modeling that arose from this need. A *class grammar* is automatically generated from a given library of source code, from the constructors and associated parameters found along its class hierarchy, to give a context-free grammar that provides access to the underlying code while hiding its implementation details.

1 Introduction

There currently exist a number of software systems for modeling and playing various types of games, including deterministic perfect information games [1], combinatorial games [2], puzzle games [3], strategy games [4], card games [5], video games [6], even complete logical game worlds [7], to name but a few. Each system defines games using a custom *game description language* (GDL), primarily for the *playing* of games. In this paper, we examine such GDLs from the perspective of *designing* games, and propose a new approach that might obviate the need to write a specific GDL for each different type of game.

I introduce the notion of a *class grammar*, which is a formal grammar derived directly from the class hierarchy of the underlying source code. The class grammar is the visible tip of the iceberg of code underneath; it provides a clean, simple interface to the underlying code that offers full functionality, while hiding the implementation details. This approach is described in the context of a new general game system called LUDII, and has potential benefits not only for game design but also for the modeling and playing of games.

The following sections compare some GDLs from a design perspective, describe the syntax, operation and implementation of the class grammar, and give some formatting guidelines for programmers for producing a cleaner grammar.

2 Game Description Languages for Game Design

The tasks of game *playing* and game *design*, although closely linked, have different needs. Game playing focuses primarily on the correctness of the underlying models and the efficiency of their implementation, while game design involves

© Springer International Publishing AG 2016
A. Plaat et al. (Eds.): CG 2016, LNCS 10068, pp. 167–182, 2016.
DOI: 10.1007/978-3-319-50935-8_16

additional aspects, such as the ease with which game descriptions can be modeled and manipulated by the designer, the expressiveness of the GDL, and how readily the design process can be automated.

Kernighan and Pike list four principles of good software design: *simplicity, clarity, generality* and *automation* [8]. I propose a similar set of properties that a GDL should possess, in order to be effective for the purpose of game design.

1. *Simplicity:* Game descriptions should be simple to write and modify.
2. *Clarity:* Game descriptions should be readily comprehensible.
3. *Generality:* The GDL should support a wide range of games.
4. *Extensibility:* The GDL should be easy to extend to support new concepts.
5. *Evolvability:* Game descriptions should combine to produce mostly valid (i.e., playable) children with characteristics of their parents.

The ideal GDL, from a design perspective, would allow the designer to quickly prototype new ideas for equipment, mechanisms and complete games, be easily extended as required, and easily automated for the purposes of play-testing, evaluation, optimization of rules and equipment, and even self-guided game design. Further, the ideal GDL should be hierarchical in nature, with useful game-related concepts called *ludemes* [9] chunked into convenient building blocks, to be easily tried in combination with other rules and equipment in other contexts.

The following subsections briefly examine some individual GDLs, and their suitability for game design, with these points in mind. Note that the focus here is on abstract and board game design, rather than video game design.

2.1   Zillions Rules File

Zillions Rules File (ZRF) is the proprietary game description format for ZILLIONS OF GAMES, a commercial program for modeling and playing Chess-like (and similar) games and puzzles [10]. Appendix A shows Tic-Tac-Toe described in ZRF, by way of example.

ZRF is a scripting language, much like a C macro, which utilises a library of pre-defined keywords for defining equipment, piece movement, and so on. It is highly structured and excellent for modeling Chess-like games, with an in-built AI that can provide a surprisingly responsive and tricky opponent for Chess variants. The syntax is reasonably straightforward and extensible for those familiar with functional programming languages.

However, games become harder to describe, and the AI less effective, the further they diverge from a Chess-like basis, e.g., the AI is effectively random for connection games, and some implementation choices, such as the lack of integer state variables and 2D-only graphics, further limit the generality of the system.[1] ZILLIONS OF GAMES has a strong following among game design hobbyists, but has had very little academic application [11].

---

[1] The 3D connection game Akron took hundreds of man-hours to model in ZRF.

2.2 Stanford GDL

The Stanford Logic Group's Game Description Language (S-GDL) [12], designed for their associated General Game Player (GGP) [1], is *the* standard GDL for academic research.[2] It is a low-level language that describes games in terms of simple, general instructions that update the game state using first order logic. This approach allows reasonable generality at the expense of clarity, and tends to be somewhat verbose. For example, the S-GDL description of Tic-Tac-Toe, listed in Appendix B, uses 384 tokens, compared to the 89 used by ZRF.

S-GDL is problematic in terms of game design. Game descriptions can be time-consuming to write and debug, and difficult to decipher for those unused to first order logic. The equipment and rules are typically interconnected to such an extent that any change to any aspect of the game would require significant rewriting. For example, one of the simplest choices that a game designer might want to experiment with is board size, but changing simply the board size from 3×3 to 4×4 in the Tic-Tac-Toe example would require modifying many lines of code and adding several more.

Extending S-GDL involves defining new versions of the grammar with the appropriate additions and dedicated implementations to support them. For example, GDL-II supports imperfect information games [13], rtGDL supports real-time play [14], and rtGDL-II supports both [14].

In terms of evolvability, games described in S-GDL lack high-level conceptual structure, so it is unlikely that ludemes will pass intact from parents to offspring. In fact, S-GDL descriptions tend to be so finely crafted that any random mutation or crossover is unlikely to yield a playable result. S-GDL, to my knowledge, has not been used except for playing known games, and in academic circles.

2.3 Ludi GDL

Ludi is a software system written for modeling, playing, evaluating and evolving combinatorial games [2]. The associated Ludi Game Description Language (L-GDL) describes games as high-level hierarchical structures of ludemes in a LISP-like format, and was developed with game design squarely in mind.

Complete games can be written and tested within minutes (sometimes seconds), and the format proved ideal for evolving games using a *genetic programming* (GP) approach [15]. Game descriptions are easy to comprehend even by lay readers, with the exception of certain pre-defined keywords that require documentation, and are easily modified. For example, changing the board size in the L-GDL Tic-Tac-Toe example shown in Appendix C simply involves changing the board size parameter from (size 3 3) to (size 4 4).

Ludi was successful as a proof-of-concept in producing the world's first computer-designed games to be commercially published [16], but only supported a small range of combinatorial games and suffered from over-specialization, with

---

[2] The acronym "GDL" in the literature typically refers to this particular language, but it is disambiguated here as "S-GDL" to avoid confusion.

a strong preference for N-in-a-row games. Lack of extensibility meant that any rule or equipment outside the scope of the language would require both the language and the program to be modified, highlighting a drawback of the standard approach of separating the language from the implementation. LUDI has not been publicly released or used outside the study for which it was developed.

2.4   LUDII Class Grammar

LUDII[3] is a complete *general game system* (GGS) [17] that builds on the principles pioneered in LUDI, but extends them to improve the key issues of generality and extensibility. This is achieved primarily through the class grammar that constitutes its GDL. The class grammar is automatically generated from the LUDII source code library, and game descriptions expressed in the grammar are automatically instantiated back into the corresponding library code for compilation, giving a guaranteed 1:1 mapping between the source code and the grammar.

Schaul *et al.* point out that: *any programming language constitutes a game description language, as would a universal Turing machine* [18, p. 12]. LUDII achieves this, to some extent, by effectively making the programming language (Java) the game description language; it can theoretically support any game that can be programmed in Java to implement its minimal API (described in Sect. 4.3). The programmer is free to implement whatever rule, equipment or behavior they want, however they want, while the user only sees the simplified view of the constructor in the grammar and not the implementation details.

LUDII has been designed with game design in mind. It is currently under development, but the aim is to provide a solid, general framework that supports as wide a range of games as possible, allowing scope for ever increasing functionality as classes in its source code library are subclassed and extended over time.

2.5   Comparison

Figure 1 shows a graphical comparison between these four GDLs, based on the five key design properties. The values shown are subjective estimates only, and are intended to highlight the relevant strengths and weaknesses of each GDL for the purpose of game design.

Simplicity is estimated by the number of tokens required to define games, on average, and the ease with which game descriptions can be modified. Clarity is estimated by the degree to which game descriptions would be self-explanatory to lay readers. Generality is based on the estimated percentage of games listed in the BoardGameGeek (BGG) online database[4] that it would be feasible to describe. Extensibility is estimated as the ease with which the language can be extended to incorporate new rules, behaviours, equipment, etc. Evolvability is estimated as the likelihood with which randomly mutating and crossing-over game descriptions will produce playable children that resemble their parents.

---

[3] LUDII is named after its predecessor LUDI but improves on it in most respects.

[4] The BGG database now lists over 80,000 games: https://www.boardgamegeek.com.

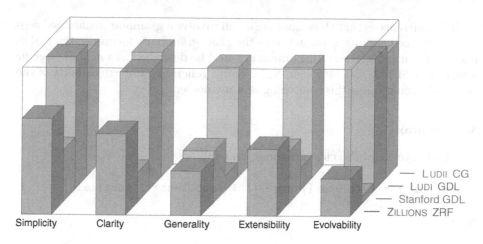

Fig. 1. Comparison of key aspects of GDLs from a design perspective.

ZRF is characterised by reasonable simplicity, clarity and extensibility. S-GDL has reasonable generality and extensibility, but poor evolvability. L-GDL has excellent simplicity, clarity and evolvability, but poor generality and extensibility. The class grammar mechanism devised for LUDII was designed to address the relative shortcomings of existing methods, and produce an approach for computer-assisted and fully automated game design that performs well across all five key design criteria. The following sections describe this approach in detail.

3   Class Grammar

The class grammar is set of *production rules* in which sequences of *symbols* on the RHS (right hand side) are assigned to a *nonterminal symbol* on the LHS (left hand side), very much like an Extended Backus-Naur Form (EBNF) grammar. It is intrinsically bound to the underlying code library, but is a *context-free grammar* that is self-contained and can be used without knowledge of the underlying code. In this section we discuss context (Sect. 3.1), syntax (Sect. 3.2), generation (Sect. 3.3), and instantiation (Sect. 3.4).

3.1   Context

The class grammar involves two main automated parsing steps.

1. *Forwards:* From source code to grammar.
2. *Backwards:* From grammar expressions back to specified source code.

The backwards step is similar in principle to existing approaches for using grammars to generate code. These include C++ code generators [19,20], Java code generators [21], *parser generators* such as ANTLR [23], and Translational BNF (TBNF) [22], in which code actions are embedded in the grammar.

The difference is that these approaches all involve a grammar maintained separately by the user or system, whereas the class grammar's forwards step makes it self-generating. The resulting grammar could be described as a *domain-specific language* (DSL) [23,24], although the potential generality and extensibility of the approach would make this something of a misnomer.

3.2 Syntax

The basic syntax of the class grammar is as follows:

```
<class> ::= { (class [{<arg>}]) | <subClass> | terminal }
```

where:

> `<class>`   denotes a LHS symbol that maps to a class in the code library.
> `(class [{<arg>}])` denotes a `class` constructor and its arguments.
> `<subClass>`   denotes a subclass derived from `class`.
> `terminal`   denotes a terminal symbol (fundamental data type or `enum`).
> `[...]`   denotes an optional item.
> `{...}`   denotes a collection of one or more items.
> `|`   denotes a choice between options in the RHS sequence.

Class names typically start with an uppercase character, but are converted to lowercase in the grammar for readability, convenience, and in keeping with the traditional form of EBNF style grammars. Appendix E shows a sample of the grammar generated from the LUDII code library.

3.3 Forward Mechanism (Generation)

The forward step of converting source code to grammar involves recursively parsing the code library from a specified root class (`Game` in this case) downwards, storing a new symbol for each new class encountered. A chain of dependency is then created from the root class, linking the arguments of each visited constructor by data type, until terminal symbols are reached. Fundamental data types and `enums` constitute terminals, while all other user-defined classes constitute *non-terminals*.

The grammar is then generated with each class name forming the LHS symbol of a production rule, of which the RHS is a sequence of constructors that instantiate that class (or subclasses derived from it) and their parameters. For example, the following abstract base class with no constructors:

```
public abstract class Start { ... }
```

and its two derived subclasses:

```
public class Place extends Start
{
    public Place(final String what, final int where)
}

public class Store extends Start
{
    public class Storepublic Store(final int who, final String what, final int count)
}
```

generate the following production rules:

```
<start> ::= <place> | <store>
<place> ::= (place (what String) (where int))
<store> ::= (store (who int) (what String) (count int))
```

The result is a summary of the class hierarchy, based on constructors and parameters, that offers full functionality while hiding the implementation details.

3.4 Backward Mechanism (Instantiation)

Each individual game is described as a *symbolic expression* (s-expression) compatible with the grammar. For example, Appendix D shows Tic-Tac-Toe described in the LUDII class grammar.

Game descriptions are parsed in a *top-down* manner [24, p. 225], with each (class ...) instance matched with its generating constructor, and parameters recursively instantiated as required. The calling app can then use the JavaCompiler and associated classes from the javax.tools library to compile the assembled code and produce an executable version of the game.

To maximise extensibility, the game author can append their own custom Java code to the end of the game description file, and call its constructors from within the description as per any other constructor defined in the grammar. This makes the approach quite extensible without the need to modify or recompile the underlying code library, with the caveat that the author of such appended code would need to be familiar with Java and would probably have to develop it outside a Java development environment.

4 Implementation

This section describes the following relevant implementation details: programming language (Sect. 4.1), algorithm (Sect. 4.2), interface (Sect. 4.3), formatting guidelines (Sect. 4.4), and version control (Sect. 4.5).

4.1   Programming Language

Java was chosen for the class grammar code base due to its ease of use, portability (it runs on any device and operating system with the appropriate Java virtual machine) and speed (it performs as well as equivalent C++ code, to within a few percent, using current compilers). Further, Java's reflection library is ideal for extracting relevant class information from the code base, and its javax.tools compilation tools are ideal for the run-time compilation of reconstructed classes.

4.2   Algorithm

The algorithm for generating the class grammar is summarised as follows:

```
public void generate(final String rootPath)
{
    setPredefinedSymbols();
    findSymbols(rootPath);
    scopeSymbols();
    expandRHSs();
    removeSuperfluousSubclasses();
    collapseSimilarConstructors();
    prioritiseOrder();
    trimRules();
}
```

First, SetPredefinedSymbols() creates predefined symbols for fundamental Java data types such as int, float, double, boolean, String, Object, and so on. findSymbols() then recursively finds additional symbols corresponding to user-defined classes and enums from the specified root. These are then *minimally scoped* to disambiguate symbols with identical names, by prepending superclass names as required. For example, multiple occurrences of class or might be scoped to start.or, move.or, end.or, etc.

expandRHSs() then creates a production rule for each symbol, with the symbol name as LHS, and expands the RHS to include the constructor(s) for this class and derived subclasses. removeSuperfluousSubclasses() removes duplicate occurrences of subclasses in the RHS except for the deepest.

collapseSimilarConstructors() combines similar constructor descriptions on the RHS where possible, identifying implicit optional parameters (discussed shortly). prioritiseOrder() prioritises package order in depth-first order, and rule order within each package so that base classes come first. trimRules() removes unused and empty rules, which might occur in partially implemented code under development.

4.3 Interface

The root `Game` class implements the following minimal API:

```
public void create(final int viewSize);
public void start(final Episode episode);
public List<Turn> actions(final Episode episode);
public Status apply(final Episode episode, final Turn turn);
public Status playout(final Episode episode);
```

Every game defined in the grammar, when compiled, *must* implement this basic functionality for play. The user therefore defines games in the grammar but executes them through the API. This decouples the grammar from its implementation, from the user's perspective, and makes it context-free. The `playout()` function is for performing optimised playouts, avoiding complete legal move enumerations, for AI implementations such as Monte Carlo tree search (MCTS) [25].

Details regarding the internal game state representation are beyond the scope of this paper, which focuses on the class grammar itself. Suffice it to say that this representation is designed to be general and efficient, but can be subclassed and overridden for the optimisation of individual cases as desired.

4.4 Formatting Guidelines

While the class grammar is conceptually decoupled from its generating code, the programmer can make the grammar cleaner and clearer by following some basic formatting guidelines.

Named Parameters. Constructor parameters that are simple (terminal) data types are explicitly labeled in the grammar by their parameter name. This makes the grammar self-documenting to some extent, easier to interpret and reduces ambiguity. For example, this:

```
<what> ::= (what (who int) (where int))
```

is more meaningful to the reader than:

```
<what> ::= (what int int)
```

It is sometimes desirable to *anonymize* named parameters, where this simplifies the grammar and does not create ambiguity; for example, the two parameters in (`add int int`) do not need naming. Such parameters can be explicitly denoted using the custom annotation `@Anon` to override the default behavior.

Conversely, parameters representing complex (non-terminal) data types are not named in the grammar by default, as the data type itself usually gives sufficient information to infer the parameter's purpose. However, this behavior can also be overridden to explicitly name such parameters using the custom annotation @Name. Note that parameter naming requires the use of Java version 8 for the relevant `reflection` call, but warrants the move to this version.

Optional Parameters. Constructor arguments can be *explicitly* specified as [optional] items in the grammar using the custom annotation @Opt. For example, the following code:

```
public Board(final Basis basis, @Opt final Modify[] modify)
```

will generate the following rule with an optional parameter:

```
<board> ::= (board <basis> [{<modify>}])
```

Parameters can also be *implicitly* made [optional] by providing multiple constructors for a class, such that parameters that occur in one constructor but not in another are interpreted as optional. For example, the following pair of constructors would produce the same rule shown above:

```
public Board(final Basis basis)
public Board(final Basis basis, final Modify[] modify)
```

The explicit approach is recommended as it is simpler and less error prone. The implicit approach, although more conceptually elegant, requires care to avoid ambiguous cases, and complicates the initialisation of default values.

Default Values. It is useful to set default values for member variables of all classes described in the grammar, in case their corresponding constructor parameters are made optional. However, this is complicated by the fact that we also want to declare them as `final` and make the instantiated objects *immutable* if possible, as per good object oriented design practice [26, pp. 73–80].

Java only allows `final` member variables to be initialised once in the class's execution flow. This is handled in the class grammar by passing parameter values up the `super(...)` constructor chain as appropriate, and instantiating missing values due to optional parameters with their default values in the appropriate constructors. Care must be taken to instantiate the same default values across all constructors for each class, for consistency.

Library Structure. The LUDII code library is organised to reflect the underlying class structure, with each Java *package* containing the base class of the same name and immediate subclasses that will create items in the RHS sequence for the corresponding grammar rule. This makes it easier to navigate and maintain the code library using the class grammar as a reference.

Abstract Classes. The programmer can influence the format of the generated grammar through judicious use of **abstract** classes. Constructors for **abstract** classes are not shown in the grammar as they cannot be instantiated by the user.

Inner Classes. The programmer is free to use inner classes, but these are private to their defining class and so will not appear in the grammar (except for **enums**).

Collections. Constructor parameters denoting arrays and Java collections, such as **Lists**, are all represented in the grammar as {...}, for the sake of brevity. The appropriate data type is reconstructed and populated with the specified items in the backwards (instantiation) step, during code compilation.

4.5   Version Control

As the LUDII code library is a work in progress, and could continue to expand for years to come, *regression testing* is important to guarantee that future additions to the library do not unduly affect existing code.

This will be achieved by maintaining a database of N deterministic playouts for each game described in the grammar, seeding the RNG with a hash code based on the game's (unique) name, and storing the moves thus generated. Any change to the library that makes any known game diverge from its stored playout record will be flagged for investigation.

5   Conclusion

While the class grammar described in this paper is based on the LUDII general game system's source code library, the basic approach – of automatically generating a context-free grammar from a class hierarchy's constructors, then instantiating expressions in that grammar by compiling the appropriately parameterised constructor calls – has general application to any domain for which such a class hierarchy can be defined.

Benefits of the approach for computer-assisted and fully automated game design include: (1) the generality implicit in effectively using the programming language (Java) as the game description language; (2) the extensibility afforded by the ease with which code can be added to the source code library and automatically incorporated into the grammar; and (3) the evolvability of games described in this high-level hierarchical manner. The class grammar is the ideal GDL for LUDII as it develops and expands over the upcoming years.

Acknowledgements. This work was funded by a QUT Vice-Chancellor's Research Fellowship as part of the project *Games Without Frontiers*. Thanks to Stephen Tavener for nudging me towards Java, which proved ideal for this task.

Appendix

A   Tic-Tac-Toe in ZRF

The following code describes Tic-Tac-Toe in the ZILLIONS OF GAMES Zillions Rules File (ZRF) format [10] (88 tokens):

```
(define add-to-empty ((verify empty?) add))
(game
    (title "Tic-Tac-Toe")
    (players X O)
    (turn-order X O)
    (board
        (grid
            (start-rectangle 16 16 112 112)
            (dimensions
                ("top-/middle-/bottom-" (0 112))
                ("left/middle/right" (112 0))
            )
            (directions (n -1 0) (e 0 1) (nw -1 -1) (ne -1 1))
        )
    )
    (piece (name man) (drops (add-to-empty)))
    (board-setup (X (man off 5)) (O (man off 5)))
    (draw-condition (X O) stalemated)
    (win-condition (X O)
        (or (relative-config man n man n man)
            (relative-config man e man e man)
            (relative-config man ne man ne man)
            (relative-config man nw man nw man)
        )
    )
)
```

B   Tic-Tac-Toe in the Stanford GDL

The following code describes Tic Tac Toe in the Stanford GDL [12] (384 tokens):

```
(role white)
(role black)
(init (cell 1 1 b))
(init (cell 1 2 b))
(init (cell 1 3 b))
(init (cell 2 1 b))
(init (cell 2 2 b))
(init (cell 2 3 b))
(init (cell 3 1 b))
```

```
(init (cell 3 2 b))
(init (cell 3 3 b))
(init (control white))
(<= (legal ?w (mark ?x ?y)) (true (cell ?x ?y b))
    (true (control ?w)))
(<= (legal white noop) (true (control black)))
(<= (legal black noop) (true (control white)))
(<= (next (cell ?m ?n x)) (does white (mark ?m ?n))
    (true (cell ?m ?n b)))
(<= (next (cell ?m ?n o)) (does black (mark ?m ?n))
    (true (cell ?m ?n b)))
(<= (next (cell ?m ?n ?w)) (true (cell ?m ?n ?w))
    (distinct ?w b))
(<= (next (cell ?m ?n b)) (does ?w (mark ?j ?k))
    (true (cell ?m ?n b)) (or (distinct ?m ?j) (distinct ?n ?k)))
(<= (next (control white)) (true (control black)))
(<= (next (control black)) (true (control white)))
(<= (row ?m ?x) (true (cell ?m 1 ?x))
    (true (cell ?m 2 ?x)) (true (cell ?m 3 ?x)))
(<= (column ?n ?x) (true (cell 1 ?n ?x))
    (true (cell 2 ?n ?x)) (true (cell 3 ?n ?x)))
(<= (diagonal ?x) (true (cell 1 1 ?x))
    (true (cell 2 2 ?x)) (true (cell 3 3 ?x)))
(<= (diagonal ?x) (true (cell 1 3 ?x))
    (true (cell 2 2 ?x)) (true (cell 3 1 ?x)))
(<= (line ?x) (row ?m ?x))
(<= (line ?x) (column ?m ?x))
(<= (line ?x) (diagonal ?x))
(<= open (true (cell ?m ?n b))) (<= (goal white 100) (line x))
(<= (goal white 50) (not open) (not (line x)) (not (line o)))
(<= (goal white 0) open (not (line x)))
(<= (goal black 100) (line o))
(<= (goal black 50) (not open) (not (line x)) (not (line o)))
(<= (goal black 0) open (not (line o)))
(<= terminal (line x))
(<= terminal (line o))
(<= terminal (not open))
```

C Tic-Tac-Toe in the Ludi GDL

The following code describes Tic-Tac-Toe in the Ludi GDL [2] (29 tokens):

```
(game Tic-Tac-Toe
    (players White Black)
    (board (tiling square i-nbors) (shape square) (size 3 3))
    (pieces (Piece All (moves
        (move (pre (empty to)) (action (push)))))))
    (end (All win (in-a-row 3)))
)
```

D   Tic-Tac-Toe in LUDII Class Grammar

The following shows Tic-Tac-Toe in the LUDII class grammar (47 tokens):

```
(game "Tic-Tac-Toe"
    (control (player "P1") (player P2") Discrete)
    {
        (board Board (square 3))
        (disc Disc1 (owner P1))
        (disc Disc2 (owner P2))
    }
    (rules
        {
            (store P1 Disc1 (count 5))
            (store P2 Disc2 (count 4))
        }
        (play
            (move
                (from (generate Store Mover))
                (to (generate Board empty))
            )
        )
        (end
            (line (length 3) (dirn Any) (owner Mover))
            (result Mover Win)
        )
    )
)
```

The description (game "Tic-Tac-Toe") has the same effect in 2 tokens, due to default parameter values. A full board without a winning line defaults to a Draw, after both players are forced to pass in succession.

E   Sample of the Class Grammar

The following listing shows an incomplete subset of the class grammar generated from the LUDII code library. Rules are grouped by package.

```
<game>        ::= (game (name String) [{<metadata>}]
                        [<control>] [{<equipment>}] [<rules>])
<metadata>    ::= (String String)

<control>     ::= (control [{<player>}] [<timeType>])
<timeType>    ::= Discrete | Real

<player>      ::= (player [(index int)] (name String))
```

```
<equipment>   ::= <component> | <container>

<container>   ::= <board> | <store>

<board>       ::= (board (label String) <basis> [{<modify>}])
<store>       ::= (store (label String) (owner int))

<basis>       ::= <hexHex> | <rect> | <square>
<hexHex>      ::= (hexHex (dim int))
<rect>        ::= (rect (rows int) (cols int))
<square>      ::= (square (dim int))

<component>   ::= <ball> | <disc>

<ball>        ::= (ball (label String) (colour int))
<disc>        ::= (disc (label String) (colour int))

<rules>       ::= (rules [{<start>}] [<play>] [<end>])

<start>       ::= <place> | <store>
<place>       ::= (place <equipment> <site>)
<store>       ::= (store <equipment> <roleType> (count int))

<play>        ::= (play <move.logic>)

<end>         ::= (end <bool> <result>)
<result>      ::= (result <bool> <roleType> <resultType>)

<roleType>    ::= None | P1 | P2 | P3 | P4 | P5 | P6 | P7 | P8 |
                  Any | All | Mover | NonMover | Opposite |
                  Next | Prev | Odd | Even
<resultType>  ::= Win | Lose | Draw | Tie | Abort
```

References

1. Genesereth, M., Love, N., Pell, B.: General game playing: overview of the AAAI competition. AI Mag. **26**, 62–72 (2005)
2. Browne, C.: Automatic Generation and Evaluation of Recombination Games. Ph.D. Thesis, Faculty of Information Technology, QUT, Brisbane (2008)
3. Shaker, M., Sarhan, M.H., Naameh, O.A., Shaker, N., Togelius, J.: Generation and analysis of physics-based puzzle games. In IEEE Conference on Computational Intelligence in Games (CIG 2013), Niagara Falls, pp. 1–8 (2013)
4. Mahlmann, T., Togelius, J., Yannakakis, G.N.: Modelling and evaluation of complex scenarios with the strategy game description language. In: IEEE Conference on Computational Intelligence in Games (CIG 2011), Seoul, pp. 174–181 (2011)

5. Font, J., Mahlmann, T., Manrique, D., Togelius, J.: A Card Game Description Language. In: European Conference on Applications of Evolutionary Computation, Vienna, pp. 254–263 (2013)
6. Schaul, T.: An extensible description language for video games. IEEE Trans. Comput. Intell. AI Games 6(4), 325–331 (2014)
7. Kulick, J.: World Description Language - A Logical Language for Agent-Based Systems and Games. Bachelors thesis, Freie Universität Berlin, Fachbereich fü Mathematik und Informatik (2009)
8. Kernighan, B.W., Pike, R.: The Practice of Programming. Addison-Wesley, Boston (1999)
9. Borvo, A.: Anatomie D'un Jeu de Cartes: L'Aluette ou le Jeu de Vache. Librarie Nantaise Yves Vachon, Nantes (1977)
10. Mallett, J., Lefler, M.: Zillions of Games: Unlimited Board Games & Puzzles(1998). http://www.zillions-of-games.com
11. Hom, V., Marks, J.: Automatic design of balanced board games. In: Artificial Intelligence and Interactive Digital Entertainment Conference (AAIDE 2007), Stanford, pp. 25–30 (2007)
12. Love, N., Hinrichs, T., Genesereth, M.: General Game Playing: Game Description Language Specification. Report LG-2006-01, Stanford Logic Group (2006)
13. Thielscher, M.: A general game description language for incomplete information games. In: AAAI Conference on Artificial Intelligence, Atlanta, pp. 994–999 (2010)
14. Kowalski, J., Kisielewicz, A.: Game description language for real-time games. In General Intelligence in Game-Playing Agents (GIGA 2015), B. Aires, pp. 23–30 (2015)
15. Koza, J.: On the Programming of Computers by Means of Natural Selection. MIT Press, Massachussetts (1992)
16. Browne, C.: Evolutionary Game Design. Springer, Berlin (2011)
17. Browne, C., Togelius, J., Sturtevant, N.: Guest editorial: general games. IEEE Trans. Comput. Intell. AI Games 6(4), 1–3 (2014)
18. Schaul, T., Togelius, J., Schmidhuber, J.: Measuring Intelligence through Games. Technical report arXiv:1109.1314v1 (2011)
19. Hall, P.W.: Parsing with C++ Constructors. ACM SIGPLAN Not. 28(4), 67–69 (1993)
20. Conway, D.: Parsing with C++ Classes. ACM SIGPLAN Not. 29(1), 46–52 (1994)
21. Pohjalainen, P.: Object-oriented language processing. In: Lightfoot, D., Szyperski, C. (eds.) JMLC 2006. LNCS, vol. 4228, pp. 104–115. Springer, Heidelberg (2006)
22. Mann, P.: A Translational BNF Grammar Notation (TBNF). ACM SIGPLAN Not. 41(4), 16–23 (2006)
23. Fowler, M., Parsons, R.: Domain-Specific Languages. Addison-Wesley, Boston (2011)
24. Ghosh, D.: DSLs in Action. Manning, Stamford (2011)
25. Browne, C., Powley, E., Whitehouse, D., Lucas, S., Cowling, P.I., Rohlfshagen, P., Tavener, S., Perez, D., Samothrakis, S., Colton, S.: A survey of monte carlo tree search methods. IEEE Trans. Comput. Intell. AI Games 4(1), 1–43 (2012)
26. Bloch, J.: Effective Java, 2nd edn. Addison-Wesley, Boston (2008)

The Number of Legal Go Positions

John Tromp[✉]

Stony Brook, USA
john.tromp@gmail.com

Abstract. The number of legal 19×19 Go positions has been determined as

208168199381979984699478633344862770286522453884530548425
639456820927419612738015378525648451698519643907259916015
628128546089888314427129715319317557736620397247064840935

A roughly $1.2\,\%$ fraction of the $3^{19 \times 19}$ total number of positions, this is more naturally expressed in ternary. Replacing the usual ternary digits 0,1,2 by +(empty), ● (black), and ○ (white) respectively, yields the following (illegal) position that counts all legal positions:

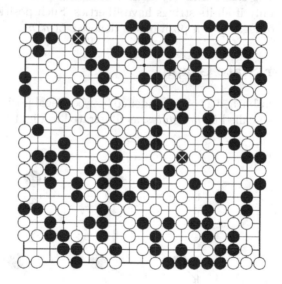

1 Introduction

Go [2,4] almost needs no introduction, but one can be found in the parent paper "Combinatorics of Go" [1], which derived a dynamic programming algorithm to compute numbers of legal positions. With the resources available at the Center for Mathematics and Computer Science (CWI) in 2006, John Tromp and Michal Koucký, who helped develop a file-based implementation, were able to count the number of legal 17×17 positions. This was announced on August 18, 2006, over 10 months after the quick succession of results for 14×14 through 16×16.

© Springer International Publishing AG 2016
A. Plaat et al. (Eds.): CG 2016, LNCS 10068, pp. 183–190, 2016.
DOI: 10.1007/978-3-319-50935-8_17

Since then we have been on the lookout for potential new sources of computing power for the final two steps of 18×18 and 19×19. We submitted many a proposal, both formal and informal, academic and commercial. It was not until early 2014 that Tromp got an offer from Piet Hut at the Institute for Advanced Studies, to use their computing cluster, which led to the results reported here. This paper focuses on these recent results and the software used to obtain them, at the expense of repeating a great deal of the underlying theory detailed in the parent paper. The reader is therefore strongly advised to have a copy of that paper handy for filling in some of the missing details.

2   Preliminaries

A position on an $m \times n$ Go board is a mapping from the set of *points* $\{0, \ldots, m - 1\} \times \{0, \ldots, n - 1\}$ to the set of colors {empty, black, white}. Points are *adjacent* in the usual grid sense—equal in one coordinate and differing by one in the other. A point colored black or white is called a *stone*. Adjacent stones of the same color form connected components called *strings*. An empty point adjacent to a string is called a *liberty* of that string. A position can arise in a game of Go if and only if all its strings have liberties. Such positions are called *legal*. The number of legal $m \times n$ positions is denoted $L(m, n)$.

3   The Border State Graph

The parent paper established a correspondence between legal positions and paths through a graph of so-called *border states*, as illustrated in Fig. 1 for a small 3×3 board.

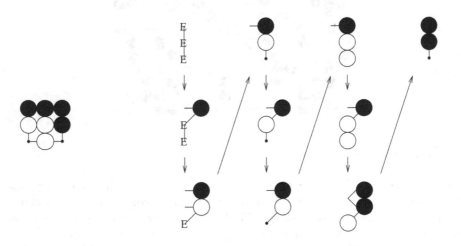

Fig. 1. A 3×3 position and corresponding path through the border state graph

We number the points of the board (plus an extra point to its right) from 0 through 9, isomorphic to the ordering of border states on the right. All the points less than a point p constitute a *partial board up to* p, and the position on these points is a called *partial position*. Each border state on the path records not only the colors of the previous $n = 3$ points ('E' denoting the board edge) but also what is needed to ensure that they have liberties when extending the partial position. This includes knowledge of which stones currently lack liberties and how they are connected in the partial position, shown as lines pointing left and possibly joining up.

The border state of a partial board up to p together with the color of p uniquely determines the *successor* border state up to $p + 1$, if legal. The *border state graph* consists of all border states and their successor transitions. An example of an illegal successor would be a white stone at $p = 3$, preventing the top left black stone from gaining a liberty. Now the problem of computing $L(m, n)$ is reduced to that of counting paths of length mn in a certain graph.

4   The Path Counting Implementation

The go counting software is publicly available at my github repository [5].

To jump right in, file modulus.h implicitly defines a list of relatively prime numbers each of the form $M_i = 2^{64} - d$, for many different small values of $0 \le d < 256$. This allows us to split up the task of computing $L(m, n)$ into many smaller independent jobs that each compute modulo some M_i. The resulting set of equations

$$L(m, n) = a_i \bmod M_i,$$

is readily solved using the Chinese Remainder Theorem [3], as implemented in the Haskell program CRT.hs. For $L(18, 18)$, a 508 bit number, we need $\lceil \frac{508}{64} \rceil = 8$ jobs, while for $L(19, 19)$, $\lceil \frac{566}{64} \rceil = 9$ jobs suffice.

File golegal is a shell script for computing modular path counts, to be invoked as

```
./golegal width modulus [y [ x [incpus [memsize [height [ncpus]]]]]]
```

For example, if we want to compute $L(13, 13)$ modulo $M_1 = 2^{64} - 3$, using 3 GB of memory and 2 cores, (and we already ran make all to create the start and legal executables), we would run

```
./golegal 13 1 0 0 2
```

This creates a top-level directory 13.1 with data sets in subdirectories yx.00.00 through yx.13.00, each one computed from the previous with multiple invocations of legal, one for each cpu. If problems arise necessitating a restart, then we can invoke golegal with appropriate values of y and x. For historical reasons, this implementation works row by row rather than column by column as in Fig. 1.

Within each yx.*.* subdirectory are the start and end timestamps, the cpu.* logs containing the standard output of all legal invocations, and finally the `fromto.*.*` directories holding the actual counts. Let us look at what happens in the sample execution

```
time ./legal 13 1 12 10 2 2 1 500M &>  13.1/yx.12.11/cpu.1
```

The shell script chose a default memory footprint of 500MB, which is allocated to hold blocks of state-count pairs. The executable starts with opening all files in `13.1/yx.12.10/fromto.*.1/` directories in order to merge their already sorted records into a single stream of state-count pairs (see `instream.c`). This stream is processed in the `legal.c` code fragment

```
for (; (mb = minstream(gin))->state != FINALSTATE; nin++,deletemin(gin)) {
  sn.cnt = mb->cnt;
  nnew = expandstate(mb->state, x, newstates);
  for (i=0; i<nnew; i++) {
    sn.state = newstates[i];
    jtinsert(jts, &sn);
  }
  if (nnew < 3) // nnew == 2
    modadd(modulus, &nnewillcnt, mb->cnt);
  if (jtfull(jts))
    dumpstates(go, jts, noutfiles++, mb->state);
}
```

The call to expandstate (in `states.c`) generates the 2 or 3 successor states, each of which is paired with the state count and inserted into the custom `jtset` data structure from `sortstates.c`. State expansions involve first unpacking the highly compressed representation (using only 3 bits per border point), then trying all 3 possible colors for the next point to record the effects on liberties and connections, and packing the results back into the highly compressed representation. The sum count of missing, i.e., newly illegal, successors is maintained in `nnewillcnt` to be logged and cross-checked. Whenever the `jtset` reaches its capacity, routine `dumpstates` from `outstream.c` is called to dump the state-count pairs to files. This involves first (radix) sorting all pairs by state, merging identical ones by summing their counts, and then partitioning them over all cpus, writing one file for each.

The partition boundaries have been precomputed in `partition.c`[1] to ensure an almost uniform distribution of states over cpus. The first line of output

```
width=13 bump=11 tot=48744371 part=24372185
```

shows the width, the bump (x-coordinate) of new states, the number of states, and the boundary between states for cpu 0 and states for cpu 1. Each state pair is written as a state delta followed by the 64 bit count. With the states being sorted, the delta is just over 1 byte on average. Each file ends with a checksum record, that uses a sentinel FINALSTATE and a count such that the sum of all counts equals zero (for the given modulus).

---

[1] This is probably the trickiest part of the code, and was still found to contain bugs during the 18×18 run (affecting efficiency rather than correctness).

In a typical file name of `13.1/yx.12.11/fromto.1.0/1.6546124577333`, the basename consists of the number of `dumpstates` calls, followed by the next state in the input stream (in octal). This helps with mid-step restarts using manual invocations of `legal`, an advanced feature best avoided.

If the memory allocated is too small then dumpstates will be called hundreds of time, which might require thousands of files to be opened for reading in the next step, creating IO bottlenecks. For the 19×19 jobs I liked to use a minimum of 20 GB.

The final lines of output are

```
(12,10) size 24313729 xsize 24391897 mod 18446744073709551613
newillegal 8421059390853372058 needy 15106516706600782168
      legal 17975594761389357431 at (12,11)
```

The first summarizes the input stream, giving the merged size and total size in number of states, as well as reminding us of the modulus used. The next shows the sum count of illegal successors, of states with some border stones in need of liberties, and of states with no such stones.

Apart from setting up the directory structure and iterating over all the steps and cpus, the `golegal` shell script also conserves space by removing files that can be considered obsolete, and takes care to protect against accidental damage by making files and directories read-only.

The perl script `gocheck` performs many checks and balances on these numbers. For instance, the total of `newillegal` + `needy` + `legal` should be congruent to 3 times the previous step's total of `needy` + `legal`. It also checks that $L(m, n) = L(n, m)$ if the latter has been previously computed, as is usually the case when $n < m$. These checks, in addition to the file checksums make it very hard for disk/memory corruption errors to go undetected. And if any of jobs manages to produce even a slightly wrong result, then Chinese Remaindering will amplify this to a huge difference in the reconstructed result, which will then no longer match the highly accurate approximation formula (see below).

5   Results

Table 1 shows the number of legal positions for 18×18 and 19×19.

The $L(18, 18)$ computation ran from summer 2014 through March 2015, taking over 50,000 CPU-hours and 4PB of disk IO, generously provided by the Intel x86 Linux Cluster of the IAS School of Natural Sciences in Princeton. It used 8 jobs with modulo indices 1,2,3,4,5,6,7,8. The smaller of two prime factors found with Dario Alejandro Alpern's ECM implementation is 7176527950749135946361.

The 18×18 result was announced on Hacker News on March 9, 2015 [6] accompanied by a request for yet more computing power to tackle 19×19.

The $L(19, 19)$ computation ran from March 9, 2015 through December 26, 2015, taking over 250,000 CPU-hours and 30PB of disk IO, generously provided

188   J. Tromp

Table 1. Number of legal $n \times n$ positions.

n	#digits	$L(n,n)$
18	153	669723114288829212892740188841706543509937780640178732810318337696945624428547218105214326012774371397184848890970111836283470468812827907149926502347633
19	171	208168199381979984699478633344862770286522453884530548425639456820927419612738015378525648451698519643907259916015628128546089888314427129715319317557736620397247064840935

by the Intel x86 Linux clusters at the IAS School of Natural Sciences in Princeton, the IDA Center for Communications Research, also in Princeton, and on a HP Helion Cloud server. It used 9 jobs with modulo indices 0,1,2,3,4,5,6,11,19. Due to delays in transferring log files, the actual reconstruction of the number didn't happen until January 20, 2016.

Factorizing $L(19,19)$ results in 8 prime factors, the first 7 of which are 5, 401, 4821637, 964261621, 2824211368611548437, 21984669650023760017596133079227 57, and 6594846468368075679414404343317404197. An interesting observation about this deconstruction is that what allows us to do this in just a few hours is that the ECM factoring algorithm is exponential, not in the number of digits itself, but in the square root thereof. Similarly, our construction of $L(19,19)$ is only possible due to the path counting algorithm being exponential, not in the number of board points, but in the square root thereof.

This final result was announced on Hacker News on January 22, 2016 [7], and has been reported on (with various inaccuracies) by the popular press [9] as well as by several enthusiast sites [8,10].

6   The Base of Liberties

If we take the mn'th root of the number of all 3^{mn} positions on an $m \times n$ board, we of course get the base of 3. If we count only legal positions, then the mn'th root can be shown to converge to some number $L < 3$. Since this single number characterizes the growth rate of stones having liberties, we call it the *base of liberties*. The parent paper showed that, conditional on some conjecture about vanishing error terms,

$$L(m,n) = A\ B^{m+n} L^{mn}(1 + O(m\phi^m))$$

for some constants A, B, $\phi < 1$, and $n = \Theta(m)$. The constants A, B, and L can all be computed as limits of expressions involving legal counts of square and almost-square boards.

$$L = \lim_{n\to\infty} \frac{L(n,n)L(n+1,n+1)}{L(n,n+1)^2},$$

$$B = \lim_{n\to\infty} \frac{L(n,n+1)}{L(n,n)L^n} = \lim_{n\to\infty} \frac{L(n,n)}{L(n,n-1)L^n},$$

$$A = \lim_{n\to\infty} \frac{L(n,n)}{B^{2n}L^{n^2}}.$$

Table 2. Legal counts of almost square boards.

n	#digits	$L(n,n+1)$
17	145	20722054276190233030395875202363901217542740727187846094339981969 3328260806703631440346520296370029734115221628675057693627459392 979397487964077
18	162	21645008927907827531439545348046842446969487357646989370951775056 3261490751122922463339745178577954008324586419548071995019779454 5 84564790800309660950831580481393
19	180	20020319408629769567144797301355785099698625915243038261123500773 4890620740154339541587081797890280045754305529783867873845704588 7 2377085128994221639240314849802261643574096842726 1

Of course L could also be approximated according to its definition as $L(n,n)^{n^{-2}}$ but the above formula offers much better convergence. Using the almost-square legal counts in Table 2, as computed by our algorithm, our best estimates using $L(19,19)$, $L(19,18)$, and $L(18,18)$ are

$$L \approx 2.975734192043357249381,$$
$$B \approx 0.96553505933837387,$$
$$A \approx 0.8506399258457145.$$

Table 3 shows the rapid convergence of $L(n,n)L(n+1,n+1)/L(n,n+1)^2$.

Table 3. Convergence to the base of liberties L.

n	$L(n,n)L(n+1,n+1)/L(n,n+1)^2$
15	2.9757341920433572924932
16	2.975734192043357249362
17	2.975734192043357249381 1
18	2.975734192043357249381 38097

Although the formula for $L(m,n)$ is only asymptotic, convergence turns out to be quite fast. Compared to the exact results in Table 1, it achieves relative accuracy 0.99993 at $n = 5$, 0.99999999 at $n = 9$, and 1.00000000000023 at $n = 13$. It is consistent with all the simulated results. For $n = 99$ it gives the same result of $4 \cdot 10^{4638}$. Accuracy is also excellent far away from the diagonal. For instance, at $L(7, 268)$, the relative accuracy is still 1.0000007, witnessing the wide range of application of the asymptotic formula.

Acknowledgements. We are indebted to Piet Hut and Lee Colbert for supporting both the 18×18 and 19×19 computations, and to Michael Di Domenico for supporting and helping script the 19×19 computation.

References

1. Tromp, J., Farnebäck, G.: Combinatorics of go. In: Herik, H.J., Ciancarini, P., Donkers, H.H.L.M.J. (eds.) CG 2006. LNCS, vol. 4630, pp. 84–99. Springer, Heidelberg (2007). doi:10.1007/978-3-540-75538-8_8
2. Wikipedia: Go (game). http://en.wikipedia.org/wiki/Go_(game)
3. Wikipedia: Chinese remainder theorem. https://en.wikipedia.org/wiki/Chinese_remainder_theorem
4. Tromp, J.: The game of Go (website). http://tromp.github.io/go.html
5. Tromp, J.: github repository. https://github.com/tromp/golegal
6. Tromp, J.: Number of legal 18×18 Go positions computed. One more to go, Hacker News, March 9, 2015. https://news.ycombinator.com/item?id=9167781
7. Tromp, J.: Number of legal Go positions computed, Hacker News, January 22, 2016. https://news.ycombinator.com/item?id=10950875
8. GoBase.org (website). http://gobase.org/
9. Johnson, L.: After 2,500 years, a Chinese gaming mystery is solved, Motherboard, January 25, 2016. http://motherboard.vice.com/read/after-2500-years-a-chinese-gaming-mystery-is-solved
10. James, M.: Number of legal Go positions finally worked out, IProgrammer, February 3, 2016. www.i-programmer.info/news/112-theory/9384-number-of-legal-go-positions-finally-worked-out.html

A Googolplex of Go Games

Matthieu Walraet and John Tromp[(✉)]

Stony Brook, USA
matthieu@walraet.net, john.tromp@gmail.com

Abstract. We establish the existence of $10^{10^{100}}$ Go games, addressing an open problem in "Combinatorics of Go" by Tromp and Farnebäck.

1 Introduction

The board game of Go is well known for its combination of simple rules [3] and profound complexity. That complexity is in part due to the large boardsize, allowing for long games and hundreds of choices at every turn. Estimates on the number of 'practical' $n \times n$ games take the form b^l where b and l are estimates on the number of choices per turn (branching factor) and game length, respectively [1]. A reasonable and minimally arbitrary upper bound sets $b = l = n^2$, while for a lower bound, values of $b = n$ and $l = \frac{2}{3}n^2$ seem both reasonable and not too arbitrary. This gives us bounds for the ill-defined number $P19$ of 'practical' 19×19 games of

$$10^{306} < P19 < 10^{924}$$

Wikipedia's page on Game complexity [5] combines a somewhat high estimate of $b = 250$ with an unreasonably low estime of $l = 150$ to arrive at a not unreasonable 10^{360} games.

But the rules also allow for less sensible games where players fill in their eyes and continue capturing each other, restricted only by the superko rule that forbids repeating the whole board position. It is this precisely defined set of all possible games that we want to bound.

Let us denote by $N(n)$ the number of Go games on an $n \times n$ board using the rules of [3]. Tromp and Farnebäck [2] established

$$10^{10^{48}} < N(19) < 10^{10^{171}},$$

and list this rather huge gap as one of the open problems.

The challenge in proving a lower bound is to make a single game as long as possible, by visiting as many of the roughly $2 \cdot 10^{170}$ legal positions as possible [4]. There will then turn out to be sufficient choices along the way to lift the game length into the exponent.

While [2] used properties of binary Gray codes to prove their lower bound, we obtain much stronger bounds by subdividing the board and iterating over all legal sub-board positions. Supporting materials can be found at [6].

© Springer International Publishing AG 2016
A. Plaat et al. (Eds.): CG 2016, LNCS 10068, pp. 191–201, 2016.
DOI: 10.1007/978-3-319-50935-8_18

2   Basic Scheme

For the 5×5 board (Fig. 1), consider the 25 points in row-major order from top left to bottom right. The central 3 control points marked 'c' split the board into two other symmetric sub-boards: the 11 point top and 11 point bottom.

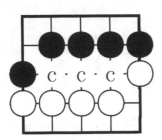

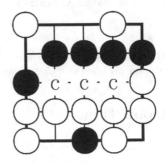

Fig. 1. Basic scheme

Fig. 2. A pair of legal sub-board positions

The 5 points of the top directly preceding the control are reserved for a black border; which means they are either black or empty. The rest of the top, consisting of 6 points, can be anything that forms a legal position in combination with the black border.

Definition 1. *For some odd board size $n \geq 3$, a legal top position is a position on $\frac{n^2-3}{2}$ points, ending in n black border points, that is legal on the sub-board. It is called* pseudo-legal *if the position is legal on the sub-board plus an empty control. Let H_n be the number of legal sub-board positions (H for half).*

We have computed and manually verified that $H_5 = 323$. Similarly, the 5 points following the control are reserved for a white border, which allow for 323 corresponding legal bottom positions, which can be defined analogously. Figure 2 shows a pair of legal sub-board positions.

In the basic scheme, we alternate setting up top and bottom positions, using the control to mark the different phases as follows (see Table 1).

To set up a position, pick any permutation of its stones (non-empty points), and play them in that order, passing in between if necessary. To complete a position setup, let us say in the black-bordered top, white plays in the control center. This "freezes" the top position, and moves the scheme into the next fill phase.

To fill up a position, say on top, first grow all white strings until they have only one liberty, possibly capturing black stones in the process. Note that the black border string is safe from capture because of its liberty in the control. Then, play black stones in any order until they fill the whole sub-board, capturing all expanded white strings in the process. The fillup phase is completed by a white

Table 1. Overview sub-boards of 5 × 5 board

control state	top sub-board	bottom sub-board
┼┼┼	setup	
┼┼◯	setup	frozen
┼◯◯	frozen	fillup
●┼┼	frozen	setup
●●┼	fillup	frozen

play on the control liberty, capturing the entire black block and clearing the sub-board.

Lemma 1. *For n odd, let T (resp. B) denote the set of legal top (resp. bottom) positions. For every permutation of T, every permutation of B, every permutation of stones and every permutation of empty points in every t ∈ T, and every permutation of stones and every permutation of empty points in every b ∈ B, there is a unique game of Go.*

An example game serves to illustrate the proof (see Figs. 3, 4 and 5).

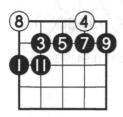

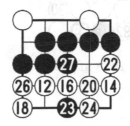

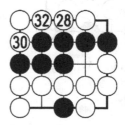

Fig. 3. W 2,6,10 pass   **Fig. 4.** B 13,15,17,19, 21,25 pass   **Fig. 5.** B 29,31 pass

With an empty control, the game sets up the first top position in some order (see Fig. 3), with consecutive stones of the same color requiring an intermediate pass by the other side. Move 11 changes the control, entering the next phase. The first top setup is unique not only in using an empty control, but also in skipping the bottom fillup afterwards, a fact that will be exploited later. Now the first bottom position is set up in some more arbitrary order. Move 27 changes the control again, to start a top fill (see Fig. 4). First White expands her strings until they have only 1 liberty (see Fig. 5).

Then Black plays the originally empty points in some order, except for having to play e5 first to vacate the other points (see Fig. 6). But one of the original

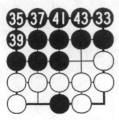

Fig. 6. W 34,36,38,40, 42 pass

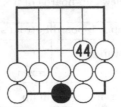

Fig. 7. Top captured

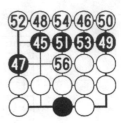

Fig. 8. B 55 pass

white stones, say at a5, can assume its place in the order. White 44 captures the entire top (see Fig. 7) while changing the control yet again, preparing to set up the next top position (see Fig. 8). Let us fast-forward to the end of the game. This will be thousands of moves later, but for notational convenience we will pretend it is move 78.

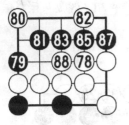

Fig. 9.   W   80,84,86 pass

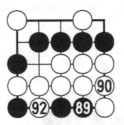

Fig. 10. B 91 pass

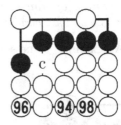

Fig. 11. B 93,95,97 pass

After the last of the top positions has been filled up and captured at move 78 we set up the first top position again, but this time, with move 88 (see Fig. 9), proceed to the fillup of the last bottom position (see Fig. 10), after which the game ends (a Black play at 'c' is prohibited by superko; see Fig. 11).

Proof. The existence of the permutation implied move sequence is clear from the sample game. What is left to show is that every move is legal, i.e. no position is repeated. By construction, every single setup phase is repetition free. In the fillup phase, say, on top, the first part of expanding white strings to a single liberty is repetition free, and so is the second part of forming a solid black block. Since capture of a white string in the second part removes white stones present at the fillup start, there is no repetition across the two parts either. Since every phase except the initial setup and final fillup, has half the board frozen in a sub-board position that gets set up only once, there is no repetition across phases either.   ●

Lemma 2. *Each combined setup and fillup of a sub-board position allows for at least* $\lfloor \frac{K}{2} \rfloor! \lceil \frac{K}{2} \rceil! \approx \pi K (\frac{K}{2e})^K$ *permutations, where K is the sub-board size in points.*

Proof. Let the position have $0 \leq k \leq K$ non-empty points. The setup allows for $k!$ permutations, while the fillup allows for at least $(K - k)!$ permutations. Minimizing the product of these gives the stated lower bound.   •

Our lemmas combine to prove

Theorem 1. *For n odd, $N(n) \geq (\lfloor \frac{K}{2} \rfloor! \lceil \frac{K}{2} \rceil!)^{2H_n} H_n!^2 \approx 2\pi H_n \left(\pi K (\frac{K}{2e})^K \frac{H_n}{e} \right)^{2H_n}$, where $K = \frac{n^2 - 3}{2}$ is the sub-board size.*

In order to apply this to $n = 19$ we need a good lower bound on H_{19}. We computed the number of legal 11×9 positions ending in an 11-stone black border as 25002241191249830032815224867294033961060, and the number of legal 8×10 positions ending in an 10-stone black border as 6838262511331611487262030859411923. Multiplying these together provides the lower bound $H_{19} > 1.7 \cdot 10^{75}$.

Corollary 1. *There are at least $(5! \, 6!)^{646} \, 323!^2 > 10^{4314}$ Go games on 5×5, and at least $(89! \, 90!)^{2H_{19}} H_{19}!^2 > 10^{10^{77}}$ Go games on 19×19.*

The theorem in fact applies to pseudo-legal sub-board positions as well but we refrain from a formal proof, as we will need the legal ones in the next section.

3   Nested Scheme

With the basic scheme, we can play games visiting all legal positions of roughly half the board. To improve our lower bounds, we need to increase the fraction of the board iterated over beyond a half. While one half of the board is frozen, we have a lot of freedom in the other half. Instead of just setting up one sub-board position there, let us run a nested scheme in advance. This requires additional main control states, to distinguish these parts. Yet, we want to limit this control to 3 points. So instead, we consider the control state in context, where the context can be the color of a point horizontally adjacent to the control (marked 'x' for don't-care), or whether a stone in the control is capturable, denoted by a triangle (see Table 2).

Figures 12 and 13 show the nested controls on 13×13 and 15×15 boards, respectively. The main control is marked 'C', and the sub-control, situated about either halfway above or halfway below the center, is marked 'c', and acts just as the basic scheme control. For $n \equiv 1 \bmod 4$, the sub-control splits the sub-board evenly into two sub-sub-boards, but for $n \equiv 3 \bmod 4$, one side is necesarily larger by 1 point. To allow for alternating positions from the two sets of legal sub-sub-board positions, we truncate the bigger set to match the size of the smaller, which we denote Q_n (Q for quarter).

Table 2. Overview sub-boards in a nested scheme

Control state	top sub-board	bottom sub-board
x —┼—┼—┼— x	setup	
x —┼—┼—○ x	play sub	frozen
x —┼—●—○ x	play sub	frozen
x ●—●—●—○ x	play sub	frozen
x ⬡—┼—○ x	last play in sub	frozen
—┼—┼—○—○ x	setup	frozen
●—┼—○—○ x	frozen	fillup
x ●—┼—┼—┼— x	frozen	play sub
x ●—○—┼— x	frozen	play sub
x ●—○—○ x	frozen	play sub
x ●—┼—⬡ x	frozen	last play in sub
x ●—●—┼—┼—	frozen	setup
x ●—●—┼—○	fillup	frozen

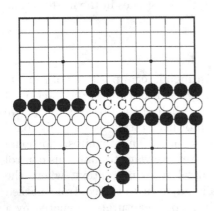

Fig. 12. Nested controls, 13 × 13

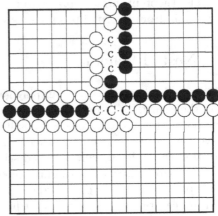

Fig. 13. Nested controls, 15 × 15

Lemma 3. *For a position $p \in T$ (resp. B), denote the possibly truncated set of legal top-left (resp. bottom-left) positions as p_L, and the possibly truncated set of legal top-right (resp. bottom-right) positions as p_R. For every Lemma 1 game, for every sub-board position p in $T \cup B$, for every permutation of p_R, every permutation of p_L, every permutation of stones and every permutation of empty*

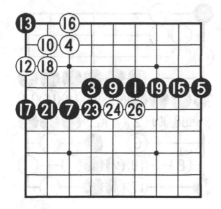

Fig. 14. W 2,6,8,14,20,22 B 11,25 pass

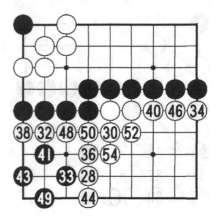

Fig. 15. W 42 B 27,29,33,35,37,...
pass

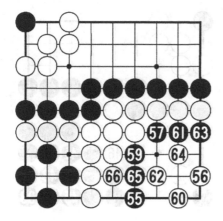

Fig. 16. W 58 pass

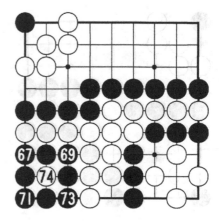

Fig. 17. W 68,70,72 pass

points in every $r \in p_R$, and every permutation of stones and every permutation of empty points in every $l \in p_L$, there is a unique game of Go.

Again we illustrate the proof with an example game.

With an empty control, the game sets up the first top position in some order. Move 23 changes the control, entering bottom play (see Fig. 14). In bottom play, vacated main control points are always filled, as with moves 24 and 26, except in the final sub-game cleanup. With the sub-control empty, we then set up a bottom-left position, ending with the sub-control move at 54 (see Fig. 15).

' Next a bottom-right position is set up, and move 66 changes sub-control to the first quarter fill (see Fig. 16). Black expands her string to a single liberty to be captured by White 74 (see Fig. 17).

White then fills the whole bottom-left and is captured by Black 91, starting a new bottom-left setup (see Fig. 18). For clarity we show move numbers modulo

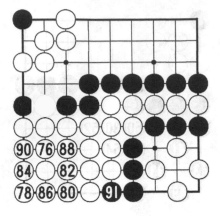

Fig. 18. B 75,77,79,81,83,85,87,89 pass

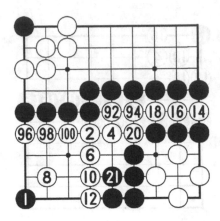

Fig. 19. B 93,95, ... pass

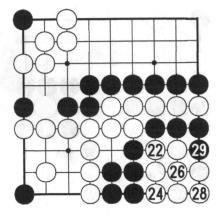

Fig. 20. B 23,25,27 pass

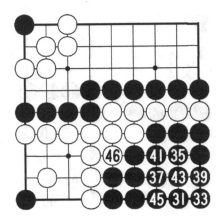

Fig. 21.   W   30,32,34,36,38,40,42,44 pass

100. The setup ends with move 21 starting a bottom-right fillup phase (see Fig. 19).

Now that the black border has one string not adjacent to the sub-control, we must take care to avoid capturing it during white string expansion (always possible due to White's multiple choice) (see Fig. 20). As in the basic scheme, we can iterate through all quarter-board positions in this sub-game (see Fig. 21).

Fast forward to the capture of the last of the bottom-left positions in this sub-game with Black 1 (see Fig. 22). We now add back the white border but skip adding white stones to the main Control. Next, we fill up the last of the bottom-right positions, effectively concluding the bottom sub-game. From move 55, we basically play a bottom fillup (see Fig. 23).

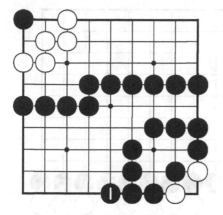

Fig. 22. many moves later

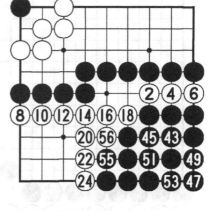

Fig. 23. B 3,5,... W 44,46,... pass

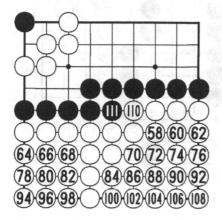

Fig. 24. B 57,59,... pass

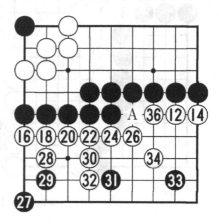

Fig. 25. B 13,15,17,19,21,23,25 pass

White 110 adds the single liberty stone to the main control, letting Black clear the whole bottom with 111. We now set up the first bottom position, freezing it with White 74 (see Fig. 24). The following top fillup will be concluded by a White capture at 'A', initiating a top sub-game (see Fig. 25).

Proof (sketch). As before, it remains to show that no position is repeated. Our previous proof of the basic scheme applies to each sub-game, up until the last sub-sub-board fillup. Then the fillup phase of sub-board is safe from repetition as the main control is left with two liberties. The last move of this fillup, its capture and the setup of next sub-board position, the fillup of the previous main position and its capture, are all protected by distinct main control codes. Thus there can be no repetition during a sub-board position freeze. Furthermore, as each of these sub-board positions gets used only once, there is no repetition across main phases.   •

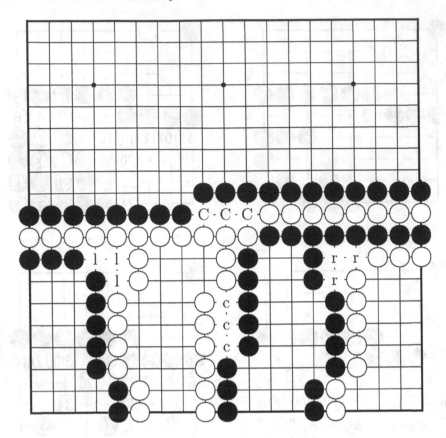

Fig. 26. Triple nesting

Lemma 4 *Each combined setup and fillup of a sub-sub-board position allows for at least $10^{\frac{33}{4}}$ permutations for $n \geq 9$, and at least $10^{\frac{402}{4}}$ permutations for $n \geq 19$.*

Proof This follows from Lemma 2. The $n = 9$ sub-sub-board positions consist of at least 15 points, giving a choice of $7! \, 8! = 203212800 > 10^{8.25}$ permutations. The $n = 19$ sub-sub-board positions consist of at least 83 points, giving a choice of $41! \, 42! > 10^{100.5}$ permutations. •

Since each of the constructed games has $2H_n$ sub-games each consisting of $2Q_n$ combined sub-sub-board setup/fills, we immediately obtain.

Theorem 2 *For $n \geq 9$ odd, $N(n) \geq 10^{33Q_n H_n}$, while for $n \geq 19$ odd, $N(n) \geq 10^{402Q_n H_n}$.*

We computed $H_9 = 95276398927407$ and $Q_9 > 10000$. We showed earlier that $H_{19} > 1.7 \cdot 10^{75}$, and computed $Q_{19} > 8.4 \cdot 10^{30}$.

Corollary 2 *There are at least $10^{10^{19}}$ Go games on 9×9, and at least $10^{10^{108}}$ Go games on 19×19, well over a "googolplex".*

4   And Beyond . . .

We need not stop nesting at 2 levels. Figure 26 shows a triple nesting, with even less uniformity in shape, and diminishing returns, of what can be estimated as $10^{10^{117}}$ games. Considering the burden of proof, and how big of a gap remains with the known upper bound of $10^{10^{171}}$, we leave that as an exercise for the reader.

5   Conclusion

The original lower bound of $10^{10^{48}}$ on the number of 19×19 games, proved in [2], uses approximately half the board to cycle through binary configurations. This paper obtains a much stronger result by improving on both aspects. The nesting subdivision construction allows a majority of the area to be used for cycling through configurations, and these can be ternary rather than binary. Combined, these improvements push the number of games beyond $10^{10^{100}}$, popularly known as a "googolplex".

Acknowledgments. Many thanks to Arnaud Knippel for comments on early versions.

References

1. Number of possible Go games, Sensei's Library (website). http://senseis.xmp.net/?NumberOfPossibleGoGames
2. Tromp, J., Farnebäck, G.: Combinatorics of go. In: Herik, H.J., Ciancarini, P., Donkers, H.H.L.M.J. (eds.) CG 2006. LNCS, vol. 4630, pp. 84–99. Springer, Heidelberg (2007). doi:10.1007/978-3-540-75538-8_8
3. Tromp, J.: The game of Go (website). http://tromp.github.io/go.html
4. Tromp, J.: Number of legal Go positions (website). http://tromp.github.io/go/legal.html
5. Wikipedia: Game complexity. http://en.wikipedia.org/wiki/Game_complexity
6. Walraet, M.: Go-games-number, Supporting materials (website). http://matthieuw.github.io/go-games-number/

An Analysis of Majority Systems with Dependent Agents in a Simple Subtraction Game

Raphael Thiele[✉] and Ingo Althöfer

Friedrich-Schiller-Universität, Fakultät Für Mathematik Und Informatik,
07743 Jena, Germany
{raphael.thiele,ingo.althoefer}@uni-jena.de

Abstract. It is common knowledge that a majority system is typically better than its components, when the components are stochastically independent. However, in practice the independency assumption is often not justified. We investigate systems of experts which are constituted by couples of dependent agents. Based on recent theoretical work we analyse their performance in a simple 2-player subtraction game. It turns out that systems with negatively correlated couples perform better than those with positive correlation within the couples. From computer chess practice it was at least known that systems of very positively correlated bots were not too successful.

1 Introduction

Consider a situation with finitely many options, for instance, a game position with finitely many feasible moves. Several agents or experts may be combined by majority voting: each agent is asked independently for her favorite option, and the option with most votes is selected. Ties are broken by fair coin flips.

Majority systems have been applied to groups of bots in different games [14], such as Chess [1], Shogi [12], and Go [8,11]. Successes were mixed. In particular, it sometimes turned out to be a problem, when the bots were too similar in their inner structure or evaluation functions.

In political sciences the name of Condorcet is famous for a jury theorem. In its basic form [7] it deals with a group of n stochastically acting experts who form a jury and have to vote on a yes/no-question. In case of independence between the experts and uniform strength, the voting decision of the group will have higher expected quality than the decision of its single members. Furthermore, the competence converges to 1, if the number of experts goes to infinity.

Non-independence of agents means that probabilities cannot simply be multiplied and added. However, under certain conditions the systems can nevertheless be analysed. In this paper we look at a situation where the group of experts (called jury) has even size and is split in independent couples. Within each couple dependencies may occur. One situation where such a structure occurs can be a group of N women and N men which form altogether N married couples.

© Springer International Publishing AG 2016
A. Plaat et al. (Eds.): CG 2016, LNCS 10068, pp. 202–211, 2016.
DOI: 10.1007/978-3-319-50935-8_19

Each woman depends on her husband and vice versa. However, dependencies between different couples may be much looser or even completely missing. In game programming, one may think of $2N$ bots from N different programmers where each programmer has designed two of the bots.

In this paper we investigate coupled groups of experts and their performance in a very basic 2-player subtraction game. It turns out that negative correlation within the couples is the best one can have. The paper is organised as follows. In Sect. 2 we present an abstract stochastic model for a simple voting situation. In Sect. 3 the simple (1,2)-subtraction game is analysed, with results for jury vs. single player and jury vs. jury. The paper concludes in Sect. 4.

2   The N-couple Model in General

First, we present the basic N-couple model by Althöfer and Thiele [2]. In the second part of this section, the main theoretical findings for the model are summarized.

2.1   Model

The jury consists of $2N$ experts. Always two of these experts form a couple. Every expert has to choose one of two given options (good or bad). Each expert of couple i picks the good option with probability $p_i \in \left(\frac{1}{2}, 1\right)$. Thus $q_i = 1 - p_i$ is the probability of the bad option. The vector $p = (p_1, \ldots, p_N)$ is called the *competence structure* of the jury.

The experts of a couple influence each other, but they decide independently of the other $2N - 2$ experts. Thus, we have correlation within the couples and independence between the couples. For each couple i we model the dependence like in Bahadur [3] and Boland et al. [5] as follows:

$$\pi_{i,0} = q_i^2 + c_i\, p_i q_i\,,$$
$$\pi_{i,1} = 2\left(p_i q_i - c_i\, p_i q_i\right)\,, \tag{1}$$
$$\pi_{i,2} = p_i^2 + c_i\, p_i q_i\,.$$

In this formulation $\pi_{i,0}$, $\pi_{i,1}$ and $\pi_{i,2}$ are the probabilities for 0, 1 and 2 good votes within couple i, respectively. The probability $\pi_{i,1}$ includes both mixed cases [(good,bad) and (bad, good)].

We model the strength and direction of the dependence between the experts in a couple i by the correlation coefficient c_i. Positive c_i mean positive correlation, negative c_i negative correlation. The vector $c = (c_1, \ldots, c_N)$ is called the *dependence structure* of the jury. However, not all correlation coefficients $c_i \in [-1, 1]$ generate valid distributions. So we need better bounds for the c_i. From Bahadur [3] we get the following tight bounds for our model:

$$-\frac{q_i}{p_i} \le c_i \le 1. \tag{2}$$

The correct votes within the couples are summarized. So the set $\{0, 1, 2\}^N$ contains all possible voting profiles for the N-couple jury. We split this set into disjoint sets $V^N_{k_0, k_1, k_2}$ with $k_0 + k_1 + k_2 = N$ and

$$V^N_{k_0, k_1, k_2} = \left\{ \{0, 1, 2\}^N \mid k_0 \text{ times } 0,\ k_1 \text{ times } 1,\ k_2 \text{ times } 2 \right\}.$$

k_0 is the number of couples with 0 good votes, k_1 the number of couples with 1 good vote, and k_2 the number of couples with 2 good votes.

With these disjoint sets we are able to calculate the probability $e^N_t(p, c)$ that exactly $0 \leq t \leq 2N$ experts choose the good option.

$$e^N_t(p, c) = \sum_{k=max\{0, N-t\}}^{\lfloor N - \frac{t}{2} \rfloor} \quad \sum_{v \in V^N_{k, 2N-2k-t, t-N+k}} \quad \prod_{i=1}^N \pi_{i, v_i}. \tag{3}$$

By adding up the probabilities of all voting profiles with at least N good votes we get the jury competence $M_N(p, c)$. Fair coin tosses resolve possible N:N-ties (first term in the following equation).

$$M_N(p, c) = \frac{1}{2} e^N_N(p, c) + \sum_{t=N+1}^{2N} e^N_t(p, c) \tag{4}$$

2.2   Theoretical Results

This subsection summarizes the main theoretical findings for the model of Subsect. 2.1. For a proof of these results see Althöfer and Thiele [2].

Theorem 1. *If $N \geq 2$ and $p_i > \frac{1}{2}$ for all i, then the following four statements hold.*

(i) *Positive correlation within the couples decreases the jury competence.*
(ii) *Negative correlation within the couples increases the jury competence.*
(iii) *The dependence structure $c^{worst} = (1, \ldots, 1)$ minimizes the jury competence.*
(iv) *The dependence structure $c^{best} = (-\frac{q_1}{p_1}, \ldots, -\frac{q_N}{p_N})$ maximizes the jury competence.*

By applying the dependence structures of Theorem 1 in Eq. (4) we get the following tight bounds for the jury competence.

Corollary 1. *If $p_i > \frac{1}{2}$ for all i, then the jury competence $M_N(p, c^{best})$ can be calculated as follows for the best dependence structure c^{best} from Theorem 1:*

$$M_N(p, c^{best}) = 1 - 2^{N-1} \prod_{i=1}^N (1 - p_i).$$

Corollary 2. *If $p_i > \frac{1}{2}$ for all i, then N couples with the worst dependence structure c^{worst} from Theorem 1 are exactly as competent as N independent experts with the respective competence structure $(p_1, ..., p_n)$.*

To prove the Condorcet jury theorem for couples, we use the following two results of Ben-Yashar and Paroush [4] and Owen et al. [13]. These theorems extend the classical Condorcet jury theorem, while allowing agents with different competences.

Theorem 2 (Theorem in Ben-Yashar and Paroush [4]). *A jury with an odd number (greater than one) of independent experts is always more competent than the expected competence of a randomly chosen expert.*

Theorem 3 (Theorem II, statement (1) in Owen et al. [13]). *If the average competence of the agents is uniformly higher than $\frac{1}{2}$ then the jury competence converges to 1, if the number of agents goes to infinity.*

Now, we have all ingredients to prove the Condorcet jury theorem for couples.

Theorem 4 (Condorcet jury theorem for couples). *If $p_i > \frac{1}{2}$ for all i, then the following two statements hold for the N-couple model.*

(i) A jury with an odd number $N > 1$ of couples is always more competent than the expected competence of a randomly chosen expert from this jury. Formally, $M_N(p, c) > \frac{1}{N} \sum_{i=1}^{N} p_i$ holds.

(ii) If the average competence of the experts is uniformly higher than $\frac{1}{2}$ then the jury competence converges to 1, if the number of couples goes to infinity.

Proof. If the Condorcet jury theorem for couples is valid for the worst dependence structure, it holds also for all other dependence structures. We transform the worst case according Corollary 2 into the independent case. Afterwards, the statements follows instantly from Theorems 2 and 3. □

3   Subtraction Games

The results of Sect. 2 give the performance in single game positions. But what happens if a majority jury has to play a whole game, with repeated voting situations? In this section we numerically analyse the situation for a simple 2-player game.

3.1   The Classical (1,2)-Subtraction Game

A heap with $m \in \mathbb{N}$ matches is given. Two players alternatingly reduce this heap by picking either one or two matches. Finally, the player who picks the last match wins. For this game the positions of win (W) and loss (L) can be calculated via backward analysis. In Table 1 we illustrate the results for the ten smallest heap sizes. It is obvious that all positions with $m \equiv 0 \bmod 3$ are loss positions.

Table 1. Win and loss positions for the (1,2)-subtraction game

Heap	1	2	3	4	5	6	7	8	9	10
Value	W	W	L	W	W	L	W	W	L	W

3.2   The (1,2)-Subtraction Game with Stochastic Experts

We have two experts which we call Agent A and Agent B. "Expert" means that Agent A chooses the winning move with probability $a > \frac{1}{2}$. Analogously, Agent B chooses the winning move with probability $b > \frac{1}{2}$. The agents play randomly, if the current position is a loss position. T. Fischer in his doctoral dissertation [6] already investigated the symmetric case $a = b$. We analyse what happens between agents of different strength. In particular, we look at situations where at least one of the agents is a majority jury.

Assume that in play between agents A and B, Agent A wins the game with probability $x_A(m)$ if it is his turn in position m. We recursively calculate the probabilities $x_A(m)$ for $m > 2$. For that we use the start values $x_A(1) = 1$, $x_A(2) = a$, $x_B(1) = 1$, and $x_B(2) = b$. Thus we get the following rules of recursion for all $m > 2$:

$$x_A(m) = \begin{cases} \frac{1}{2}\left[1 - x_B(m-1)\right] + \frac{1}{2}\left[1 - x_B(m-2)\right], & \text{if } m \equiv 0 \bmod 3 \\ a\left[1 - x_B(m-1)\right] + (1-a)\left[1 - x_B(m-2)\right], & \text{if } m \equiv 1 \bmod 3 \\ (1-a)\left[1 - x_B(m-1)\right] + a\left[1 - x_B(m-2)\right], & \text{if } m \equiv 2 \bmod 3 \end{cases} \quad (5)$$

Analogously, for Agent B we get:

$$x_B(m) = \begin{cases} \frac{1}{2}\left[1 - x_A(m-1)\right] + \frac{1}{2}\left[1 - x_A(m-2)\right], & \text{if } m \equiv 0 \bmod 3 \\ b\left[1 - x_A(m-1)\right] + (1-b)\left[1 - x_A(m-2)\right], & \text{if } m \equiv 1 \bmod 3 \\ (1-b)\left[1 - x_A(m-1)\right] + b\left[1 - x_A(m-2)\right], & \text{if } m \equiv 2 \bmod 3 \end{cases} \quad (6)$$

From the recursions it is clear that the x_A- and the x_B-values mutually depend on each other.

3.3   Jury vs. Single Agent

We apply the model of Subsect. 3.2 by assuming Agent A to be a jury. The jury is modeled according to the N-couple model of Subsect. 2.1. In this subtraction game the good option is the move which leads to an L-position (loss for the opponent). Consequently, the bad option is the move which leads to a W-position. To simplify, we assume that all experts have the same individual competence p and all couples have the identical dependence parameter c. The jury chooses her move by simple majority voting. Thus the probability a is equal to $M_N(p, c)$ from Eq. (4) in Subsect. 2.1. Agent B gets the same individual competence like the other single experts ($b = p$).

A fair coin flip decides whether Agent A or Agent B has the first move in the game. This is necessary because the heap size m can be a win or loss position. Thus the agent has an advantage if it is a win position and a disadvantage by a loss position. In combination with Eqs. (5) and (6) we are able to calculate the probability $w_A(m)$ that A wins the subtraction game with initial heap size m.

$$w_A(m) = \frac{1}{2}x_A(m) + \frac{1}{2}\left[1 - x_B(m)\right]$$

In the four diagrams of Fig. 1 we illustrate the influence of the individual competence p, the dependence c, and the number of couples N on the probability $w_A(m)$. The initial heap size is always $m = 40$. For a better overview we only plot the best case $c = -\frac{1-p}{p}$ (negative correlation) and the worst case $c = 1$ (both drawn with solid lines). Furthermore the independent case $c = 0$ is also plotted (dotted line). All other combinations with $c < 0$ are located above the dotted line while the combinations with $c > 0$ are located below (we checked this for several parameters; a formal proof, however, is still missing).

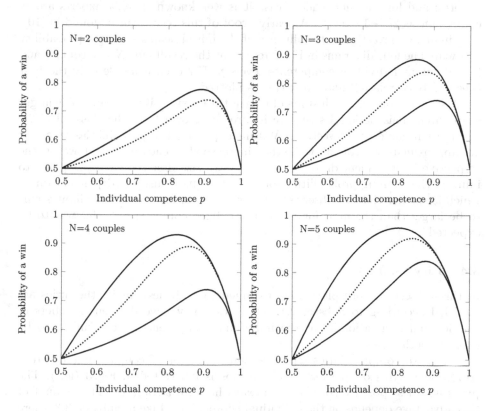

Fig. 1. Probability of a jury win in the (1,2)-subtraction game with heap size $m = 40$ for a jury with N couples against a single agent (best and worst case given by solid lines, independent case dotted)

In the best case the success rate $w_A(m)$ of the jury rises first with increasing individual competence. The probability of success decreases again after her maximum in p_{best}, because now also the opposing single agent makes wrong moves more and more seldomly. If we increase the number of couples N (from 2 to 3 to 4 to 5) then the maximum point p_{best} drops (from 0.89 to 0.84 to 0.81 to 0.79). We conjecture that p_{best} converges to $\frac{1}{2}$ if N goes to infinity. Also, the related success probabilities of win rise with an increasing number of couples, but the differences decrease. (We mean that the difference between 2 and 3 couples is approximately 0.1 while the difference between 4 and 5 couples is only about 0.02). For $N = \infty$ we know by Theorem 4 that $a = M_N(p, c) = 1$. So Agent A plays optimal while Agent B makes mistakes. Altogether it is obvious that for fixed initial heap size m this probability converges to some limit value (near 1 for large m) if N goes to infinity.

The statements for the best case are applicable also to the worst case, except for one minor difference. A jury with $N = 2k$ couples wins always with the same probability as a jury with $N = 2k - 1$ couples (for $k \geq 1$). This is because by Corollary 2 in the worst case N couples are as competent as N independent experts; and for the independent case it is well-known that $2k$ experts are as competent as $2k - 1$ experts. An early proof of this result can be found in [10].

Finally, we investigate the influence of the initial heap size on the probability of a win. The four diagrams in Fig. 2 represent the results for $N = 3$ couples and four different individual competence levels p. For each example only the best (negatively correlated) and worst case is plotted.

A staircase pattern with stairs of length three exists, if the heap size is larger than three. This period-3 structure is already known from the classical (1,2)-subtraction game of Subsect. 3.1. Within a period, the probabilities of a win are approximately identical, while they increase after each period. However, the respective improvement drops with rising heap size. For the heap size going to infinity, the winning probabilities converge to some constant (dependent on p) which is smaller than 1. Observe that, for instance, for $p = 0.8$ this limit seems to be larger than the limit for $p = 0.9$. For fixed couple size N this was to be expected.

3.4   Jury vs. Jury

In this subsection both players are assumed to be juries. Again, the juries are modeled according to Subsect. 2.1. The juries may have different numbers of couples and correlations. But the individual competences are assumed to be equal in both juries.

First, we compare juries with the same number of couples, but different correlations. An example for such scenarios is illustrated in Fig. 3 (left). The juries with less positive correlations always have an advantage. The amount of this advantage depends on the individual competence. Like in Subsect. 3.3, there exists a medium individual competence p_{best} with a maximal advantage.

In a second run, we freeze the correlation and change the number of couples. For the 2 extremal correlations we present the results in Fig. 3 (right). The

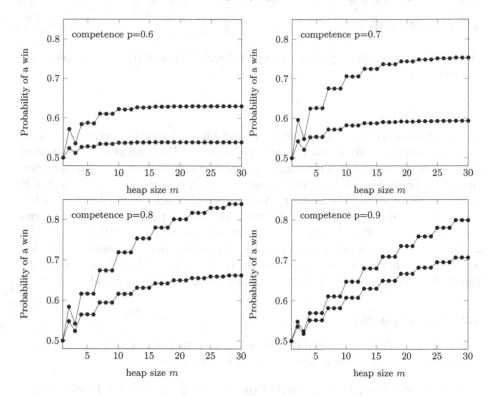

Fig. 2. Probability of a jury win in the (1,2)-subtraction game for a jury with $N = 3$ couples against a single agent (best and worst case)

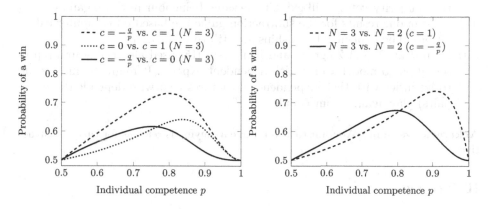

Fig. 3. Different juries against each other for a heap of size $m = 40$

advantage is with the bigger jury. Interestingly, for $p < 0.8$ the advantage for the larger jury is higher in case of negative correlations, and for $p > 0.8$ the advantage for the larger jury is higher in case of positive correlations.

4   Conclusion

We conclude the paper by a summary (Subsect. 4.1) and three open questions (Subsect. 4.2).

4.1   Summary

We investigated the (1,2)-subtraction game with stochastically acting agents. In each win position there is exactly one winning move. Each agent was assumed to choose this optimal move with a fixed probability higher than $\frac{1}{2}$. In this subtraction game larger heap sizes favor stronger agents. Concerning voting schemes, it turns out that a team with majority voting is better than a single agent when the team consists of independent couples with arbitrary dependence within the couples. The main finding, however, is that negative correlation within the couples is the best that can happen - and couples with strong positive inside correlation are not more helpful than a single agent. In the spirit of the Condorcet's jury theorem we found that a larger number of couples is always helpful.

4.2   Open Questions

Below we formulate three open questions. We are convinced that there are many more, but these three are most relevant at this moment.

(i) We only investigated the simplest subtraction game with the feasible moves 1 and 2. Subtraction games with other possible moves or more than two feasible moves could be also interesting. However, we are firmly convinced that majority voting will exhibit the same behaviour in those games.

(ii) Most of our results for the subtraction game are based on computer calculations. The explicit relationships are still to be proven.

(iii) Kaniovski [9] and Zaigraev and Kaniovski [15] used also Bahadur's representation to model a jury with dependent experts. It might be interesting to let juries with their dependency structures (pairwise dependence for all pairs) play against "our couple juries".

Acknowledgement. We want to thank three anonymous referees for there constructive reports.

References

1. Althöfer, I.: Selective trees and majority systems: two experiments with commercial chess computers. In: Beal, D.F. (ed.) Advances in Computer Chess, vol. 6, pp. 37–59. Ellis Horwood, Chichester (1991)

2. Althöfer, I., Thiele, R.: A condorcet jury theorem for couples. Theor. Decis. **81**, 1–15 (2016)

3. Bahadur, R.R.: A Representation of the joint distribution of responses to n dichotomous items. In: Solomon, H. (ed.) Studies in Item Analysis and Prediction, pp. 158–168. Stanford University Press, California (1961)

4. Ben-Yashar, R., Paroush, J.: A nonasymptotic Condorcet jury theorem. Soc. Choice Welfare **17**(2), 189–199 (2000)
5. Boland, P.J., Proschan, F., Tong, Y.L.: Modelling dependence in simple and indirect majority systems. J. Appl. Probab. **26**(1), 81–88 (1989)
6. Fischer, T.: Exakte analyse von Heuristiken für kombinatorische Spiele. Doctoral dissertation, Friedrich Schiller University Jena (2011). http://www.althofer.de/dissertation_thomas-fischer.pdf
7. Grofman, B.: A comment on 'democratic theory: a preliminary mathematical model'. Public Choice **21**(1), 99–103 (1975)
8. Jiang, A., Soriano Marcolino, L., Procaccia, A.D., Sandholm, T., Shah, N., Tambe, M.: Diverse randomized agents vote to win. In: Ghahramani, Z., Welling, M., Cortes, C., Lawrence, N., Weinberger, K. (eds.) Advances in Neural Information Processing Systems, vol. 27, pp. 2573–2581. Curran Associates, Inc. (2014)
9. Kaniovski, S.: Aggregation of correlated votes and Condorcet's Jury theorem. Theor. Decis. **69**(3), 453–468 (2010)
10. Lam, L., Suen, S.Y.: Application of majority voting to pattern recognition: an analysis of its behavior and performance. Trans. Sys. Man Cyber. Part A **27**(5), 553–568 (1997)
11. Manabe, K., Muramatsu, M.: Boosting Approach for Consultaton by Weighted Majority Vote in Computer Go. IPSJ Symposium Series 2011, vol. 6, pp. 128–134 (2011)
12. Obata, T., Sugiyama, T., Hoki, K., Ito, T.: Consultation algorithm for computer shogi: move decisions by majority. In: Herik, H.J., Iida, H., Plaat, A. (eds.) CG 2010. LNCS, vol. 6515, pp. 156–165. Springer, Heidelberg (2011). doi:10.1007/978-3-642-17928-0_15
13. Owen, G., Grofman, B., Feld, S.L.: Proving a distribution-free generalization of the Condorcet Jury theorem. Math. Soc. Sci. **17**(1), 1–16 (1989)
14. Sato, Y., Cincotti, A., Iida, H.: An analysis of voting algorithm in games. In: Computer Games Workshop at ECAI 2012, pp. 102–113 (2012)
15. Zaigraev, A., Kaniovski, S.: A note on the probability of at least k successes in n correlated binary trials. Oper. Res. Lett. **41**(1), 116–120 (2013)

Do People Think Like Computers?

Bas van Opheusden[✉], Zahy Bnaya, Gianni Galbiati, and Wei Ji Ma

Center for Neural Science and Department of Psychology, New York University,
New York City, USA
svo213@nyu.edu

Abstract. Human cognition inspired the earliest algorithms for game-playing computer programs. However, the studies of human and computer game play quickly diverged: the Artificial Intelligence community focused on theory and techniques to solve games, while behavioral scientists empirically examined simple decision-making in humans. In this paper, we combine concepts and methods from the two fields to investigate whether human and AI players take similar approaches in an adversarial combinatorial game. We develop and compare five models that capture human behavior. We then demonstrate that our models can predict behavior in two related tasks. To conclude, we use our models to describe what makes a strong human player.

1 Introduction

Developing a computer program to play a given game as well as the best human players was a significant challenge for early computer scientists, even predating the term *artificial intelligence* [1,2]. Much of the initial progress in game-playing AI was inspired by examining human gameplay and formulating games as *search problems* [3]. Subsequently, the Artificial Intelligence community focused on developing algorithms, approaches and concepts in order to improve computer game play for more games in more domains (Checkers [4], Poker, Chess [5] and Go [6–8]), while generally ignoring potential similarities to human thought processes. Meanwhile, psychologists, neuroscientists and economists have built successful models for human reasoning in simple decision tasks, while ignoring games with large decision spaces [9,10]. Recent approaches have begun using human game play to train stronger AI agents [7].

In this paper, we present AI-based computational models for the behavior of non-expert human players in a simple, adversarial, full-information game. Our models formalize hypotheses for the cognitive processes by which a human player makes a decision on a given task; the models we consider simulate human responses to game positions, making similar decisions to human players. We aim to determine whether modern AI concepts such as heuristic search [3] are useful in explaining human play.

We compare the ability of our models to predict subjects' choices during regular game play. We further show that our main model can predict behavior in two related tasks. Finally, we investigate how strongly the playing strength of our subjects is related to our main model's algorithmic properties, such as search depth, tree size, and the quality of the heuristic function.

© Springer International Publishing AG 2016
A. Plaat et al. (Eds.): CG 2016, LNCS 10068, pp. 212–224, 2016.
DOI: 10.1007/978-3-319-50935-8_20

2 Experimental Methods

We collected data from human subjects playing a simple board game. Two players take turns placing pieces on a 4 by 9 board (Fig. 1A). The black player makes the first move. The goal is to place four consecutive pieces in a row, column, or diagonal. We chose this game because the rules are few and easily learned, it is unfamiliar to our subjects, and it is sufficiently hard to master without being computationally intractable.

We performed two experiments on human subjects with a total of four tasks: (1) playing full games against a human opponent, (2) playing against AI opponents with different playing strengths, (3) deciding between two alternative moves on a given board position (2AFC) (Fig. 1B), and (4) evaluating their winning chances in a given board position (Fig. 1C).

Experiment 1: We recruited 40 subjects and divided them into 20 pairs. Subjects in each pair played multiple games against each other without time constraints, switching colors after every game. The experiment terminated after subjects had played for one hour and finished their last game.

Experiment 2: We recruited 40 additional subjects to perform three tasks. For the first 30 min, subjects played games against AI opponents, switching colors after every game. To make it less likely for subjects to latch onto any particular opponent's idiosyncrasies, and to keep play challenging for all subjects, we selected opponents from a set of 30 AI agents with different playing strengths. We switched to a stronger opponent every time the subject won a game, and to a weaker opponent whenever they lost. In the second task, subjects saw board positions and chose between two marked candidate moves (Fig. 1B). We selected the positions and candidate moves to create difficult choices for subjects. In positions where both candidate moves had the same game-theoretic value, the subject's choice indicates a subjective preference. On trials where one move was strictly better than the alternative, the subject's choice can be used to measure their playing strength. The third and final task, *board evaluation*, required subjects to rate board positions from 1 ('losing') to 7 ('winning') from the perspective of the current player. In the second and third task, each subject completed 84 trials.

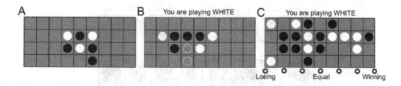

Fig. 1. A: Example of a game position. **B:** On a trial of the 2AFC task, subjects see a board position with two possible moves, and indicate their preference. **C:** On a trial of the evaluation task, subjects see a board position and estimate their winning chances on a 7-point scale.

3   Models of Human Behavior

Our goal is to build a computational model that mimics how human subjects play our game. A model of behavior is an algorithm that, given a board state s, selects a move $a \in A(s)$ from the set of available moves $A(s)$. To account for variability in human choices, our models contain multiple sources of stochasticity. Since players may vary in their decision processes and cognitive abilities, our models have parameters, which we fit to individual subjects. In this section we discuss the following seven items: heuristic function, sources of variability, myopic model, main model, conv-net model, opt-rand model, and fitting the model parameters.

3.1   Heuristic Function

Most of our models rely on a *heuristic function* that assigns a value to each board position. Our heuristic function is a weighted sum of five features. Each feature is counted separately over a player's own pieces and their opponent's pieces. The first feature, which we call the *center* feature and denote by $f_0(s, c)$, measures the number of pieces of color c on the 12 central squares of the board s. The other four features (Fig. 2), denoted by $f_i(s, c)$ with $i = 1, \ldots, 4$, count how often the following patterns occur on the board (horizontally, vertically, or diagonally).

1. *Connected 2-in-a-row:* two adjacent pieces with sufficient empty squares around them to complete 4-in-a-row.
2. *Unconnected 2-in-a-row:* two non-adjacent pieces which lie on a line of four contiguous squares, with the remaining two squares empty.
3. *3-in-a-row:* three pieces which lie on a line of four contiguous squares, with the remaining square empty. This pattern represents an immediate winning threat.
4. *4-in-a-row:* four pieces in a row. This pattern appears only in terminal boards.

We handpicked these features to reflect heuristics that are intuitive given the goal of the game. We tested additional features, but none of them improved the main model's fit to human play. However, a more systematic approach to select these features is a natural direction that we leave for future work.

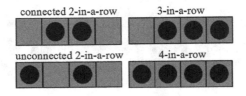

Fig. 2. Patterns in the heuristic function. The four features in our heuristic function. Each feature counts how often one of these patterns occurs on board (horizontally, vertically, or diagonally).

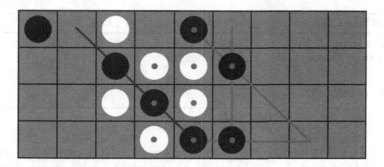

Fig. 3. Heuristic function. In this position, white is to move. Black has 5 pieces on the central squares, white has 4 (marked with blue dots). Black has two connected two-in-a-rows (purple), one unconnected two-in-a-row (orange) and one three-in-a-row (green). White has no instances of any pattern. The value of this board state, from white's perspective, is therefore $H(s) = -w_0 - w_1 - 2w_2 - w_3$. (Colour figure online)

We associate a weight w_i to each of the five features, and write the heuristic function as

$$H(s) = c_{\text{self}} \sum_{i=0}^{4} w_i f_i(s, \text{own color}) - c_{\text{opp}} \sum_{i=0}^{4} w_i f_i(s, \text{opponent color})$$

where $c_{\text{self}} = C$ and $c_{\text{opp}} = 1$ whenever the player is to move in state s, and $c_{\text{self}} = 1$ and $c_{\text{opp}} = C$ when it is the opponent's move. The scaling constant C is a fitting parameter which can vary between subjects. Figure 3 demonstrates a calculation of the heuristic function in an example board state, taken from human play.

The weight parameters $W = \{w_0, w_1, \ldots, w_4\}$ vary between subjects. They encode differences in subjects' preferences, such as their relative inclination to make direct threats (3-in-a-row) over indirect strategic maneuvers (unconnected 2-a-in-row).

3.2 Sources of Variability

Unlike deterministic AI agents, realistic models for human behavior must support variability. Our models are required not only to identify the subject's most likely move given a position, but also to assign some probability to their noisy and inconsistent decisions.

We introduce three sources of variability in our models. (a) *Value noise*: We add Gaussian noise to the heuristic value of each state, reflecting a human tendency to choose almost arbitrarily between two moves of roughly equal value. (b) *Feature dropping*: When counting instances of any one of our patterns, we exclude with probability λ every possible location-orientation combination where that pattern may occur. This mechanism represents lapses of attention, where a subject overlooks a pattern in some region on the board. We denote this

---

Algorithm 1. Myopic-model(State s, Parameters $\{\lambda, W, lapse\}$):

1 **if** *lapse* **then**
2 $\quad\lfloor$ **return** *random-move*

3 **else**
4 $\quad\lfloor$ **return** $\text{argmax}_{a \in A(s)} H_\lambda(T(s, a)) + \mathcal{N}(0, 1)$

---

modified heuristic function by $H_\lambda(s)$. (c) *Lapse rate*: On each move, there is some probability that the model makes a completely random move, capturing human moves with no apparent rationale behind them. The lapse rate, feature dropping rate (λ), and feature weights are all model parameters. We now describe the five specific models that we test.

3.3 Myopic Model

After checking for a lapse, the *Myopic* model (shown in Algorithm 1) uses a heuristic function with value noise and feature dropping to evaluate every possible move on a given board position; it then selects the move with the highest value. We use $T(s, a)$ to denote the resulting state by applying action a to state s.

3.4 Main Model

Our main model (described in Algorithm 2) builds a partial game tree similar to algorithms such as Minimax, alpha-beta pruning, and Monte-Carlo Tree Search. Each state is represented as a node in the tree. Each node n has a value estimate $V(n)$ and a set of successors $Succ(n)$.

On each execution, the model initially determines whether a lapse occurs, in which case it makes a random move (lines 1–2). Otherwise, the model builds the root node to represent the current state (line 3) and repeats a procedure to build a partial tree. On each iteration, the algorithm selects a node in the tree for further exploration (line 4). The *selectnode* procedure recursively selects the successor node with the maximal heuristic value until it reaches a leaf node. The selected node is *expanded* (line 5) by the *expand(n)* procedure, which generates successor nodes of the selected node n and assigns each of them a value using the modified heuristic function H_λ. Successor nodes with value less than the best move minus a threshold are pruned from the game tree; the remaining nodes are added to the partial tree.

The *backpropagate* procedure (line 6) recursively updates the values of the predecessor nodes up to the root of the tree. Each node value is assigned the maximum value of its successors. The algorithm iterates for a random number of iterations, with a fixed probability to stop each iteration. Finally, the model returns the move with the highest value (line 7).

Algorithm 2. Main-model(State s, Parameters $\{\lambda, W, lapse, stop\}$):

1   **if** *lapse* **then**
2   **return** *random-move*

3   root = node(s)
4   **while** !*stop* **do**
5   n=selectnode(root)
6   expand(n)
7   backpropagate()

8   **return** $\text{argmax}_{n_i \in Succ(root)} V(n_i)$

3.5   Conv-net Model

We develop an alternative model based on convolutional neural networks, which have recently been used successfully to play Go [7, 8]. Our convolutional neural network (CNN) model treats the game as a classification problem, learning to assign 1 of 36 labels to a board, represented by a $4 \times 9 \times 2$ binary tensor. The network has three layers: an input layer, a hidden convolutional layer, and an output layer. The convolutional layer contains 32 $4 \times 4 \times 2$ filters with rectified linear activation functions. There is no pooling layer between the convolutional layer and the fully output layer. The output layer is a fully connected layer, to which two nonlinearities are applied: the first is a softmax function to convert the output to a probability distribution over the 36 possible labels, the second is a filter that forces zero probability to be assigned to occupied squares.

We fit the CNN model using stochastic gradient descent with Nesterov momentum. To reduce overfitting, we introduce random dropout ($p = 0.75$) between the hidden layer and the output layer and an early stopping condition during training. We use a five-fold cross-validation scheme with the same splits as used for fitting the main model, setting aside 60 % of the data as training data, 20 % as validation data used for the early stopping condition, and 20 % as final test data. Because we did not collect sufficient data to fit the network to each subject individually, we aggregate the data across all subjects for training and report the average log-likelihood per subject. Additionally, we apply reflections to augment the training data to achieve a sufficiently large training set.

3.6   Opt-rand Model

The opt-rand model is a mixture between optimal (i.e., minimax) and random play with only one parameter: the mixture weight. Because human subjects do not have access to the minimax values of each state, we consider the opt-rand model psychologically implausible. However, it still serves as an important control to verify whether our models predict only the subjects' frequency of making mistakes, or more general preferences.

3.7   Fitting the Model Parameters

We use maximum-likelihood estimation to infer the parameter values Θ that maximize the likelihood function $\prod_{(a_t,s_t)\in D} P(a_t|s_t,\Theta)$ where D is the set of all actions performed by a subject in all the states they encountered. Because computing the likelihood analytically or numerically is intractable, we instead estimate the log probability of a subject's move in a given board position using inverse binomial sampling [12]. We use a uniformly unbiased estimator with variance equal to the Cramer-Ráo bound, and optimize the log-likelihood function with *multilevel coordinate search* [13]. We report log-likelihoods for all models with five-fold cross-validation.

4   Results

We compare our models and show which of them best describe subjects' choices. To demonstrate that all parts of our main model are important, we compare our model to *lesion* models generated by removing model components (in Sect. 4.1). Next, we show two specific patterns in human behavior that our model accurately predicts (in Sect. 4.2). We then show that our model is able to predict the subjects' responses in two related tasks (in Sect. 4.3). Finally, we use the model to explain differences in the decision process between stronger and weaker subjects (in Sect. 4.4). We find that the model, fitted to stronger subjects' choices, uses larger trees and has less noise.

4.1   Predicting Human Choices with Our Models

Fig. 4A depicts the cross-validated log-likelihood of our models (*Main, Myopic, Conv-net* and *Opt-Rand*) for each subject, playing against a human opponent. We also plot the log-likelihood of a completely random model (*chance*). Our models' log-likelihoods are better than chance, demonstrating their ability to predict subjects' responses.

We find that our main model predicts subjects' choices better than the *Myopic* model, suggesting that people indeed build decision trees. The Conv-net model also performs worse than the main model, but this primarily reflects its tendency to overfit training data. All our models perform much better than the *Opt-Rand* mixture model, demonstrating their ability to predict more than only the subjects' error rates.

We next perform a lesioning comparison, examining the relative contribution of different components in our main model by removing them, one at a time. We remove either the pruning rule, the feature-drop procedure, or any of the five features. All of the lesioned models perform worse than the original (Fig. 4B), indicating that these model components are necessary to the main model's ability to predict human behavior. The most and least important features are the *3-in-a-row* and the *center*, respectively. This also demonstrates that the pruning and feature-drop are necessary to capture the subjects' selective attention, either to specific patterns on the board or to a subset of the decision tree.

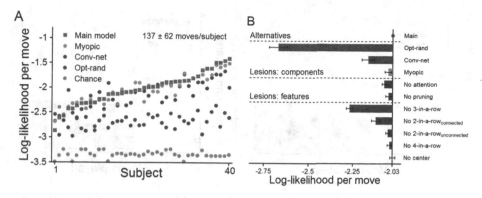

Fig. 4. (A) Log-likelihood of our models for each subject. Our main model performs better than chance, Opt-Rand, Conv-net and the Myopic model. **(B)** Log-likelihood of our models and lesions, averaged across subjects. For each model, the error bars denote the standard error of the mean log-likelihood difference with the main model. The main model performs best, although some lesion models come close.

4.2 Summary Statistics

We have shown that our main model predicts the subjects' choices better than alternative models. Here, we compare the model prediction directly to the subjects' choices, using two *summary statistics*. For each move played by each subject, we measure (1) the distance from the square they moved on to the center of the board, and (2) the number of pieces on the 8 neighboring squares. We plot the average of these statistics as a function of the number of moves played in a game (Fig. 5). We also measure these statistics for moves played by the model in the same positions, as well as random moves. On average, subjects move closer to the center and on squares with more neighboring pieces than random. The model closely matches these two aspects of human play.

4.3 Generalizing Predictions of Our Model

We demonstrate our model's ability to generalize beyond predicting the subjects' choices during full games by inferring parameters for each individual subject from their choices during games, and predicting their 2AFC choices and board evaluations without additional fitting.

To predict a choice on a 2AFC trial, we execute our tree search model as usual, except that we restrict the successor nodes of the root node to the two candidate moves and omit the pruning step. To predict board evaluations, we execute our model and take the value of the root node. If the model lapses, we set this value to 0. Then, we map this value into the subject response interval $[1, 7]$ using score $= 3 + 4 \tanh(value/20)$.

The average accuracy of the 2AFC prediction across subjects is $56.1 \pm 1.1\%$ (Fig. 6A), and the average correlation between the predicted and observed

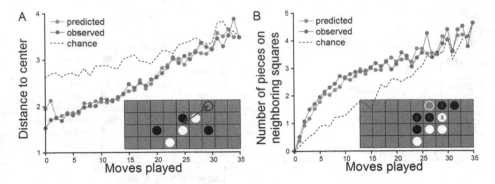

Fig. 5. The predicted and the observed behavior on (**A**) the average distance from the move played by a subject to the center of the board. (**B**) The number of pieces on neighboring squares. Our model reproduces both these patterns. The insets illustrate how these metrics are defined for a given board and a subject's move (open circle).

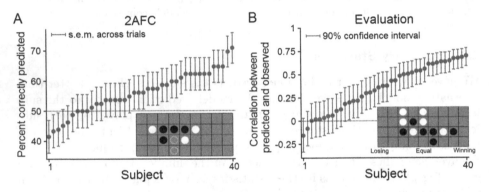

Fig. 6. (**A**) Percentage of correctly predicted choices on the 2AFC task for each subject. (**B**) The correlation coefficients between each subject's board evaluations and evaluations predicted by the model. In both cases, we fitted the model parameters on subjects' choices during games against AI opponents. Both predictions are better than chance for almost all subjects.

evaluations is $\rho = 0.36 \pm 0.04$ (Fig. 6B). The prediction is better than chance for 34 out of the 40 subjects in the 2AFC task and for 38 subjects in the evaluation task.

To put these results into context, we develop an *oracle* model, which selects the optimal move on each 2AFC task (with random tie-breaking). On the board-evaluation task, the oracle responds 1, 4 or 7 for winning, drawn and losing positions, respectively. Overall, the oracle model predicts subjects' choices slightly worse than our main model (percent correct 2AFC: $55.3 \pm 0.6\%$, correlation predicted/observed evaluation: $\rho = 0.30 \pm 0.03$, Fig. 7).

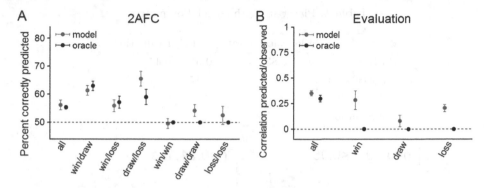

Fig. 7. (A) Performance of our main and oracle models on each category of candidate moves. **(B)** Correlation between predicted and observed evaluations on positions with the same game-theoretic value. In both cases, our model performs on average slightly better than the oracle model. Importantly, our model predicts subjects' preferences when there is no correct decision.

To explain our model's advantage over the oracle model, we compute the percent of correctly predicted 2AFC choices for the main and oracle models for each category of trials (win/win, win/draw, etc.).

For trials where one move is strictly stronger, our model performs comparably to the oracle model, showing that our model does capture the subjects' error rates. For trials where both moves are equally strong, the oracle predicts at chance, but our model performs better, demonstrating that our model predicts the subjective preferences. In the board-evaluation task, we compute the correlation between predicted and observed evaluations across all trials in a category. Again, the oracle model predicts at chance, but our model can predict the subjective evaluations, for either winning or losing positions (but no drawn).

4.4 Playing Strength

The model parameters that we infer for each individual subject reflect how human thought processes differ between subjects, allowing us to examine the differences between strong and weak players. We measure a subject's playing strength by combining 4 metrics: (1) the Elo rating [14] computed from their results in games against AI opponents, (2) the frequency at which they make errors in their games, (3) the percentage of correct choices in the 2AFC task, and (4) the correlation of their board evaluations with the game-theoretic values. All 4 performance metrics correlate with each other across subjects as shown in Table 1.

The playing strength of heuristic search algorithms depends on properties such as the size and depth of the game tree or the 'quality' of the heuristic function. Because our model is stochastic, we can also improve its playing strength by reducing noise. Among these factors, which is responsible for differences in human playing strength?

Table 1. Player strength correlation matrix

	Elo	Success rate	2AFC	Evaluation
Elo	1	0.83	0.61	0.47
Success rate		1	0.47	0.44
2AFC			1	0.43
Evaluation				1

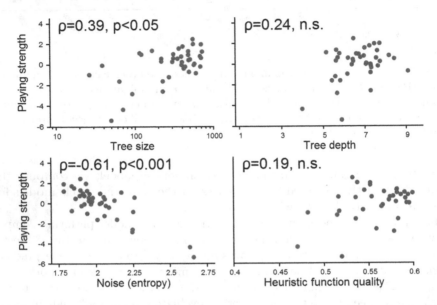

Fig. 8. Correlation between playing strength and size of decision tree, depth of leaf nodes, entropy of the predicted distribution, and heuristic quality. We use *Spearman* correlations to mitigate the effect of outliers. Stronger players build larger trees and have less noise but do not necessarily have better heuristics or search deeper.

For each subject in Experiment 2, we infer model parameters from their choices in games against AI opponents. We let the model with these parameters simulate moves in all positions from the games in Experiment 1. We measure the size of the decision tree built by the model, the average depth of the leaf nodes, the entropy of the model's move distribution, and the correlation between the heuristic function $H(s)$ and the game-theoretic value.

In Fig. 8, we plot these 4 metrics against the playing strength of each subject. The tree size and entropy correlate with playing strength, but the depth of search and heuristic function quality do not; stronger players search more, have more precise board evaluations, and make fewer attentional lapses.

5 Summary and Future Work

We described a model inspired by heuristic search that mimics humans playing a simple combinatorial game. We fitted the model's parameters to individual subjects to capture differences in playing styles. We also suggested alternative models and compared our model to lesions in order to show that the components of our model are necessary to predict human behavior. We then showed that our model predicts subjects' choices in 2AFC tasks and board evaluations. We analyzed player strengths and conclude that stronger players build larger trees and have less noise.

For future work, we plan to investigate whether our models can also describe choices of expert players. We plan to run multiple sessions of Experiment 2 to measure improvements in the subjects' playing strength and investigate which aspects of our model (tree size and depth, noise or heuristic quality) change as a result of experience. We also plan to investigate the encoding of board states in human memory by asking subjects to memorize and then reconstruct board positions, similar to what was done previously in Chess [15]. We are also interested in finding physiological and neural correlates of our model. We plan to record response times, eye movements, and neural activity as measured by an *fMRI* scanner, and use that as further evidence that our model captures the cognitive processes humans use to play games.

References

1. Turing, A.M.: Computing machinery and intelligence. Mind **59**, 433–460 (1950)
2. Shannon, C.E.: XXII. Programming a computer for playing chess. London, Edinb. Dublin Philos. Mag. J. Sci. **41**, 256–275 (1950)
3. Pearl, J.: Heuristics: Intelligent Search Strategies for Computer Problem Solving. Addison-Wesley, Reading (1984)
4. Schaeffer, J., Culberson, J., Treloar, N., Knight, B., Lu, P., Szafron, D.: A world championship caliber checkers program. Artif. Intell. **53**, 273–289 (1992)
5. Campbell, M.A., Joseph, H., Hsu, F.H.: Deep Blue. Artif. Intell. **134**, 57–83 (2002)
6. Coulom, R.: Efficient selectivity and backup operators in monte-carlo tree search. In: van den Herik, H.J., Ciancarini, P., Donkers, H.H.L.M.J. (eds.) CG 2006. LNCS, vol. 4630, pp. 72–83. Springer, Heidelberg (2007). doi:10.1007/978-3-540-75538-8_7
7. Silver, D., Huang, A., Maddison, C.J., Guez, A., Sifre, L., van den Driessche, G., Schrittwieser, J., Antonoglou, I., Panneershelvam, V., Lanctot, M., Dieleman, S., Grewe, D., Nham, J., Kalchbrenner, N., Sutskever, I., Lillicrap, T., Leach, M., Kavukcuoglu, K., Graepel, T., Hassabis, D.: Mastering the game of Go with deep neural networks and tree search. Nature **529**, 484–489 (2016)
8. Clark, C., Storkey, A.: Training Deep Convolutional Neural Networks to Play Go. J. Mach. Learn. Res. **37** (2015)
9. Glimcher, P., Fehr, E.: Neuroeconomics: Decision Making and the Brain. Academic Press, London (2013)
10. Camerer, C., Loewenstein, G.: Behavioral economics: past, present, future. In: Advances in Behavioral Economics. Princeton (2004)
11. Auer, P., Cesa-Bianchi, N., Fischer, P.: Finite-time analysis of the multiarmed bandit problem. Mach. Learn. **47**, 235–256 (2002)

12. de Groot, M.H.: Unbiased sequential estimation for binomial populations. Ann. Math. Stat. **30**, 80–101 (1959)
13. Huyer, W., Neumaier, A.: Global optimization by multilevel coordinate search. J. Global Optim. **14**, 331–355 (1999)
14. Elo, A.E.: The Rating of Chessplayers, Past and Present. Arco Pub. (1978)
15. Chase, W.G., Simon, H.A.: Perception in chess. Cogn. Psychol. **4**, 55–81 (1973)

Author Index

Printed in the United States
By Bookmasters